VIOLENT WEATHER: HURRICANES, TORNADOES & STORMS

Other TAB Books by the Author

VIOLENT WEATHER: HURRICANES, TORNADOES & STORMS

BY STAN GIBILISCO

TAB BOOKS Inc.
BLUE RIDGE SUMMIT, PA 17214

To Beverly

FIRST EDITION

FIRST PRINTING

Copyright © 1984 by TAB BOOKS Inc.
Printed in the United States of America

Library of Congress Cataloging in Publication Data

Gibilisco, Stan
Violent weather.

Bibliography: p.
Includes index.

1. Weather—Popular works. 2. Storms—Popular works.
I. Title.
QC981.2.G53 1984   551.5′5   84-8873
ISBN 0-8306-1805-8 (pbk.)

Cover photograph courtesy of NOAA.

Contents

Acknowledgments

I wish to thank the following people and institutions for their help in obtaining photographs for this book: the Hansen Planetarium; Edmund Scientific Company; the National Oceanic and Atmospheric Administration; the National Hurricane Center; the Environmental Research Laboratory; the National Aeronautics and Space Administration; the United States Naval Observatory; the Rochester, Minnesota, *Post-Bulletin*; Gary Campisi of Omaha, Nebraska; and my relatives and parents. I also want to thank my wife Beverly for her emotional support and tolerance while I wrote this book.

Introduction

When we think of the inconvenience, destruction, and death that weather has dealt the human race, it seems ironic that we owe our existence to bad weather.

Many millions of years ago, the climate on the earth was moderate. The earth's interior, and its atmosphere, had stabilized. Life developed, and the dominant dinosaurs evolved. The dinosaurs were perfectly suited to the habitat of Planet Earth: they were the absolute biological rulers of the world. The largest mammal was about the size of a field mouse; anything bigger would have been easily seen and devoured in mindless hunger by the giant lizards.

Then something happened to the climate: it started to get cooler. Coldblooded lizards couldn't keep warm. Some of them moved toward the equator, but most died from the cold. Only a few descendants of the dinosaurs remain today in tropical and subtropical regions.

The day-to-day weather got worse. Rain and wind storms swept in from the oceans, flooding the land and stripping it of vegetation. Blizzards raged across the continents. Survival no longer required brute strength, but intelligence and dexterity. Because the mammals were warmblooded, they could survive the cold. They grew more sophisticated and diverse over the ensuing millions of years. Most scientists today believe that this evolutionary process led ultimately to homo sapiens—man. We are the product of harsh climate and severe weather.

At any given time, there are hundreds of places where the weather is foul at best. Most of the time, there is at least one hurricane raging across an ocean or hammering at the shores of an island or continent. Somewhere, somebody is shivering in a blizzard, baking in brutal heat, or cleaning up after a flash flood. We have the intelligence to survive all of these weather disasters, however; we can forecast, prepare for, and rebuild after all kinds of storms.

Our ability to forecast the weather is enhanced by the availabilty of sophisticated equipment like the radiosonde, the weather satellite, and other devices. Storm forecasting, however, is an ancient art.

A few years ago, a group of scientists discovered some wreckage on a mountain in the region of the Tigris and Euphrates rivers. The debris appeared to be the remains of a wooden boat. Who would put a boat on a mountain?

More recently, a whole city was uncovered in a valley in the same region. The city had been buried under silt for thousands of years. It seems that the silt covered up the city almost before the residents knew what was happening to them.

It is believed that in the area called Mesopotamia (now known as Turkey, Syria, and Iraq), people first began to settle in groups and grow crops rather than hunt animals and eat wild fruits. People stopped being nomadic. Vegetable food provided more calories and nutrition for a given expenditure of human effort than animal food. To grow plants for food, it was necessary to stay in one place and cities arose, making our species more vulnerable to mass destruction by natural disasters.

The buried city is believed to have been one of the first communities in the world. It was evidently also one of man's first urban areas to be destroyed by a storm. The storm was catastrophic: the rainfall must have been heavier—much heavier—than anything we have seen in modern times. The most vicious hurricane would seem like a shower by comparison to that storm.

The flood was so great that a whole city was buried under millions of tons of dirt, and a boat ran aground on a mountainside. Theologians say that the event almost destroyed mankind, and that the repercussions have been passed down to this day. Scientists won't necessarily go that far, but there is plenty of evidence that an unprecedented storm did strike the cradle of civilization.

Archeological research has revealed some astonishing facts. The people of ancient times were extremely intelligent. Thousands of years ago, Eratosthenes believed that the earth was round, and accurately measured its diameter. The people of ancient Egypt had calendars as accurate, or more so, than ours today, in spite of our atomic clocks, massive telescopes, and other sophisticated instruments.

It is not unreasonable to suppose that somebody in Mesopotamia, several thousand years ago, was able to forecast the weather. Maybe there were numerous adept meteorologists. It seems they thought there was going to be a lot of rain, and they were right! Scientific evidence supports the theory that some people knew what was about to happen. They survived. Someone, or some group of people, built a boat that ended up on the side of a mountain.

History is full of stories about floods, hurricanes, blizzards, and other natural temper tantrums. Bad weather, in some form, is part of the climate of every place in the world. No place on Earth is paradise—at least from a meteorological standpoint.

There is good reason to believe, as we have just seen, that our weather is gentler than it was a few millenia ago. Still further back in time, when the earth had not yet settled down following the creation of the solar system, the weather was unimaginably violent. Today, we can survive a hurricane, tornado, blizzard, flood, or drought. We might not have lived through the tempest that destroyed Mesopotamia, and we certainly could not have endured the conditions on this planet a billion years ago. What will the future bring? Will things keep getting better, or will they again become adverse?

This book is about bad weather. It is about storms of all kinds, as well as prolonged weather problems such as droughts, floods, cold spells, and heat waves. We should be concerned about adverse weather, since man evolved because of it, and has died because of it.

You will see how the sun, air, water, and movement of the earth influence our weather. You will see what conditions favor good weather and what brings bad weather. You will see how we can forecast a storm hours or days before it strikes.

We will look into the mysteries of one of the most dreaded of all storms, the hurricane. Hurricanes have changed the course of events from the time of the wars between the Japanese and the Mongol Empire, and they still inflict destruction on us today. There will be more killer hurricanes before we learn how—or if—we should try to stop them.

What causes severe thunderstorms? You will find out why they occur, and when and where they are likely to form. You will see how you can protect yourselves against hail, high winds, and lightning.

Tornadoes are the most violent of all storms. They can reduce a building to a pile of rubble in seconds. How and when do tornadoes form? How can we protect ourselves from their winds and pressure changes? What is it like to be struck by a tornado and survive the experience? We will look at the causes and the sometimes bizarre effects of these storms.

The weather of winter and spring does not have the concentrated violence that the winds of hurricanes and tornadoes do. Blizzards and other widespread storms, however, while not always getting a lot of publicity, cause much hardship to people in the temperate latitudes. You will find out what causes winter and spring storms, and what you can do to protect yourselves and your property against them.

Prolonged heat, cold, wet, or dry spells can do more damage than the worst storm. Long-term bad weather is not as immediately dramatic as the storms, but the cost is often far greater. Even today, millions of people face starvation in Africa because of drought, and the continents of North America and Asia are suffering from prolonged and repeated cold, dry weather.

What will happen in the next decade, century, millenium, or era to the weather on our planet? Can we survive? We should be confident that we can. Our species grew up with bad weather. You will find out what various scientists think will happen to our climate in the coming ages. Climatic change is slow; that fact may bring us some comfort, but we should consider the long-term situation.

We would not exist if there were no bad weather. That is what makes intelligence evolve. We worry about the weather, and we have good reasons for worrying. Our predecessors did the same. That is why we are here now.

Chapter 1

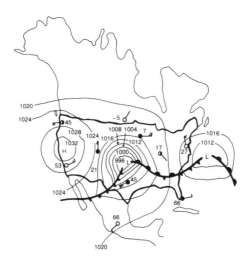

Winds and Clouds

In many ways, we are like dwellers on an ocean floor. We carry on our lives at the bottom of a dense, swirling, sometimes dangerous sea consisting of about 78 percent nitrogen, 21 percent oxygen, and 1 percent other substances like carbon dioxide, argon, neon, water vapor, dust, and various natural and manmade pollutants. The sea of air rises thousands of feet—many miles, in fact—above our heads. The sea of air gives us life; we could not survive more than a few seconds outside of it. The sea of air may also take life from us. It can dry or batter our food crops or flood our homes. It can freeze our skin or make us burn with fever. It can bury us with ice crystals, tear apart our places of shelter, and jolt us with thousands of volts of electricity. The sea of air is turbulent and sometimes perilous.

Our earth is a stormy place. We have all had some dramatic weather-related experience. Those who live in the center of a continent are familiar with the blizzards of winter and the droughts and violent storms of summer. Coastal dwellers know the fury of storms that come from the great saltwater expanse and batter the shore with wind and waves. Those who dwell at lower latitudes know the brutal heat and dryness of the desert, or the violent whirlwinds that come from the tropics. High-latitude inhabitants must deal with the variability of their seasons from short spells of day long warmth to months of cold. Severe weather exists, in some form, everywhere on earth; no place on this planet is heaven.

SIGNS OF A TEMPEST

Until recent decades, we have had almost no understanding of the idiosyncrasies of that turbulent sea of air we live beneath. Before the advent of sophisticated instruments for observing weather phenomena and effects, some people who had dwelt for many years in a particular place became familiar with the weather patterns and developed an innate ability to forecast storms. A thermometer, a barometer, and a keen sense of direction were their only means of sensing changes that might foretell an approaching tempest.

You can buy a barometer in a department store for a few dollars, listen to your favorite radio station or watch the 6 o'clock news and weather, and set the barometer according to the latest data from the National Weather Service. If the barometer suddenly falls, you might suspect that a storm is coming. Actually, the barometer is one of the oldest storm-forecasting instruments, and mariners have used them for centuries. A barometer works because all storms are associated with areas of low pressure: pockets in which the air is rarefied. As the low-pressure center approaches, the barometer reading falls.

Even without a barometer, you can often tell when a storm is approaching. The wind changes direction in front of a low-pressure system. In the tropics of the northern hemisphere, the prevailing east wind turns and blows from a northerly quarter. At northern temperate latitudes, the west wind shifts and comes from the south or southeast; this is called a *backing wind.* It turns counterclockwise.

In the southern hemisphere, the wind also shifts in front of a storm, but in the opposite direction; an east wind becomes southerly, and a west wind shifts to a north wind. The shift is not counterclockwise, or backing; it is clockwise, or *veering.* Mariners who crossed the equator were befuddled by this apparent contradiction for many years. Why should the wind foretell fair weather, but the barometer warn of foul weather? Some seamen died in the process of finding out.

An approaching storm system is often indicated by rising temperature and humidity, but not always. The appearance of high, thin clouds, gradually becoming lower and thicker, portends disturbed weather, but some storms show no such warning signals. The rate of cloud movement may increase or decrease, but the barometer always falls.

Weather experts, or *meteorologists,* have more sophisticated apparatus for forecasting the weather. Satellites continually orbit the earth, their television cameras scanning the surface for signs of storms. Large storm systems, which may harbor violent thundershowers, tornadoes, high winds, heavy snows, or other adverse conditions, have a characteristic signature that the meteorologist recognizes immediately.

As a storm system comes near a weather station, the meteorologist can look at it with a radar set. Large balloons, equipped with instruments to measure temperature, humidity, pressure, wind direction, and wind speed, can be sent aloft to detect atmospheric changes that might indicate severe or inclement weather on the way. Daring pilots can fly their aircraft into a storm and see for themselves how bad it is. Meteorologists in various cities share their information, and from this combined effort intricate diagrams are made, showing the currents, temperature regions, pressure zones, and other details of the sea of air.

By using all of our weather instruments, and by gathering together all of the data that we have obtained over several decades, we are beginning to get familiar with how our sea of air behaves. There are large-scale air currents and small-scale air currents; the large-scale patterns are relatively constant, while the small-scale ones can change in days, hours, or minutes. All of the weather that affects us—hurricanes, tornadoes, blizzards, and droughts—occurs within about 10 miles of the surface of the earth, but our weather is ultimately generated by forces and influences that extend far into space.

THE DEPTH OF THE AIR

In the seventeenth century, an inventor named *Evangelista Torricelli* built a device that demonstrated how the air exerts pressure on everything. Torricelli built a *mercurial barometer.* You may have seen this device, or even built one in a science class. A simple mercurial barometer can be constructed from a glass tube closed off at one end, a small flask, and a quantity of mercury (Fig. 1-1).

Torricelli believed that a 50-mile-high sea of air caused the pressure that supported the mercury column. Today, we know that this is true. While our sea of air does not abruptly end at an altitude of 50 miles—it has no well-defined "surface"—we know that it does exist in rarefied form even at heights greater than 50 miles. Scientists define the atmosphere in terms of layers (Fig. 1-2).

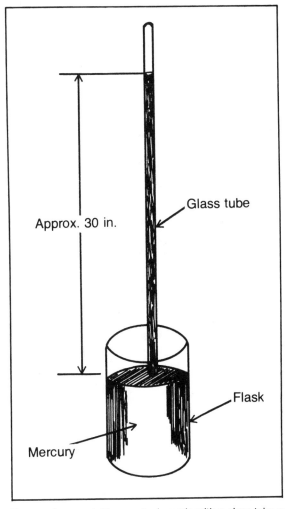

Fig. 1-1. A mercurial barometer is made with a glass tube a little over 30 inches long, a flask, and some mercury.

Interplanetary space is an almost perfect vacuum. There are some molecules, sparsely distributed, but the pressure is practically zero. These molecules are in constant, rapid motion, heated by the radiation from the sun. This region is called the *exosphere*, which means "outside the sphere." The exosphere is not really part of the atmosphere of our planet. Some of the molecules in our atmosphere do, however, come from space. They are captured by the gravitational field of our planet. Other molecules escape from our atmosphere into the exosphere.

At an altitude of about 250 to 300 miles, the near vacuum of the exosphere gives way to a slightly increased concentration of gases. These gases exist largely in the form of ions. The high-energy ultraviolet and X-rays from the sun cause the electrons to wander from atom to atom. Some atoms have too many electrons, and others have too few; so the air at high levels is electrically charged. This region is known as the *ionosphere*. It extends down to an altitude of about 40 miles.

The ionization at altitudes of 40 to 300 miles is not observed at all levels. Instead, it tends to occur in layers. Four discrete layers of ionization are recognized; they are called the D, E, F1, and F2 regions, as shown in Fig. 1-2. (Some evidence exists that there might be a fifth, thin layer above the 300-mile level, which has been called the G layer.) It is these zones of ionized air that cause radio waves to be returned to the earth on the shortwave frequencies.

If the solar radiation becomes extremely strong, the ionosphere glows above the magnetic poles. In North America, we sometimes see this glow at night, and call it the *aurora borealis* or *northern lights*. In the southern hemisphere it is called the *aurora australis*. The ionosphere does not have weather as we know it, although the aurora is a sort of storm consisting of highly agitated atoms.

Below the ionospheric D layer, extending down to an altitude of about 10 miles, is the *stratosphere*. The air here is free from the turbulence generated by the storms at the surface, and it is also free from the ion activity that dominates at higher levels. There are winds in the stratosphere, however, which have been detected by high-flying aircraft and weather balloons. Little is known about the air currents in the stratosphere, but they sometimes have a profound effect on weather at the earth's surface.

After a great volcanic eruption, fine particles of dust are blown into the stratosphere, where they circulate for months or even years. This dust reflects some of the light and heat from the sun, cooling the earth. A large eruption in Mexico, in 1982, may be partially responsible for the exceptionally severe winter of 1983-1984 in the midwestern United States and Canada. Volcanic dust in the stratosphere has been blamed for the famous cold summer of 1816, when frosts coated New England at least once during every month, and snows fell as late as June. (In the event of a large-scale nuclear war, radioactive fallout might be blown into the stratosphere in much the same way, settling back to the earth over a period of several years. This could pose a long-term threat to many forms of life on the planet we call home.) The stratosphere may have no weather of its own, but it affects the weather at the floor of the sea of air.

At the bottom of the stratosphere, high-speed air currents circle the globe. These wind bands dictate whether your winter will be warm or cold, and whether your summer will be wet or dry. During and after World War II, high-flying aircraft encountered extreme headwinds or tailwinds, with speeds that reached more than 200 miles per hour.

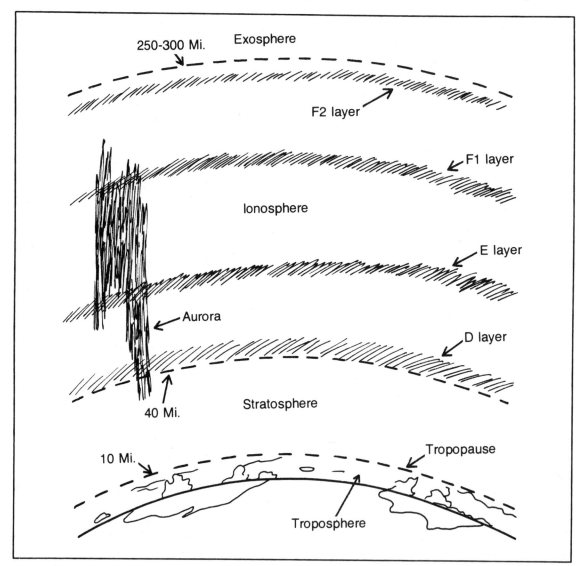

Fig. 1-2. The atmosphere is about 300 miles thick. All of the weather occurs in the lower 10 miles, or troposphere.

Pilots learned how to avoid these westerly winds when flying west, and how to take advantage of them when traveling east. Because of their influence on airplanes, and jets in particular, these wind bands have become known as the *jet streams*. I will have more to say about jet streams later in this chapter.

Below the stratosphere, extending to ground level, is the part of our atmosphere where storms rage. This layer is called the *troposphere*. The boundary between the troposphere and the stratosphere is sometimes called the *tropopause*. Clouds boil up in the troposphere, fed by hot, rising air from the surface, and sometimes reaching all the way to the tropopause and the jet streams. These great clouds, called *cumulonimbus*, produce heavy rain, hail, high winds, lightning, and tornadoes at the bottom of our ocean of air.

AIR CIRCULATION AROUND THE WORLD

There would be no weather if our planet had no atmosphere; no winds could blow, no rain could fall. There would likewise be no weather if the earth received no heat from the sun. The sun warms the earth to a greater extent in some areas than in others, and the air seeks to equalize this imbalance by *convection*. This is what makes the winds and clouds.

The equatorial regions of the world receive more heat from the sun than they can radiate back into space. The polar areas are just the opposite: they radiate more energy than they get from the sun. The polar/equatorial temperature difference is the result of the astronomical fact that the sun's average angle is more direct at the equator than at the poles. Thus the polar regions have become ice shrouded, and the equatorial zone has not. The different surface characteristics increase the temperature differential still further: snow and ice reflect much solar energy and absorb little, while vegetation and dark soil reflect little energy and absorb much.

If the air did not act to equalize this temperature discrepancy, at least to some extent, the tropics would glow red hot, and the poles would be incredibly frigid. Figure 1-3 shows a simple model to explain how the air transports heat. The air over the tropics, especially near the equator, is heated in contact with the earth. Therefore, it rises, because warm air always rises. The air over the arctic and antarctic is cooled by contact with the cold surface, and thus it falls, because cold air always descends. The result is that air flows from the poles toward the equator along the planet's surface, and from the equator toward the poles at high altitudes.

According to the model of Fig. 1-3, we should expect to have a prevailing northerly surface wind in the northern hemisphere, and a prevailing southerly surface wind in the southern hemisphere, with no surface winds at the equator or at either pole. This is not what we observe, however, because Fig. 1-3 is an oversimplification. The air flow around the earth is affected not only by temperature differences, but by geography and the fact that the earth rotates on its axis.

In the actual atmosphere, there are three major convection zones in each hemisphere, rather than the one shown in Fig. 1-3. This occurs because the convection pattern of Fig. 1-3 is inherently unstable. Ascending air is found at or near the equator and at about 60 degrees north and south latitude. These areas are semipermanent low-pressure systems, and the weather is characterized by abundant cloudiness and rainfall. Descending air is found at or near the poles and at about 30 degrees north and south latitude. The descending air results in semipermanent high-pressure systems, with comparatively fair weather. This convection pattern, neglecting the effects of the earth's rotation, is shown in Fig. 1-4.

The pattern at Fig. 1-4 is still an oversimplification of actual matters. The earth does rotate, and the rate of rotation is rapid enough to greatly alter the wind direction. In the northern hemisphere, the winds are turned toward the right; in the southern hemisphere, the winds are turned toward the left. This occurs because of the *Coriolis force* or *Coriolis effect,* which is observed on any rotating sphere.

CORIOLIS FORCE

The earth is roughly spherical in shape. It turns once on its axis in approximately 24 hours.

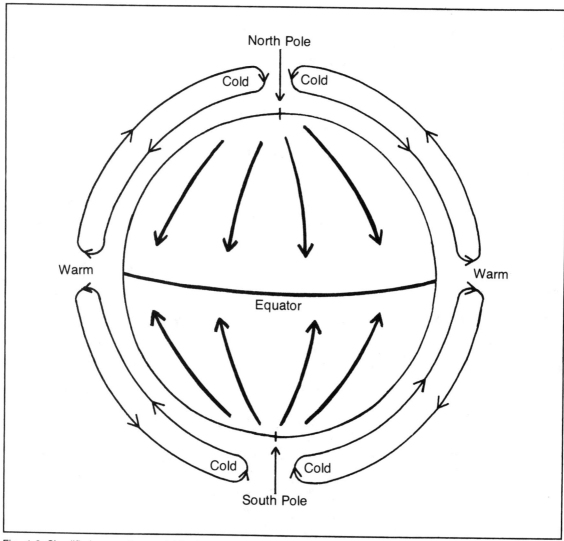

Fig., 1-3. Simplified convection model for the atmosphere. Heavy arrows show surface winds.

The *angular speed* of the earth is 360 degrees per 24 hours; this amounts to 1 degree every 4 minutes. The angular speed of the earth is independent of latitude; any point on the earth's surface makes one complete rotation around the axis every 24 hours, but the actual speed at which a point on the earth moves, from west to east, depends on its latitude.

If you were to stand at the North Pole or the South Pole, you would not move at all as the earth spins. If you were to stand at the equator, you would whiz along at about 1,040 miles per hour. At 45 degrees north or south latitude, the ground moves along at about 740 miles per hour. The lower the latitude, the faster the actual speed of the earth— and of the atmosphere near the earth. If the earth were to suddenly stop spinning, you would probably not notice it at all if you were standing at the pole, but at the equator, there would be a great gust of wind from the west, as well as other inertial effects which you can no doubt imagine.

Between the equator and about 30 degrees north latitude, the air at the surface tends to flow toward the equator, from a zone of relatively high pressure to a zone of lower pressure. The same thing happens between the equator and 30 degrees south latitude. As the air reaches progressively lower latitudes, the tangential speed of the earth's surface increases. Therefore, the air tends to drag toward the west, because the earth is speeding up underneath it. We find easterly winds in the tropics for this reason.

Between about 30 and 60 degrees north or south latitude, the air at the surface tends to flow away from the equator and toward the pole, from the 30-degree high-pressure belt toward the 60-degree low-pressure belt. As the air moves poleward, the earth slows down underneath it. Thus, the air races out ahead of the earth, in the same direction the planet rotates. We find westerly winds at the temperate latitudes.

Between 60 degrees north or south latitude and the pole, the air flow is generally away from the

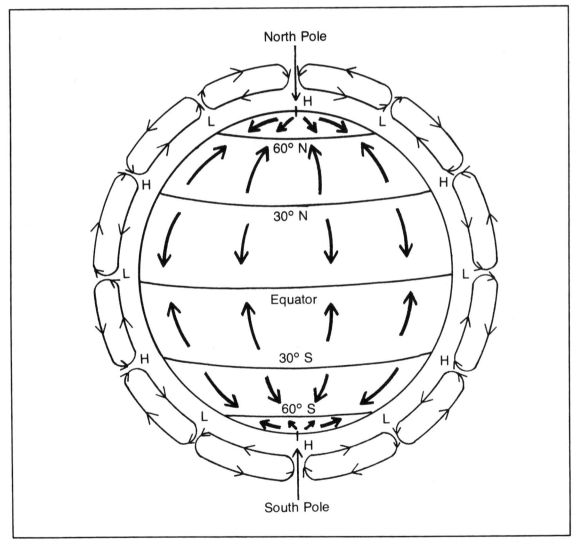

Fig. 1-4. Convection model for the actual atmosphere, neglecting the effects of the earth's rotation. Heavy arrows show surface winds.

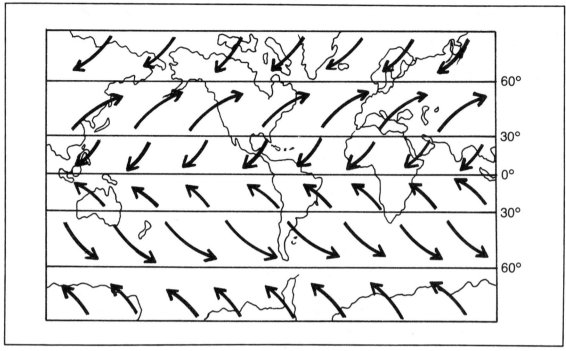

Fig. 1-5. General wind circulation, considering the effects of the earth's rotation.

pole. The effect here is the same as it is in the tropics; the earth speeds up under the air as it flows into lower latitudes. We find easterly winds in the arctic and antarctic.

The prevailing winds of the tropics, the temperate zones, and the polar regions sometimes shift because of changes in the locations of the pressure belts. In general, however, the tropics and polar regions have east winds, called *trade winds* or *polar easterlies,* and the temperate zones have west winds, or *prevailing westerlies.* This six-belt pattern is illustrated in Fig. 1-5.

The Coriolis force is responsible for more than the deflection of the prevailing winds into east-west paths. This force can, at times, cause the air to twist into a *vortex.* Sometimes the vortex is a huge, slow-turning frontal cyclone, covering millions of square miles. Sometimes the vortex is a medium-sized, fast-turning storm called a hurricane, typhoon, cyclone, or willy-willy (depending where in the world you happen to live). Sometimes the vortex is a small, incredibly violent maelstrom called a tornado or twister. All rotating storms get their

spin from the Coriolis force.

You have probably noticed the Coriolis force as you finish a bath. If you haven't, take a bath and watch the little tornadoes form and dissipate over the drain as you let the water out of the tub. At first, the tornadoes form hesitantly, appearing almost threadlike, snaking around and dissipating quickly. As the water level gets lower, the intermittent vortices become a continuous mini-tornado, widening and becoming straighter. Finally, the spiral becomes very wide and low. These vortices behave very much like real tornadoes. They are so similar, in fact, that scientists have used water tubs, equipped with special drains, in storm reasearch.

If you ever get the opportunity to take a bath at the equator, you will find that vortices hardly ever form over the drain of the tub as you let the water out; when vortices do form, they are short-lived and weak. In the northern hemisphere, the vortices will almost always turn counterclockwise, although a few go clockwise. In the southern hemisphere, the vortices almost always turn clockwise. The same is true of tornadoes and waterspouts. It would seem that atmospheric cyclones are governed by the same forces as are bathtub vortices.

Why does the water spiral around as it goes down the drain of your tub? It happens for the same reason that frontal cyclones, hurricanes, and tornadoes rotate: Coriolis force. No matter how small or large the scale, this force is always present. Miami, Florida, moves around the earth's axis more rapidly than Nome, Alaska. South Miami moves faster than North Miami, and the southern edge of your bathtub drain moves faster than the northern edge.

If you look closely at Fig. 1-5, you will notice something peculiar about the wind at the 30-degree and 60-degree latitudes, both in the northern hemisphere and in the southern hemisphere. The winds blow in opposite directions on either side of these latitude lines, giving the air an incentive to spiral around—clockwise at 30 degrees north and at 60 degrees south, and counterclockwise at 60 degrees north and at 30 degrees south. The air also spins around the poles, clockwise in the arctic and counterclockwise in the Antarctic. These latitudes are characterized by persistent eddies of air. The eddies at the 60th parallel, north and south, pull air inward, and the vortices near the 30th parallel and the north and south poles throw air outward.

Figure 1-5 is a generalization of the actual way our atmosphere circulates, but even this view is a bit too simple. Because of the tendency of the air to rotate near 30, 60, and 90 degrees north and south latitude, we find persistent cyclonic and anticyclonic vortices on our planet. The *cyclonic vortices* are known as semipermanent lows; the *anticyclonic vortices* are called semipermanent highs. Figure 1-6 shows the approximate locations of these vast weather systems. (The polar highs are not shown because of the nature of the map projection.)

SEMIPERMANENT LOWS AND HIGHS

The equator has abundant rainfall because of persistent low pressure. The equatorial low is also known as the *intertropical convergence zone (ITCZ)*. The ITCZ extends around the globe in an unbroken, sinuous band. It does not rotate because there is little or no Coriolis acceleration at low latitudes. The ITCZ moves north of the equator during the

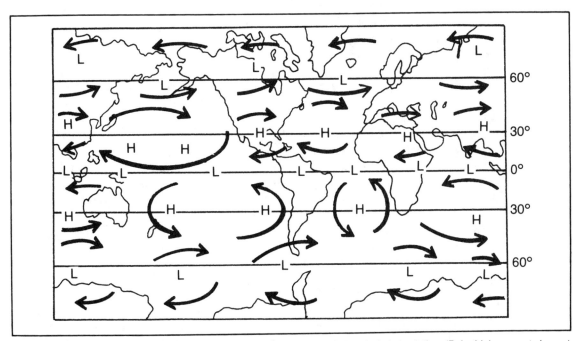

Fig. 1-6. Actual semipermanent highs and lows of the world and the associated wind circulation. (Polar highs are not shown.)

northern summer and south of the equator during the southern summer, except in the Atlantic Ocean where it remains just north of the equator all year long.

The equatorial climate is cloudy and wet most of the time because of the upward air movement in the ITCZ. Much of the world's thundershower activity occurs here. The ITCZ is thought by some meteorologists to generate the tropical depressions, storms, and hurricanes that have battered subtropical coasts since the beginning of history. If the ITCZ moves exceptionally far—10 or 15 degrees of latitude—from the equator in some part of the world, the Coriolis acceleration can twist it into a tight vortex. This spinning system attains an identity of its own, and if it gets intense enough, we call it a tropical storm and give it a name.

The earth has regions in which high atmospheric pressure prevails. These areas have fair weather most of the time. These high-pressure regions are found in the Arctic and Antarctic, and near 30 dgrees north and south latitude.

The world's great deserts are found near 30 degrees north latitude: in northern Africa, southern California, Arizona, New Mexico, Texas, the Middle East, most of Australia, and the highlands of Tibet. This is the result of the continual high pressure in these places. The polar regions are also extremely dry; some scientists consider the Arctic and Antarctic to be the greatest of all deserts.

The Azores-Bermuda high-pressure system in the North Atlantic is well known in the United States. Its effects are especially felt during summer, when hot southwesterly winds blow along the Atlantic coast, and wet easterly and southeasterly winds produce the rainy season in Florida and along the coast of the Gulf of Mexico. Similar high-pressure zones are found in the South Atlantic, the Indian Ocean, the North Pacific, and the South Pacific. The terrible hurricanes and typhoons, which are small low-pressure systems, follow the peripheral circulation of the great oceanic highs. Hurricane forecasters in the United States keep a close eye on the position, shape, and strength of the Azores-Bermuda high during the storm season of June through November.

The semipermanent oceanic highs were well known to those who sailed between Europe and the New World or the Orient. Seamen, becalmed in the hot, fair weather near 30 degrees north or south latitude, sometimes remained motionless for days. Rations ran short. The men got hungry and began to eat the food intended for the horses they had brought with them. The horses had to be thrown overboard. Even today, you occasionally hear of the "horse latitudes."

A set of intense, persistent low-pressure systems dominates the climate of the world near 60 degrees north and south latitude. These great lows spawn the frontal cyclones that sweep from west to east across the continents at temperate latitudes. One such low, which is largely responsible for the changeable weather in the United States and Canada, is called the *Aleutian low*, since it is centered just off the southern coast of Alaska. The Aleutian low brings moist ocean air eastward, where it meets the mountains of the Pacific Northwest and produces the heavy rains and snows that people in this area know so well. In winter, the Aleutian low generates frontal cyclones in a seemingly endless procession, drenching the west coast of North America with one storm after another. Some of these cyclones rival hurricanes in size and intensity.

Another well-known semipermanent low exists near Greenland and Iceland. This low, like its Aleutian cousin, hurls smaller, frontal cyclones toward the east and southeast. The *Greenland-Iceland low* intensifies during the fall and winter, and the climate of Europe is not unlike that of the Pacific Northwest during these months. Some winter gales in England, like their counterparts in the Pacific Northwest, produce devastating floods and damaging winds.

The Aleutian and Icelandic lows, although well known, cannot rival the chain of semipermanent cyclonic systems that dominate the southern hemisphere between 40 and 70 degrees south latitude. The Tierra del Fuego region, at the southernmost tip of South America, is almost constantly blasted by gales. The stormy strait of Magellan, named after the European explorer who sailed through the region on his quest to circumnavigate the world, is still feared by sailors today.

The westerly winds of the southern hemisphere blow almost unimpeded around the globe between 40 and 50 degrees south latitude, earning this region the nickname "the roaring forties." The air circulates clockwise around the northern edges of the intense semipermanent lows to the south. On the bleak, snowy coasts of Antarctica, cyclonic winds have been known to reach speeds of 200 miles per hour in late autumn and early winter, when the semipermanent low-pressure circulation reaches its greatest intensity. It is little wonder that our race has never tried to set up a civilization there!

The low-pressure region around 60 degrees north latitude is the source of most of the weather *fronts* that make our weather change so markedly from day to day. *Frontal cyclones* constantly sweep around the earth from west to east in the temperate latitudes of the northern hemisphere. Figure 1-7A is a satellite view of our planet as seen from high above the North Pole. The storms move counterclockwise with the circulation to the south of the semipermanent low at about 60 degrees latitude.

In the southern hemisphere, the pattern is very much the same. The southern hemisphere contains much less land area at temperate latitudes, and far fewer people experience the effects of frontal cyclones in this part of the world. The pattern is, nevertheless, almost the same as in the northern hemisphere. The circulation is clockwise around the globe as seen from far away in space (Fig. 1-7B).

A temperate frontal cyclone can produce severe thunderstorms in the summer months, accompanied by hail, strong winds, torrential rains, and tornadoes. In winter, frontal cyclones intensify and spread their power over a larger area, causing ice storms, blizzards, and bitter cold temperatures, as well as prolonged heavy rains. The frontal cyclones are the largest storm systems on our planet, in terms of total energy and size. During its lifetime, a frontal cyclone will expend as much energy as the greatest hurricane. A single system can affect the whole United States at once. There may be heavy snow in Wisconsin; high winds and rain along the eastern seaboard; tornadoes in Georgia and Alabama; and cold, windy weather in the western states—all because of a single frontal cyclone.

JET STREAMS AND THE POLAR FRONT

The general circulation around the semipermanent lows is counterclockwise in the northern hemisphere and clockwise in the southern. The air circulation around the highs is just the opposite resulting in a west-to-east flow in the temperate latitudes, with which most of us are familiar. The semipermanent lows near 60 degrees latitude are in constant competition with the highs near 30 degrees latitude. The lows dominate the weather much of the time between 45 and 60 degrees latitude; the highs control the weather much of the time between 30 and 45 degrees. The dividing line, or boundary, between the influence of low and high pressure is quite sharp, and it changes position with the seasons.

During the Pacific battles of World War II, aviators occasionally found themselves moving unusually fast or slowly. This effect was quite dramatic at times; the air speed was different from the ground speed by as much as 200 miles per hour. These aviators had discovered the *jet stream*. Today, airliners flying in the middle latitudes are sometimes considerably ahead of schedule or behind schedule because of the jet stream, which flows from west to east and marks the boundary between the semipermanent pressure systems. The jet stream is recognized as a major factor that contributes to our weather. North of the jet stream in the northern hemisphere, polar air masses dominate, and south of the jet stream, tropical air prevails. The situation is reversed in the southern hemisphere. A semipermanent front encircles the whole planet near 45 degrees north latitude. A similar front exists near 45 degrees south latitude.

The jet streams flow at an altitude of several miles and vary greatly in width and speed. The jet streams do not flow straight around the world at the 45th north and south parallels; instead, they meander and change position constantly. In either hemisphere, the semipermanent cold front, called

Fig. 1-7A. The northern hemisphere as it would be seen from high above the north pole.

Fig. 1-7B. A similar view of the southern hemisphere (courtesy U.S. Department of Commerce, NOAA).

the polar front, makes unending attempts to invade the tropics, pushing the jet stream toward the equator. The tropical air fights back, however, limiting the progress of the polar front. The tropical air may even conduct its own invasions, causing the jet stream to move toward the pole. Neither air mass ever wins this perpetual war; the jet stream is caught in the middle.

The polar front generally changes position almost every day. The polar air mass expands during the winter months and shrinks in the summer, as we would expect. The jet stream thus lies closer to the equator in the winter than in the summer. Much of the United States and all of Canada are in the grip of the severe polar air mass during the winter. Most of Europe and much of Asia suffer the same fate. In the southern hemisphere, much less land area is invaded by the polar front from Antarctica, but this is simply because most of the inhabited lands in that hemisphere lie far from the pole. The notable exception is the tip of South America, where the windy, rainy, raw climate bears testimony to the power of the south polar air mass.

Sometimes certain areas are spared the domination of the polar air mass for weeks or even months during the winter season. Then the people say they are having a warm winter. A "January thaw" takes place, and they might even get "spring fever!" Then the jet stream shifts position and temperatures drop again, sometimes by as much as 80 degrees Fahrenheit in a single day.

At other times, the polar front moves unusually close to the equator in a particular part of the world, and a prolonged cold wave occurs, pushing the thermometer to record low readings. An event of this type occurred in December, 1983, during one of the most severe early winters on record. The midwestern United States had readings that stayed below zero for days in a row. Heating bills skyrocketed. In Florida and Texas, oranges froze. In Miami, people had basked in warm sunshine all month until Christmas, when they woke up to find a bitter wind blasting down from the north.

The polar front, like an army, does not invade the tropics everywhere at the same time. The United States may suffer while Europe stays comfortable. While Anchorage, Alaska, experiences record high temperatures, New York City might register a high of zero degrees Fahrenheit for the day. On the morning of December 26, 1983, the temperature in Miami, Florida, was colder than it was in Moscow, U.S.S.R. The jet stream dipped toward the south over the United States, forming what meteorologists call a *trough* (Fig. 1-8A).

A similar war of the air masses takes place in the summer, except that the tropical air goes on the offensive. The cold polar front reverses and becomes a warm tropical front. The warm air conducts its invasion in a less forceful, but often more persistent, manner than the polar air. The jet stream is therefore more stable in summer than in winter. The southern United States, and much of southern Europe, settles into a weather pattern that stays fairly constant from early June through August and into September.

At times, the tropical air pushes the jet stream unusually far toward the pole, and a large part of North America or Europe stays under its influence for weeks. The jet stream moves along with the tropical front over the land, and forms what meteorologists call a *ridge* (Fig. 1-8B). The barometric pressure rises and stays high. The weather becomes hot—sometimes dangerously hot. This kind of situation dominated the summer weather during 1983, pushing temperatures to all-time record highs and drying out farm crops.

Meanders in the Jet Stream

Why does the jet stream flow in such an irregular way? Why doesn't it just go straight around the world at one latitude? The instability of the jet stream is controlled by the same force that makes the air spiral around low and high pressure centers.

Scientists have conducted an experiment to demonstrate this effect, using a rotating dish pan, ice, water, and a heating element. *The dish pan is filled with water of a moderate temperature. A

---

*This experiment, and the theory involved, is described in detail by E. R. Reiter in his book *Jet Streams* (Doubleday & Co., Inc., 1967), pp. 107-112 and Plates VIII and IX.

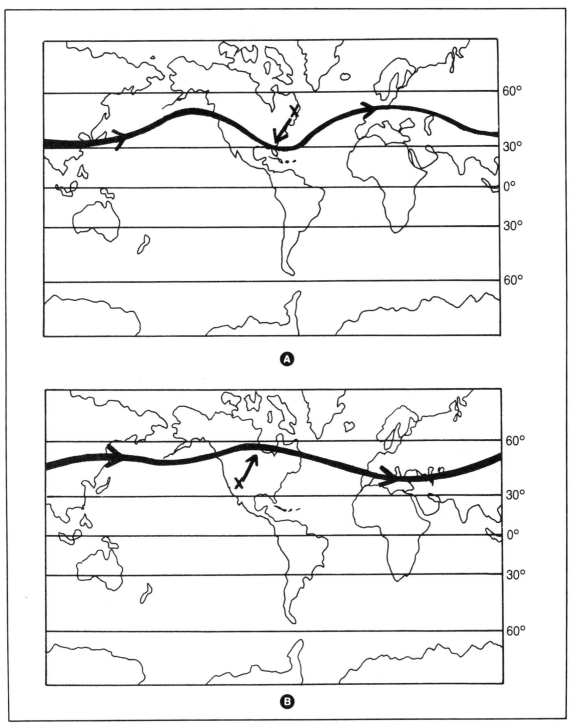

Fig. 1-8. At A, a jet stream trough produces a cold wave over much of the United States. At B, a jet stream ridge is responsible for prolonged hot spells.

container of ice water is placed at the center of the pan, and the heating element is placed under the periphery of the pan, all the way around (Fig. 1-9). This sets up a battle between cold water and hot water. Sawdust, or some other fine substance that will float, is sprinkled on the surface of the water, facilitating observation of the water circulation. The dish pan is then spun around.

Although the dish pan is disk-shaped, and not spherical like the earth, the forces imposed on the water are very similar to the forces that occur in the atmosphere of our planet. The center of the dish pan just rotates, as does the pole of the earth. The outer edge of the pan has considerable speed, as does the equator. The dish pan develops its own little jet stream somewhere between the center and the periphery, and it flows in the direction of rotation, as can be seen by watching the sawdust. If the dishpan is rotated fast enough the little jet stream develops irregularities that greatly resemble the meanders of the real jet stream. The warm peripheral water and the cold central water carry on an unending struggle.

If the temperature of the heating element is increased, simulating the conditions of summer, the jet stream becomes smaller, moving in toward the center of the dish pan. If the heat is turned down and extra ice is placed in the container at the center,

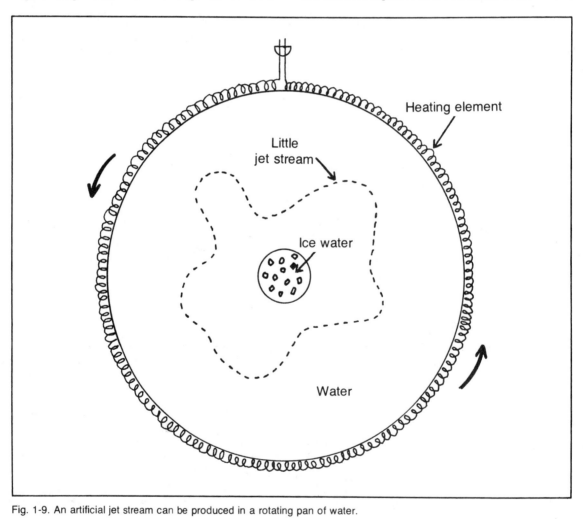

Fig. 1-9. An artificial jet stream can be produced in a rotating pan of water.

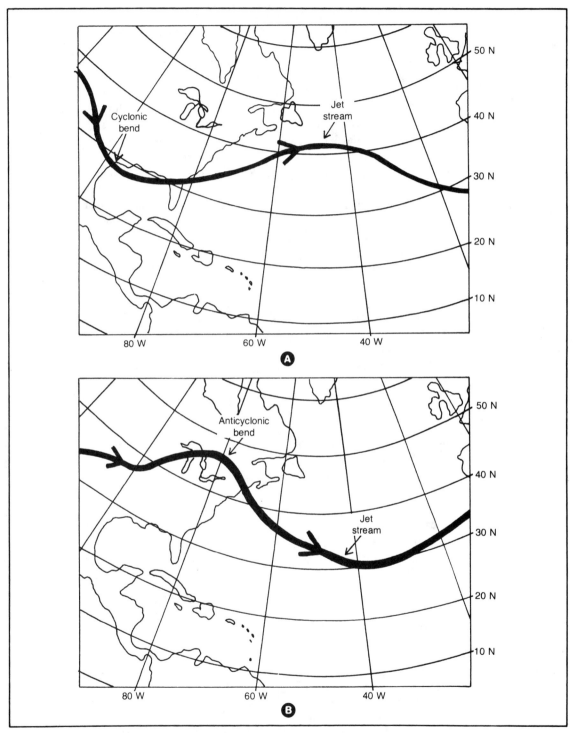

Fig. 1-10. At A, a cyclonic bend in the jet stream. At B, an anticyclonic bend.

the little jet stream moves toward the periphery of the pan, just as the real jet stream moves toward the equator in the winter.

The jet stream flows in an irregular way because of inherent instability that results from the rotation of the earth. The bends in the jet stream are called *cyclonic* if they turn toward the left (counterclockwise) in the northern hemisphere or toward the right (clockwise) in the southern hemisphere. A bend is termed *anticyclonic* if it turns toward the right in the northern hemisphere, or toward the left in the southern hemisphere. When the polar air mass pushes toward the equator, a cyclonic bend is produced in the jet stream; when the tropical air mass advances on the pole, an anticyclonic bend is produced. Figure 1-10 illustrates these types of situations as they occur in the northern hemisphere.

Cold low-pressure systems that exist on the poleward side of a cyclonic trough in the jet stream tend to be stable and persistent. The same is true of warm high-pressure systems that exist on the equator side of an anticyclonic ridge. Troughs and ridges can form over the oceans or over the continents. The general tendency is for persistent ridges to develop over the oceans during winter and over land in the summer. Troughs are more likely to form over the continents in the winter. The continental ridges bring warm, dry, fair weather, and sometimes they produce dreaded heat waves. Troughs generate stormy weather.

When Air is Pulled Apart

The jet stream varies in width and speed, as well as in direction. These variations cause air to be pushed together, or *compressed,* in some places causing an increase in pressure. In other places, the air is pulled apart, and the pressure goes down. Either of these situations can result from changes in the width of the jet stream, its speed, or both. When air is pushed together, it is said to be *converging;* when it is pulled apart, it is *diverging.*

Directional convergence and divergence are shown in Fig. 1-11; *speed* convergence and divergence are illustrated in Fig. 1-12. Directional effects take place only at bends in the jet stream,

but speed effects can occur whether there is a bend or not. It is divergence that makes storms, because divergence creates a drop in pressure.

If the air in a particular part of the jet stream diverges to a great enough extent, the pressure drops so much that the Coriolis force causes the air to spin. Clouds form, and the weather becomes foul. The system is carried along, from west to east, by the jet stream. Warm tropical air moves toward the pole ahead of the system, and cold polar air flows in behind the low-pressure center (Fig. 1-12). A *frontal cyclone* is born.

A frontal cyclone, also known as a *low,* can form anywhere along the jet stream, provided that there is enough divergence of the air. The most intense frontal cyclones are generated when there is not only strong divergence in the air, but also a cyclonic bend in the jet stream. If the jet stream is already turning counterclockwise when a frontal cyclone forms, the circulation is given an extra push. If an existing frontal cyclone encounters a

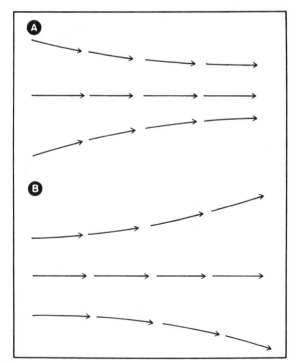

Fig. 1-11. Directional convergence (A) and divergence (B). Wind direction is shown by the arrows.

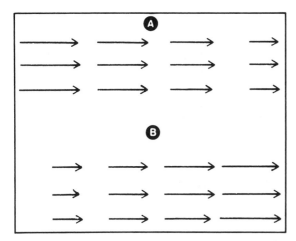

Fig. 1-12. Speed convergence (A) and divergence (B). Wind speed is indicated by the lengths of the arrows.

cyclonic bend in the jet stream, intensification is likely, and the chances of severe storms—blizzards in winter or heavy showers, hail, and tornadoes in summer—are enhanced.

Frontal cyclones are always accompanied by clouds. As a low-pressure system approaches, the first signs are usually high, thin clouds. The clouds thicken and become lower, until the sky is iron gray and rain or snow falls. If the center of a frontal cyclone in the northern hemisphere passes to the south, the weather becomes slowly chillier, and the winds shift from south to east, then to the north and northwest. If the center of the system passes polewards, the rain or snow abates; the sky clears, and the temperature rises. The wind shifts to the southwest. A day or two later, the sky becomes cloudy again. In the summer, fair-weather clouds give way to the towering thunderheads called cumulonimbus. In the winter, freezing rain or snow falls from bleak, low, fast-moving gray clouds. The temperature drops sharply as the wind shifts to the west, and then to the northwest or north. It is often possible to forecast the weather simply by recognizing the clouds and watching for changes in their thickness, altitude, and direction of movement.

TROPICAL WEATHER SYSTEMS

The mid-latitude jet stream, marking the battle front between the tropical and the polar air masses, is responsible for the changeable weather in the temperate zone. In the tropics, far from the influence of the mid-latitude jet stream, the prevailing winds are from east to west. The weather in the tropics is remarkably stable from day to day; the trade winds blow at a nearly constant speed of 10 to 20 miles per hour, and fair-weather cumulus clouds dot the sky. Near the equator, these clouds tower higher and higher, producing the daily afternoon rains of the jungle and the squally downpours of the intertropical convergence zone (ITCZ). The weather in the mid-tropical latitudes—about 10 degrees to 25 degrees north and south—is not always benign, however; the tropics are plagued by their own special breed of cyclone.

The ITCZ normally does not battle with the high-pressure air masses near 30 degrees north and south latitude, but the equator receives far more energy from the sun than it can radiate into space. Sometimes the normal atmospheric circulation is not enough to maintain equilibrium. It is then that the ITCZ makes its effects felt in the form of a *tropical cyclone.* The system begins as a trough, with cyclonic deflection of the trade winds. Clouds and rain accompany this so-called easterly wave, and the system moves from east to west.

If intensification occurs, a closed, rotating low-pressure system, called a *tropical depression,* forms, and the precipitation becomes heavier. The circulation may then become concentrated, producing the high winds and torrential rains of a tropical storm or hurricane.

Hurricanes serve a vital purpose—they help transfer heat from the equator toward the poles. Hurricanes also provide much-needed rainfall in the normally dry areas of Texas and Mexico, but the great ocean storms often inflict terrible destruction because of their high winds, which can reach sustained speeds of 200 miles per hour or more, and because of the rough and high seas that are generated by the winds and the low barometric pressure. We will look in detail at the nature of tropical cyclones in Chapter 2.

POLAR WEATHER SYSTEMS

Relatively little is known about the weather

near the poles, simply because hardly anybody lives there, or goes there to make detailed observations.

The North Pole is covered by an ocean that is completely frozen over for much of the year. The water keeps the temperature at the North Pole more moderate than at the South Pole, which lies near the center of a large continent. Although the coldest temperature in the northern hemisphere has never dipped to -100 degrees Fahrenheit, the thermometer in Antarctica has fallen to -128 degrees. This is so cold that anyone venturing outdoors must wear special protective gear like electric socks and mittens. Coffee shatters as it is poured onto concrete.

The poles are dominated by high-pressure systems. This is especially true at the landlocked South Pole. These air masses produce fair weather much of the time, along with light easterly winds. At the North Pole, the high-pressure system sometimes weakens, and the winds change or reverse direction. The sky becomes overcast, and the weather foul.

Both polar regions are characterized by very dry weather; they generally receive less than 10 inches of precipitation each year. This qualifies the Arctic and Antarctic regions as true deserts.

As we move away from either pole, we begin to encounter the effects of the low-pressure belts near 60 degrees latitude. Cloudy skies, frequent fog, and abundant precipitation occur. The winds increase in speed and become more variable. In summer, the low-pressure belt in either hemisphere moves slightly closer to the pole; in winter, it moves toward the equator.

The weather in the Arctic and Antarctic, although dominated by high pressure most of the time, is not gentle. Ask anyone who has lived for a while in the wilderness of central or northern Alaska, or who has worked at one of the scientific installations in Antarctica. Blinding snow, fierce winds, and unbelievably low temperatures are commonplace.

WEATHER MAPS

Because of the endless movement of weather systems throughout the world, especially in the temperate latitudes, conditions vary greatly from place to place. Before wire or radio communications were available, a person living in New York City could only guess at the weather in Philadelphia, Cleveland, Chicago, Minneapolis, or Omaha. Certain weather forecasting techniques were used, but the most important information—what lay to the west—could only be obtained by mail. The mail carriers could not outrun a screaming blizzard back then any more than they can today. The conditions at any given place could change within minutes.

After the telegraph was invented and wires crisscrossed the nation, connnecting the major cities, it was possible to get weather information almost instantly. Storms swirled across the Great Plains, the Ohio Valley, and into the mountains of Pennsylvania, however, they tore the wires down and surprised the inhabitants of the coast again and again. Then came the invention of the wireless telegraph. Only a few of the more violent frontal cyclones managed to rip down the massive antenna structures and cut off communications, but the sun occasionally helped by producing ionospheric disturbances, which ruined radio-propagation conditions.

Today, every city has a weather station that is linked via wire, high-frequency radio, and satellite to a central office. The meteorologist in Rochester, Minnesota, can find out in a matter of seconds what is going on in Eureka, California. The data from a particular place includes temperature, dewpoint, extent and type of cloud cover, type of precipitation (if any), wind direction, wind speed, and barometric pressure. All of this information is fed into a computer, and the computer transforms it into a detailed graphical representation of the weather over the whole country at that moment.

The conditions at each city are indicated on the weather map by a set of symbols known as a *station model*. The station model always shows the temperature, cloud cover, wind direction, and wind speed. A station model is placed on the map at the location of each major weather center. Equal pressure lines, called *isobars*, are drawn to represent various pressure levels in *millibars*. (Isobars are usually drawn at intervals of 4 millibars, equivalent

Table 1-1. Pressure in Millibars versus Inches of Mercury.

Millibars	Inches	Millibars	Inches
900	26.57	1000	29.53
904	26.69	1004	29.65
908	26.81	1008	29.76
912	26.93	1012	29.88
916	27.05	1016	30.00
920	27.17	1020	30.12
924	27.28	1024	30.24
928	27.40	1028	30.35
932	27.52	1032	30.47
936	27.64	1036	30.59
940	27.76	1040	30.71
944	27.87	1044	30.83
948	27.99	1048	30.94
952	28.11	1052	31.06
956	28.23	1056	31.18
960	28.35	1060	31.30
964	28.46	1064	31.42
968	28.58	1068	31.54
972	28.70	1072	31.65
976	28.82	1076	31.77
980	28.94	1080	31.89
984	29.06	1084	32.00
988	29.17	1088	32.13
992	29.29	1092	32.24
996	29.41		

to about 0.12 inches of mercury. The pressure in millibars can be converted to inches of mercury by using Table 1-1).

The isobars on a weather map show clearly the locations of the cyclones and anticyclones. In the vicinity of high- and low-pressure systems, the isobars are curved. If the system is intense, several closed isobars will exist around the center. The wind blows more or less parallel to the isobars, especially when the isobars are close together. Closely spaced isobars mean that the pressure gradient is steep, and high winds are likely.

The temperature data on a weather map gives an indication of the locations of fronts. Most severe weather occurs near cold fronts, which are usually found in that part of a low-pressure system nearest the equator. The isobars are usually bent sharply along the line of a cold front. If the isobars are close together and very sharply bent, the cold front is intense, and stormy weather probably exists. Weather fronts are plotted as lines with bumps or barbs that indicate the type of front and the direction of movement.

The common weather map symbols are shown in Fig. 1-13, and a hypothetical weather map, similar to the type you might see in a major daily newspaper, is shown in Fig. 1-14. In the illustration, a strong midwinter low-pressure system is sweeping across the lower midwest, and an intense cold front is pushing eastward across Texas. You might very well surmise that the weather is not very pleasant in the Dallas-Fort Worth area! A look at the barbs on the station model for that city shows that the wind speed is 55 to 60 knots—nearly hurricane force. It's not a good day for a picnic in Texas.

The weather maps used by meteorologists are more complicated than the map shown in Fig. 1-14. Computer-generated maps show such things as lines of equal temperature (*isotherms*) or weather conditions at various altitudes, but the simple map found in the daily newspaper is sufficient for you to get a good idea of what is happening throughout the continent. You can tell with reasonable accuracy where the storms are; if you know the position of the jet stream, you can forecast where the storms will pass.

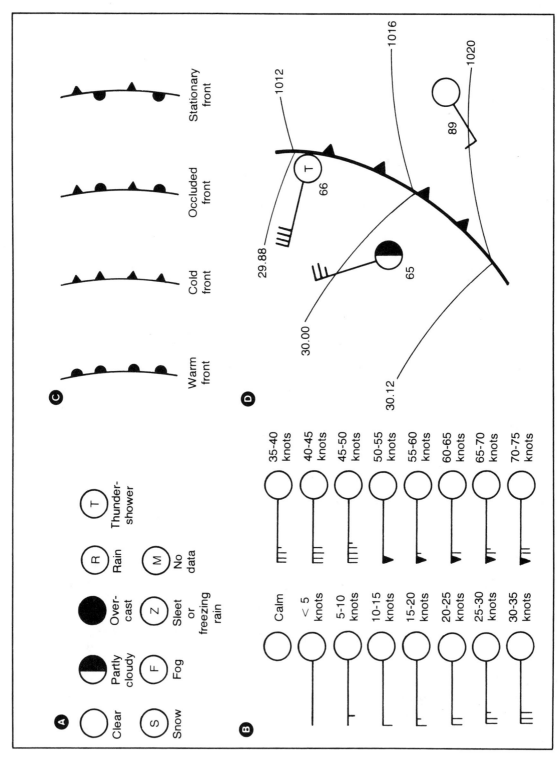

Fig. 1-13. Sky condition symbols (A), wind speed symbols (B), frontal symbols (C), and a local weather map (D).

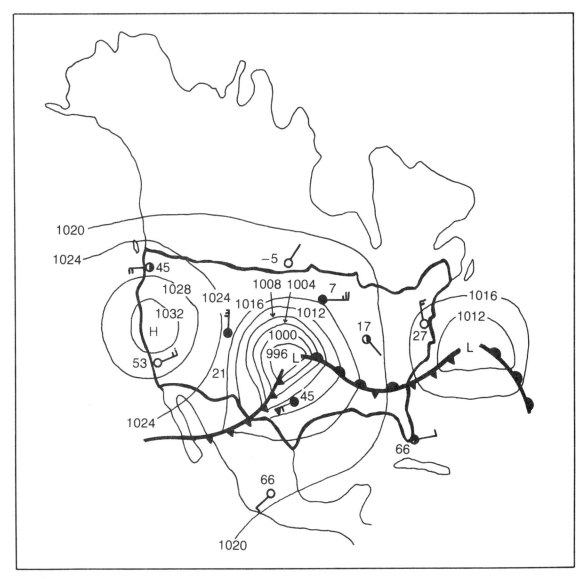

Fig. 1-14. A simple weather map showing a hypothetical storm over the lower Midwest.

Most temperate low-pressure systems move along from west to east at 20 to 40 miles per hour. This speed takes them about 500 to 1,000 miles in a single day, with an average of perhaps 700 miles. A storm system that is over Kansas and Missouri at noon on Tuesday might be over Ohio at noon on Wednesday, and by Thursday evening it will be on its way out to sea.

On the poleward side of a temperate low-pressure center, the movement of the system acts against the cyclonic rotation of the wind around the center. The winds on the north side of a northern-hemisphere low are usually not too strong, although they can sometimes reach speeds of 40 to 50 miles per hour in gusts. Snow is likely on the weak side of a temperate low in the winter, and cloudy or rainy weather prevails in the summer.

On the other side of the center (the southern

half of a northern-hemisphere temperate low), the forward progress of the system adds to the cyclonic rotation of the wind, and severe storms are more likely to develop. The westerly winds that sweep the Great Plains in winter and early spring are legendary; so are the strong wind storms that repeatedly pound the Pacific Coast. In the summer, severe thunderstorms and squall lines form on the strong sides of low-pressure systems.

THE FORCE OF THE WIND

Wind is an almost universal characteristic of our weather. It is almost never totally calm. The wind, as we have seen, tends to flow nearly parallel to the isobars on the weather map. The closer the isobars are spaced, the more nearly parallel the wind runs, and the stronger it gets as it spirals inward toward the center of a low-pressure system. Strong winds sometimes blow over a very large geographic area; sometimes they are quite localized.

Normally, the wind does not blow hard enough to have too much effect on things. Occasionally, we get an exceptionally windy day or a brief rush of strong wind as a thundershower approaches. Once in a while, the wind becomes strong enough to affect natural and manmade things. Rarely, high winds cause massive damage.

Early in the nineteenth century, an admiral in the British Navy, Sir Francis Beaufort, noticed that winds of various speeds produced consistent and visible effects on land and at sea. Not everyone has an anemometer mounted on the roof of our house, but you can get a good idea of the wind speed by observing what it does to trees, dust, buildings, or the surface of the sea.

You have probably heard an expression such as "Beaufort force 7" to describe the wind. This means a wind of 32 to 38 miles per hour, or 28 to 33 knots. That's a strong breeze. On land, a wind of this speed causes the trees to sway; the air whistles through telephone and utility wires. Opening an umbrella is a risky proposition. At sea, the waves break and throw spray. A wind of less speed produces less force, and the effects are not as dramatic. A

stronger wind creates more force and more violent effects.

It is possible to estimate the wind speed, in miles per hour or in knots, by observing the effects on land or at sea using a scheme called the *Beaufort scale*. Table 1-2 shows the Beaufort scale for land, and Table 1-3 shows the Beaufort scale for sea. The numbers range from 0 (dead calm) to 12 (hurricane-force winds).

Perhaps you have wondered why a 40-mile-per-hour wind does almost no damage to trees and buildings, while an 80-mile wind, only twice as fast, can snap trees at the trunk, shatter window panes, and create general havoc. The wind is moving air, and moving air produces measurable forces against objects that get in the way. This force can become exceedingly great at high wind speeds: in some cases it can be more than 100 pounds per square foot. The pressure of the wind increases in proportion to the square of the velocity, which is why high winds can do so much damage. An 80-mile wind is four times as powerful as a 40-mile wind. A 160-mile wind has 16 times the destructive force of a 40-mile wind.

Imagine that you tip your house sideways so that some of the walls are horizontal. Suppose that you find a horizontal wall and mark it off with a pencil into square feet. Now what will happen if a 100-pound person stands inside every 1-foot square? If the wall is 8 by 20 feet, you will have 160 people, weighing a total of 16,000 pounds (8 tons) standing on the wall. The wall will probably collapse under this load. An extremely severe thunderstorm, tornado, or hurricane can produce this kind of force on a building. Unless the walls are made of reinforced concrete, or at least of cinder blocks, a building can be demolished by winds of such speeds.

In some municipalities, such as Dade County, Florida, buildings must meet certain wind-resistance requirements. In the case of Dade County, the hurricane of 1926 resulted in this legislation, but many places that are exposed to the possibility of hurricanes have no such building codes.

Table 1-2. Beaufort Scale for Winds on Land.

Beaufort Number	Wind Speed, mph	Observed Effects
0	0	Smoke rises vertically.
1	1-3	Smoke shows direction of wind, but wind vanes do not.
2	4-7	Wind can be felt on face. Leaves move slightly.
3	8-12	Leaves in continual motion. Small flags blow outward.
4	13-18	Dust is raised. Papers are blown. Small branches move.
5	19-24	Small trees sway gently. Branches in motion.
6	25-31	Large tree branches move. Telephone wires whistle.
7	32-38	Entire trees moving. Some difficulty standing in wind.
8	39-46	Gale. Twigs break off trees. Hard to walk.
9	47-54	Strong gale. Branches break off trees.
10	55-63	Whole gale. Trees blown down. Some structural damage occurs.
11	64-73	Storm. Damage is considerable and widespread.
12	74 or more	Hurricane-force winds. Devastation occurs.

When a strong wind blows against a building, considerable force is produced directly against the wall or walls facing most nearly into the wind. This is a simple positive force. There are however, other forces generated by winds blowing around an object. As the air flows over the roof, the pressure does not increase, but instead goes down producing a negative force as the air inside the building pushes upward against the roof. If the wind gets strong enough, part or all of the roof can be ripped off because of this force. Similar negative forces are produced on walls that face sideways to the wind; windows are sometimes blown out by this pressure. Some negative pressure also occurs on the wall or walls facing away from the oncoming wind.

STORM FORECASTING

You can forecast storms with more accuracy than you probably realize. You can watch the weather map in the local newspaper or on the evening television news broadcast. If it appears that a low-pressure system will pass somewhat to your north, there is a fair chance of storm activity. The more intense low-pressure systems are the most likely to cause severe weather. You can tell how intense a low is by checking its *central barometric pressure*.

If a wintertime low has a central pressure of 1000 millibars (29.5 inches) or less, there is a good chance of severe weather developing. If the pressure is 992 millibars (29.3) inches or less, the chances of blizzard conditions are excellent. In the summer, a central pressure of 1004 millibars (29.7) inches portends trouble on the strong side of the system. If the central pressure is 1000 millibars (29.5 inches) or less, severe weather is very likely along and near the cold front.

You can forecast an approaching storm or cold front by observing only the barometric pressure, whether it is rising or falling, and the direction of the wind. (To get an immediate idea whether an aneroid barometer is rising or falling, tap it lightly. The needle will jump up or down.) Some common patterns, and the most likely type of weather to be expected in the temperate latitudes of the northern hemisphere, are given in Table 1-4. Keep a close watch on the weather map to get a better idea.

The forecasts in Table 1-4 are more reliable in the winter than in the summer. Wintertime blizzards cover large areas almost continuously, but summertime thunderstorms are very localized.

Your storm forecast will be most accurate if you keep track of the satellite pictures. The satellite view is shown every day in most newspapers, and on many television stations during the weather report. Large low-pressure systems frequently enter the United States from the Pacific Ocean. If an especially massive system moves in (Fig. 1-15), you can be sure that stormy weather will occur in many parts of the country during the next three or four days.

Table 1-3. Beaufort Scale for Winds at Sea.

Beaufort Number	Wind Speed, knots	Observed Effects
0	0	Surface is mirror-smooth (glassy), although swells may exist.
1	1-3	Small ripples form.
2	4-6	Small waves form.
3	7-10	Large wavelets appear. Some wave crests break.
4	11-16	Moderate-sized waves form and break consistently.
5	17-21	Moderate-sized waves form; some spray occurs.
6	22-27	Large waves form with whitecaps and spray.
7	28-33	Waves produce foam and considerable spray.
8	34-40	Gale. Very large waves form with foam and white streaks. Much spray.
9	41-47	Strong gale. High waves form with dense foam streaks parallel to wind.
10	48-54	Whole gale. Very high waves form with crests. Visibility becomes poor.
11	55-63	Storm. Very high waves and poor visibility, almost zero.
12	64 or more	Hurricane. Air filled with foam; monstrous waves; air and sea seem to blend.

Table 1-4. Some Common Weather Signs and the Probable Forecast in Each Case.

Barometer Reading	Barometer Movement	Wind Direction	Probable Forecast
30.0-30.2	None	SW-NW	Fair weather for next day or two.
30.0-30.2	Rising rapidly	SW-NW	Fair for a day or two, then rain or snow.
30.2 +	None	SW-NW	Fair for an indefinite period of time.
30.2 +	Falling slowly	SW-NW	Fair for a day or two with warming trend.
30.1-30.2	Falling	S-E	Becoming cloudy with rain or snow in a day or two.
30.1-30.2	Falling	SE-NE	Rain or snow within a few hours.
30.0 +	Falling	E-N	Rain or snow within a day, with rising wind.
30.0 −	Falling slowly	SE-N	Continuing rain for a day or two.
30.0 −	Falling rapidly	SE-N	Deteriorating weather; rain or snow with high winds likely.
29.8 −	Falling rapidly	SE-N	Severe storms likely within several hours.
29.5 −	Falling or steady	SE-NE	Blizzard imminent in winter; violent storms likely in summer.
29.8 −	Rising rapidly	Veering to W-NW	Improving weather and falling temperatures.

THE WEATHER EYES

We take weather satellites for granted. It is strange to think that as recently as 1959 there wasn't a single one of them up there. The tracking of storm systems, especially hurricanes, was much more difficult then than now. The space age came quickly, however, and within less than two decades, weather satellites literally fill the skies.

The first weather satellite that provided pictures of the earth and cloud formations in the troposphere was TIROS. It was launched in April, 1960. The TIROS satellite was small, shaped like a can of tuna, and about 2 feet high and 4 feet wide. Nine more TIROS satellites were launched after the first one. Since then, many other weather satellites have been put into various types of orbits so that meteorologists can keep constant watch on the

weather everywhere in the world. You might recognize some of them by their names or acronyms, such as ESSA, GOES, LANDSAT, ITOS, and Nimbus.

The strange and varied orbits of weather satellites might, at first, seem confusing, but actually there are just two kinds of orbits in which modern weather satellites are placed: the *geostationary orbit* and the *polar orbit*.

Geostationary Satellites

The first weather satellites, because they were in low orbits, went around the earth quite fast: a complete revolution took only about 90 minutes. Today, satellites orbit at much higher altitudes, and they take longer to go around the earth. (The higher an object orbits a planet, the longer it takes to go around.) When a satellite is put into orbit at a distance of 22,500 miles above the earth's surface, the orbital period is exactly 24 hours. This is called a *synchronous orbit*. Satellites in synchronous orbit above the equator are known as *geostationary satellites*, because they are always above the same place. You have probably heard of the GOES (Geostationary Operational Environmental Satellite) spacecraft.

A geostationary orbit is convenient, and it is not surprising that our planet is literally ringed with satellites in geostationary orbits. Three satellites,

placed in geostationary orbits at longitudes separated by 120 degrees, allow continuous viewing of the whole planet except for the immediate polar regions. The GOES satellites are equipped with cameras that can see in infrared light as well as at visible wavelengths. Figure 1-16 is a typical view of the earth as seen from a GOES.

Polar-Orbiting Satellites

The first TIROS satellites orbited the earth at a low altitude, and at an angle of 48 degrees to the equator. To look at a certain part of the world, it

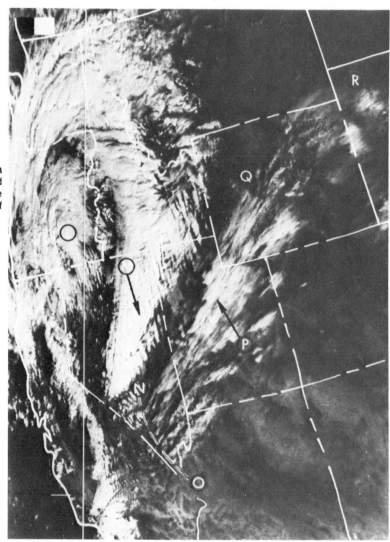

Fig. 1-15. Satellite photo showing a storm system entering the United States from the west. Markings can be ignored (courtesy U.S. Department of Commerce, NOAA).

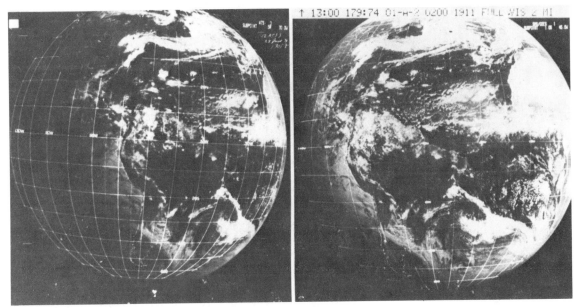

Fig. 1-16. The earth as seen from a geostationary satellite. The image at left was taken in visible light and the image at right in infrared (courtesy U.S. Department of Commerce, NOAA).

was necessary to wait until the satellite came within a few hundred miles of that location. Places north or south of the 55th parallels couldn't be seen at all. Later, as rocket technology improved, the TIROS satellites and their descendants were placed in orbits that allowed viewing at all latitudes. Such an orbit is called a *polar orbit*.

Polar-orbiting spacecraft circle the earth at an angle of almost 90 degrees to the equator. The orbit is synchronized, not with the earth's 24-hour rotation, but with the revolution of the earth around the sun. This keeps the satellite in the sun all the time so that the solar cells receive constant light 24 hours a day, 365 days a year.

As the earth turns underneath a polar-orbiting satellite, different parts of the world come into view. Over the course of half a day, a composite picture of the whole world can be obtained. Such a combination of small photographs, put together to show a large area, is called a *mosaic*. Figure 1-7 is a mosaic that shows the clouds of the northern hemisphere (A) and the southern hemisphere (B), as they would be seen from far above either pole.

The modern TIROS craft, like the GOES, have cameras that can see in both visible light and in-

frared. Figure 1-17 is a North-Polar mosaic of the earth in both visible and infrared light. Polar-orbiting satellites can be used to provide mosaics in any desired form, and of any portion of the earth.

Close-up Views

Today's sophisticated weather satellites can see in much greater detail than the first TIROS. The cameras can view the whole earth or a large part of it, as shown in Figs. 1-7, 1-16, and 1-17, or they can zoom in on a particular weather system. Several frontal and tropical cyclones can be seen in Fig. 1-17.

The magnification of the visible light and infrared cameras can be adjusted to obtain more or less resolution. The greater the magnification, the better the resolution. Figure 1-18 shows how we can zoom in on a weather system. The top photograph shows weather systems over the eastern United States and the Gulf of Mexico. In this photograph, the resolution is 2½ miles. This means that the smallest discernible features are 2½ miles across. In the view at the lower left, the resolution is 1¼ miles. In the photograph at lower right, the

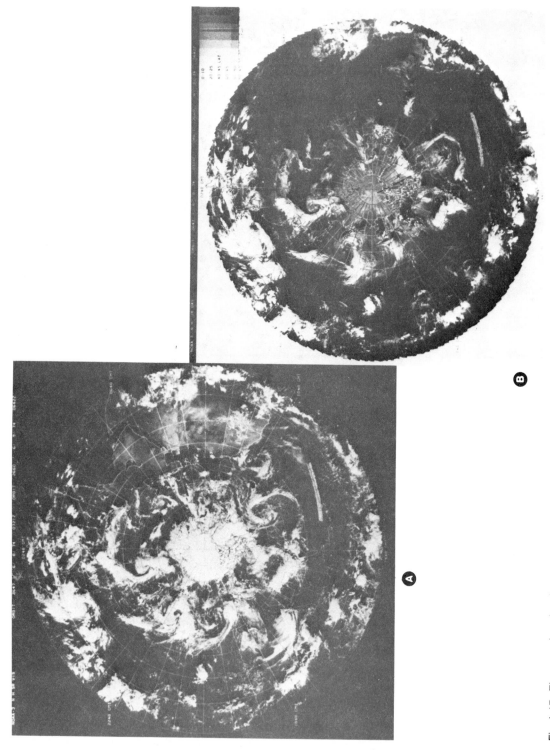

Fig. 1-17. These northern hemisphere mosaics were obtained by a polar-orbiting satellite. The view at A is in visible light, and the view at B is in infrared (courtesy U.S. Department of Commerce, NOAA).

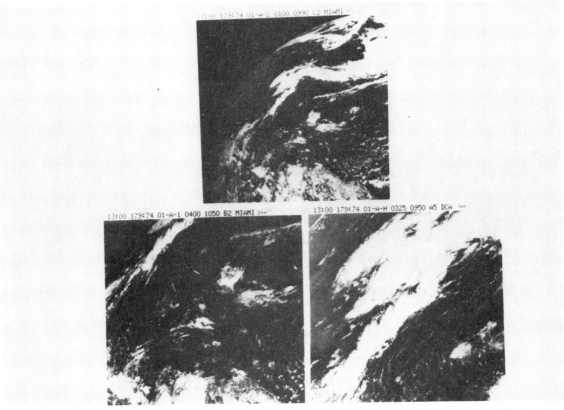

Fig. 1-18. Three satellite views of the eastern United States, using various degrees of magnification and resolution (courtesy U.S. Department of Commerce, NOAA).

resolution is ⅝ mile, or about 3300 feet. Even more detail can be obtained if necessary to allow meteorologists to view individual thunderstorms, the eyes of hurricanes, and local features of all types of weather systems.

Data Collection

Weather satellites do more than just take pictures of clouds. Geostationary weather satellites are equipped with radio receivers and transmitters. Weather information is collected from stations on the surface, including rain gauges, tide gauges, ships, seismometers, manned weather stations, and automatically controlled weather stations. A single satellite can be used to compile all the data from thousands of different stations every hour. The satellite can get the information from a particular station by sending a command to the station.

Some stations send information to the satellite whenever unusual or severe weather conditions occur. The satellite sends all of its information to a central Command and Data Acquisition Station.

Suppose, for example, that an intense earthquake takes place somewhere in the South Pacific Ocean. The impulses are recorded by seismometers, and the information is sent to the geostationary satellite. People in areas threatened by a *tsunami* (or so-called tidal wave) will know of the danger within minutes following the quake. Using computers, meteorologists can predict when the tsunami will arrive at the coasts of Hawaii, California, Alaska, Central America, South America, Japan, and Australia. Further data from various stations allows continuous updating of the predictions, and the computers can provide an indication of how severe the tsunami will be at various locations.

CLOUDS

For centuries people have been fascinated by clouds. They have noticed that certain kinds of clouds indicate the approach of bad weather, and other clouds prognosticate continued good weather. The earliest sky sign of an approaching storm, for example, is often a thin, high layer of clouds.

Causes of Clouds

Clouds form when the relative humidity is 100 percent: that is, when the air is saturated with water vapor. The temperature at which clouds form depends on how much water vapor is in the air. The more water vapor the air contains, the higher the temperature at which clouds can form.

The temperature of the air decreases steadily as you get higher above the ground, but the amount of water vapor does not necessarily decrease with altitude. The relative humidity, therefore, often rises with altitude. If it rises to 100 percent at a certain level, clouds will form there.

The development of clouds is accelerated by *atmospheric updrafts,* when moist air ascends to great heights. Many land areas at or near the equator, such as the Amazon basin and the jungles of Africa, are covered by clouds quite a lot of the time because of strong upward air currents. Most parts of the world near 30 degrees north and south latitude have descending air, and consequently the cloud cover is sparse.

In very dry air, clouds may not form at any altitude. Azure, cloudless skies are typical of areas where the climate is arid. In moist air, clouds almost always develop. Tropical regions of the world, especially near the equator where the humidity is high, are characterized by frequent cloudiness. The higher the relative humidity, the lower the height at which clouds begin to form. On an extremely muggy or rainy day, clouds are usually observed at low altitudes, and in the extreme case, they may even form on the ground. We then have fog.

Meteorologists and aviators often speak of the *cloud ceiling.* This is the altitude, measured with respect to the earth's surface in that locale, of the bottom of the lowest layer of clouds.

In between the extreme cases of very dry and very moist air, clouds form in an almost infinite variety of shapes and patterns. Meteorologists have ten different classifications for tropospheric clouds.

Cloud Types

Clouds are named according to their relative altitude and their general shape. Clouds can occur at altitudes from sea level up to about 12 miles in the troposphere. These are the clouds that affect our weather and may indicate the approach of a storm. Some clouds, called *nacreous* and *noctilucent* clouds, form in the stratosphere and are not associated with storms at the surface of the earth.

The highest clouds range from 20,000 feet to more than 50,000 feet above sea level. They are named with words that begin with *cirr,* from the Latin word *cirrus,* meaning curly. The wispy, cotton-candylike cirrus clouds are familiar to us all (Fig. 1-19). High, smooth clouds are called *cirrostratus.* They give the sky a milky appearance (Fig. 1-20) and frequently cause a ring around the sun or moon. An old adage says that a ring around the sun or moon means rain is on the way; today, we know that low-pressure systems are often preceded by high, thin clouds like cirrostratus. Some high clouds have a rather congealed or puffy look. These are known as *cirrocumulus* clouds (Fig. 1-21).

The middle-level clouds are between about 6,000 feet and 20,000 feet above sea level and are given the prefix *alto,* which is Latin for high. Middle-level clouds may have a flattened appearance, in which case they are called *altostratus.* Altostratus clouds are somewhat lower and thicker than cirrostratus, but otherwise the two cloud types are very much alike. Middle-level clouds with a puffy look are known as *altocumulus* (Fig. 1-22).

The lowest clouds occur at altitudes less than 6,000 feet. These clouds may be given the prefix *strat,* meaning flat. Low clouds sometimes extend all the way to the ground, in which case fog occurs (Fig. 1-23). Low, flat clouds are called *stratus* clouds. If rain falls from them, they are called *nimbostratus. Stratocumulus* are low, rolling, gray

Fig. 1-19. Cirrus clouds form at altitudes of several miles.

Fig. 1-20. Cirrostratus clouds, illuminated at night by city lights.

Fig. 1-21. Cirrocumulus clouds, blown about by high-level winds.

clouds, seen on an overcast and gloomy, but dry day typical of much of the United States in the late autumn. The cottonlike puffs of fair-weather cumulus are easy to recognize (Fig. 1-24).

One type of cloud forms at low, medium, and high levels, often extending from a few thousand feet to the top of the troposphere. This type of cloud is the violent *cumulonimbus*. Severe thunderstorms are always associated with these clouds. Cumulonimbus clouds may stand alone in an otherwise practically clear sky, creating a fantastic spectacle. They may form in small groups or large, fast-moving squall lines. Cumulonimbus clouds form in an unbroken, doughnut-shaped mass around the eye of a tropical storm, producing continuous downpours.

Of course, several kinds of clouds can form at the same time at different altitudes. There may be as many as three different layers of clouds in the atmosphere.

Imagine it is a cloudy, dark day, and you board an airplane bound for a distant place. You know the airplane will fly high. As you take off and settle into your seat for the long ride, the pilot's voice comes over the speakers. He tells you that the cruising altitude will be 37,000 feet. (That's 7 miles.) The plane climbs into the low, dismal nimbostratus cloud bank. The clouds are so thick that you can hardly see the wings of the plane. The sky lightens gradually. The plane bursts into the clear, only to reveal another, higher cloud layer. You recognize it as altocumulus. Even at this altitude the sky is totally overcast. The plane climbs higher and enters the second deck of clouds. The sky lightens further. Now it gets very bright. You emerge from the second deck into the blinding sun.

34

Fig. 1-22. Altocumulus clouds obscuring the sun in late afternoon (A) and the moon at night (B).

Fig. 1-23. When clouds reach ground level, the result is fog.

Fig. 1-24. Cumulus clouds form at low altitudes.

Fig. 1-25. From an airliner, it is often possible to see several different types of clouds at the same time.

Far off in the distance you can see a third, still higher, layer of clouds. As you squint into the sun, you can make out a cumulonimbus thundershower about 40 miles away, and some cirrostratus at about the same distance. The altocumulus clouds, through which you have just passed, recede underneath the airliner, which is still gaining altitude (Fig. 1-25).

Of course, clouds do not always fall neatly into one of the ten common classifications. There might be some doubt, for example, whether a certain cloud is a cumulus or altocumulus cloud. Not all clouds of a given type look exactly the same. The wind speed at the cloud level, the angle from which

the sun or moon is shining, the extent of cloud cover at higher or lower altitudes, and other factors affect the way the clouds look.

Some clouds are unusual or interesting enough to have special names, even though, theoretically, they can always be put into one of the ten formal categories.

As cumulus clouds build up in the heat of the summer, towering higher and becoming wider at the base, they are called *cumulus congestus*. The sky is almost overcast, because the clouds nearly merge together. When rain finally begins to fall from cumulus congestus clouds, they become cumulonimbus.

Fig. 1-26. Wave clouds over the Andes in South America, as seen from space (courtesy NASA).

The base of a cumulonimbus cloud can have various different features. If the cloud seems to have pouches or rounded protrusions, it is called *mammatus*. These clouds are associated with extreme turbulence.

A cyclonic vortex will occasionally form within a cumulonimbus cloud, the spinning air column extending below the base. If the vortex is strong enough, water vapor condenses and we see a *funnel cloud*. If the funnel cloud reaches the ground or water surface, it is called a tornado or a waterspout.

When high winds are present at relatively low altitudes, we sometimes observe the ragged, fast-moving, dark clouds called *fractocumulus* or "scud." These clouds are literally torn-up shreds of cumulus or cumulonimbus. The small fractocumulus clouds often move very fast as the high winds push them along. You have probably seen these clouds near violent storms.

Fractocumulus clouds usually look dark, because they hang in the shadows of the higher, thicker cumulonimbus. Fractocumulus clouds sometimes contain an unusual amount of dirt, making them look dark even when the sun shines directly on them. This is the result of strong updrafts in the past history of a thunderstorm. Dark fractocumulus clouds near a dissipating thundershower give reason to suspect that there has been a tornado or a violent wind storm.

Mountains are known to produce marked and sometimes bizarre local effects in the atmosphere, at altitudes ranging from a few thousand feet up to several miles. As moist air passes over a mountain range, strange-looking, lens-shaped or undulating clouds may form on the leeward side of one or more of the peaks. These are known as *lenticular clouds* or *wave clouds* (Fig. 1-26). Wave clouds are generally a combination of altostratus and cirrostratus, although they sometimes become large and thick enough to produce rain, thus qualifying them for the status of cumulonimbus.

Not all clouds are made by nature. High-flying jet aircraft produce their own form of cloud: the *vapor trail*. A vapor trail, if it persists long enough, is spread out into cirrostratus or cirrocumulus clouds by the high-altitude winds. Rockets produce similar clouds as they ascend through the upper part of the troposphere. In recent decades, more aircraft have been flying in the upper troposphere, and some scientists think this has had an effect on cloud cover, especially over the midwestern United States. Whether that is significant, or whether it is good or bad, is not known with certainty.

Another example of partially man-made clouds is found in and near major urban areas. This, of course, is *smog.* The term smog is derived from the words "smoke" and "fog." There are actually several different kinds of smog. There is little doubt that smog is bad for the environment, but there is considerable disagreement over just how much damage smog has caused on our planet.

Sometimes you will see what looks like a cloud, but really isn't. A forest fire can produce blue-white or gray smoke that looks like a cloud from a distance. In some places, brush fires can produce smoke that inhibits visibility and causes general darkening of the sky. For example, in the late winter and early spring in Miami, dry weather has been known to result in large fires in the Everglades to the west. If the wind blows from the west, as it often does in Miami during the winter and spring, the whole city is covered by dense smoke. It smells like burning leaves and looks like fog.

Blowing dust or sand, as well as blown smoke, can take on the appearance of threatening clouds. Sand, smoke, or dust occasionally fill the air over vast regions. Massive forest fires in the western states have darkened the skies as far east as the Atlantic seaboard. Strong winds over a large area, during a period of dry weather, can carry the topsoil for hundreds of miles, blackening the sky over a vast region.

Some clouds of debris are produced by volcanic eruptions. After the recent eruptions of Mount St. Helens, much of the United States was affected by the volcanic dust that was thrown up and carried along by the jet stream. Volcanic dust in fact, has been blamed for cooling trends lasting several years. The famous cold summer of 1816 and the cold winter of 1983-1984 were believed by some scientists to have been caused by a prolonged reduction in the amount of heat received by the earth. In both cases, massive volcanic eruptions threw tremendous amounts of dust into the upper troposphere and stratosphere.

Clouds Warn of Storms

Certain clouds, or combinations of clouds, warn of the threat of foul or severe weather. Other clouds reassure us that the weather will stay fine for a while. You can usually get a good idea of what to expect, at least for a day or two, just by looking at the clouds.

Small, puffy cumulus clouds, with little or no clouds at higher altitudes, generally mean that the weather will remain good for 24 to 36 hours. If the clouds begin to build up during the late morning or early afternoon, however, you should take your umbrella if you plan to be outside later. Gradually rising and thickening cumulus do not usually portend severe weather, although heavy rains sometimes occur. This kind of weather pattern is typical in the tropics and subtropics during much of the year and in the temperate latitudes in the summer.

A distant, but advancing, storm system causes gradually increasing instability in the upper troposphere. You have probably noticed that jet airliners don't always lay vapor trails. A clear, deep-blue sky, in which airplanes produce no vapor trails or trails that die out quickly, indicates stability in the upper air, and the continuance of fair weather. The first noticeable sign of an approaching low-pressure area is the tendency for airplanes to lay progressively longer vapor trails. Finally, they persist for so long that they stretch from horizon to horizon after planes pass overhead. The upper troposphere gets more amenable to cloud formation as water vapor condenses more readily.

As the storm system moves nearer, high cirrus

clouds appear. They get gradually thicker until the sky is nearly filled with high clouds. At temperate latitudes, the clouds thicken toward the western horizon. The apparent movement of the clouds is usually from the western side of the compass toward the eastern side. In the tropics, clouds thicken toward the east; the apparent movement may be in any direction.

As the atmosphere becomes more unstable, cumulus congestus clouds begin to form. The wind shifts, backing several compass points. In the temperate latitudes, the prevailing westerlies give way to gentler breezes that come from the direction of the equator. In the tropics, the trade winds blow more or less from the pole, and they get stronger and more gusty than usual.

Eventually, rain or snow begins to fall. At temperate latitudes, the temperature may rise several degrees over a period of a few hours. Then the sky lightens, the rain or snow abates, and moderate weather prevails. If the storm system is intense, however, these conditions will not last very long.

In the tropics, conditions are difficult to predict without satellite information. The approaching system could be nothing more than a weak tropical wave, or it might be a vicious hurricane.

For those who live in the latitudes where frontal cyclones prevail, the event just described is recognized as the passage of a warm front. When a warm front has moved by an area in the temperate zone, a cold front almost always follows. The cold front causes large cumulonimbus clouds to form in the summer. In the winter the wind sometimes reaches hurricane speeds and persists with this violence for hours, as snow blows in a blinding white sheet. The temperature falls dramatically as the front overruns the countryside—sometimes by as much as 30 degrees Fahrenheit in a half hour in summer, or 80 degrees in a single day in winter.

As a cyclone approaches in the tropics or subtropics, the changes in temperature are unnoticeable. The sky gets alternately gloomy and bright. If the storm is not intense, rain falls, accompanied by gusty winds. The rain may be light, or the accumulation might be several inches. If the storm is intense, the weather eyes will inform us of the danger far in advance. Before we had satellites and reconnaissance aircraft, people in the path of a severe hurricane had almost no warning before the winds and tides of the eyewall were upon them.

As a low-pressure system moves away, the weather improves rapidly. Behind a temperate low, brisk winds blow from the pole, and the weather is dry. Within a few days, the pattern will be repeated as another low approaches and passes. Behind a tropical storm, conditions gradually improve as the winds and rains ease.

You can learn to recognize the signs of an approaching cyclonic storm by watching the winds and clouds, and by checking the barometer, the weather map, and the satellite photographs. You can predict the path of a low-pressure system in the temperate latitudes if you know the location of the jet stream. In this chapter, you have seen how our atmosphere circulates, and how this circulation affects our weather. In the following chapters, we will look more closely at the various kinds of severe weather that affect us all.

Chapter 2

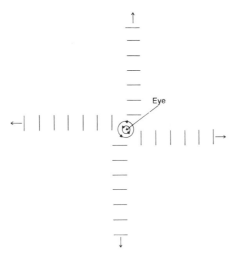

Eye

Hurricanes: Devil Winds of the Sea

The date: September 10. The time: 6:20 P.M. Eastern Standard. The weather forecast contains a passing statement that a tropical depression, west of the Cape Verde Islands, off the west coast of Africa, is being closely watched. It shows signs of strengthening. Such announcements are heard often during late summer and early fall, and there is no immediate cause for alarm. By 11:00 P.M. that day, the depression has become a tropical storm, with winds in excess of 39 miles per hour. It is the fourth such storm of the year and is given the name *Debby*.

The following morning Debby is rapidly gaining strength and may soon become a full-fledged hurricane, with winds of more than 74 miles per hour. The center of Debby is specified as 11.5 degrees north latitude and 40.4 degrees west longitude, far out in the open Atlantic. Debby is, at the moment, a threat only to shipping interests in that area.

By the evening of September 11, Debby packs winds of 85 miles per hour, and has thus become a minimal hurricane. Conditions favor greater strengthening. The storm is moving almost directly westward at 20 miles per hour. The telvision newscasters show a satellite photograph of Debby; she appears as a wispy pinwheel of clouds with a faint, small black dot near the center—a defined eye (Fig. 2-1).

We will now keep ourselves constantly informed, as will millions of residents of the eastern and Gulf coasts, of the progress of Debby. All "Cape Verde-type" hurricanes, such as Debby, pose a threat to the United States, as well as Mexico and much of Central America. The eye of Debby, at its present low latitude, moves in an almost westward direction, but it is almost certain that the storm will eventually curve toward the northwest.

By the morning of September 12, Debby has the full attention of the National Hurricane Center. She has strengthened with phenomenal rapidity, reminiscent of Hurricane Allen in 1980. The maximum sustained winds are estimated at over 180 miles per hour, with gusts as high as 200 miles per hour. On a scale of intensity from one to five, Debby is a strong five. Residents of the Windward

Fig. 2-1. Satellite photograph of a fully developed hurricane. The eye is easily visible. (courtesy NOAA/National Environmental Satellite Service.)

Islands have seen many hurricanes; they begin their preparations for the arrival of Debby with ritualistic precision. They know what a hurricane can do. A direct hit by Debby might, they know, carry away everything.

By the evening of September 12, the eye of Debby is located near latitude 12.0 north and longitude 52.9 west. The islands of Grenada, St. Vincent, St. Lucia, and Barbados await the arrival of Debby's full fury, as seas reach 70 feet and breakers pound with unrelenting violence on the eastward beaches. The normally gentle trade winds shift to the north with an ominous gustiness.

Then, one after the other, the islands are plunged into isolation from the rest of the world as the eyewall of the storm reaches them.

TALES OF DESTRUCTION

We have all heard stories and seen pictures of the incredible devastation that occurs in severe hurricanes. The first reports from Barbados and nearby islands trickle out via emergency-powered amateur radio stations. Almost every building on these islands has been flattened or gutted. Thousands of people are homeless. Hundreds are dead or missing.

The vortex of Debby begins to curve slightly northward. The eyewall, or most destructive part of the hurricane, is about 100 miles in diameter. St. Lucia gets a brief rush of tornadic winds and heavy rain, but escapes the main part of Debby. The hurricane has slowed its forward motion to about 15 miles per hour as she lumbers into the Caribbean Sea, heading in the general direction of Haiti and the Dominican Republic. Further reports now come from Barbados, which received a direct hit: trees have been stripped of their bark and leaves, the landscape is completely barren and desolate; it looks as if there has been a nuclear holocaust. Disoriented and distraught, the homeless wander through the debris. The water supply is contaminated, and people are becoming ill.

The fate of the Gulf Coast and eastern seaboard of the United States now depends on a number of factors. The so-called *steering currents,* which direct the hurricane path, are difficult to determine and predict. Computers at the National Hurricane Center in Miami, Florida, work around the clock, continually updating the status and position of Debby. Sustained winds are near 200 miles per hour. The eye is about 15 miles across; hurricane-force winds cover a roughly circular area with a diameter of 150 miles.

The hurricane slams into the island of Hispaniola with sustained winds so fierce that all the measuring apparatus is destroyed. Estimates of the peak gusts range from 220 to 250 miles per hour. Debby is being called the hurricane of the century. The residents of Florida begin to prepare for a potential onslaught. The entire Gulf Coast nervously watches the progress of the storm.

The high hills of Hispaniola weaken Debby, and as she emerges into the northern Carribbean, her intensity has decreased. Weather forecasters know this is typical, and residents of the southeastern United States are warned against complacency. The threat is far from over.

THE FORCE OF WIND AND WATER

The strongest winds in a hurricane are often impossible to measure. The device generally used to measure wind speed is the three-cup *anemometer* (Fig. 2-2). This device spins as the wind is caught in the concave parts of the cups. The greater the wind speed, the faster the device rotates. If the wind is too strong, however, the anemometer is ripped to pieces, and the building or tower on which the device is mounted may be demolished. The

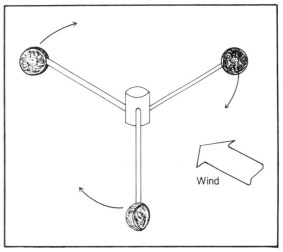

Fig. 2-2. The three-cup anemometer rotates as the wind blows past. The rate of rotation is proportional to the wind speed.

greatest officially recorded wind speed is a gust of 231 miles per hour that, ironically, did not occur in a hurricane, but instead took place on the summit of Mount Washington, in New Hampshire. Hurricane gusts have probably reached speeds of nearly 250 miles per hour in extreme cases, but such ferocious winds rarely pass over a meteorological station, and if they do, the anemometer is torn apart.

Hurricane winds are usually specified in terms of the *maximum sustained wind.* Peak-gust speeds are hard to determine, but probably are from 20 to 40 percent greater than the sustained wind speed. How much force results from a wind of 200 miles per hour? That is difficult to imagine for those who have not been through the experience. In a typical severe thunderstorm in the midwestern or eastern United States, wind speeds of 50 miles per hour are not uncommon, and gusts may reach more than 75 miles per hour. In such storms, trees are uprooted and ripped limb from limb; house roofs may be damaged or completely torn off; telephone wires are blown down; small aircraft are overturned; even automobiles may be wrecked. The force of the wind increases in proportion to the square of the velocity, so that a doubling of the wind speed represents a fourfold increase in its force. A sustained wind of 200 miles per hour, such as in Hurricane

Debby, is 16 times as violent as the average severe midwestern thunderstorm. It simply defies the imagination—until it strikes you!

The most severe part of a hurricane occurs over a rather small area, generally less than 200 miles across. The forward progress of the average hurricane, however, is only about 12 to 14 miles per hour. Thus, even a small hurricane will subject some places to severe winds for several hours. The largest hurricanes, if they are slow-moving may besiege a single place with killing winds for more than 24 hours.

The wind of the hurricane is often extreme, but it is not the most deadly effect of such a storm. The lowered barometric pressure in a hurricane causes the level of the ocean to rise. The spiraling winds in the storm literally pile the water up into a dome at the center. When this dome of water reaches a shoreline, the elevation of the tide is greatly exaggerated. In some cases it may rise as much as 30 feet. The extent of the rise in tide is dependent on many factors as a hurricane approaches.

The water may rise rapidly, in the form of one or more gigantic waves. As the water moves ashore, debris is carried along with it, increasing the destructive force. Water is denser than air and causes far more pressure when it encounters buildings and other man-made structures. The pounding waves, superimposed on the rising tide, rise even higher than the so-called *storm surge*.

Ancient people, seeing this chaotic deterioration of the air and sea during the hurricane, could ascribe it only to the wrath of some supreme being. The word "hurricane," in fact, is believed by some to translate to "devil wind" in some primitive Caribbean tongues. Hurricanes in the Pacific Ocean are called *typhoons*. In the Indian Ocean, they are generally called *cyclones*. In Australia, hurricanes are sometimes called *willy-willies*. All of these terms mean the same thing; terror and destruction, completely beyond the control of man.

Where will the hypothetical devil wind, that I have named Debby, strike the continent of North or Central America? Will the storm veer off harmlessly into the ocean? As you examine the weather map with its high and low pressure systems, it seems that there should be some way to foretell, at least approximately, where the devil wind called Debby will go. The art of hurricane-path forecasting is improving continually, but there is still a lot of uncertainty.

Debby may strike the coast of the continent anywhere from Honduras to Newfoundland, or she might miss North America completely. The exact path of a hurricane depends on many things, but the most significant influence on storm tracks may be inferred from Nature's purpose in creating the storms. The tropics receive more heat from the sun than they radiate into space. The polar regions radiate more heat than they get from the sun. The difference must be made up somehow, and hurricanes are a major vehicle for the transfer of such thermal energy from the tropics toward the poles. Hurricanes frequently curve northward sooner or later in the northern hemisphere and southward in the southern hemisphere.

Meteorologists are constantly working to improve their methods of tracking hurricanes and predicting their paths. The same basic principles apply to all hurricane regions in the world. The arrangement of continental weather systems, the presence of land masses, and the temperature of the ocean all play a crucial role in the ultimate track that a hurricane will follow. Certain variables also determine where a storm will form, how it will evolve, how long it will last, and how it will ultimately die. These factors are all within our scientific reach. We are learning more about hurricanes and how to protect our lives and property from their effects. We may someday even be able to control the great storms.

THE BERMUDA HIGH

At all times of the year, but especially during the summer in the northern hemisphere, the prevailing winds over the north Atlantic are dependent primarily on an almost stationary, persistent center of high pressure. Because this high is usually centered near the Azores or the island of Bermuda, it is often called the Azores-Bermuda high, or simply the Bermuda high. This system is responsible for much of the weather that occurs along the east coast of the United States in the summer. The Bermuda high results in a hot southwesterly wind over the New England area during July and August, bringing temperatures that often exceed 100 degrees Fahrenheit. The system also causes the regular easterly trade winds throughout the regions of lower latitude.

In other parts of the world, similar high-pressure systems exist over the tropical oceans. Near the equator, the pressure is rather low, but at about 30 degrees north and south latitude, highs form. In the northern hemisphere, the circulation around the high-pressure system is in a clockwise direction; in the southern hemisphere it is counterclockwise. The tropical oceanic highs produce easterly winds between about 0 and 30 degrees north and south latitude. Poleward from the high-pressure systems, westerly winds occur.

Near the equator, the belts of tropical easterly winds meet. This is a region of low pressure and light winds. Thundershowers often form in this zone. Because the trade winds converge here, the region is known as the intertropical convergence zone (ITCZ). In ancient times, this region was called the *doldrums*, because ships were often becalmed for lack of wind. The ITCZ describes a somewhat sinuous band around the earth near the equator, but sometimes considerably north or south of it (Fig. 2-3). In the Atlantic, the ITCZ is north of the equator; in late summer and early fall, it is quite far to the north of the equator.

Hurricanes develop when the intertropical convergence zone gets far enough from the equator to allow significant Coriolis rotation. In the northern hemisphere, this rotational force takes place in a counterclockwise direction. In the southern hemisphere, it occurs in a clockwise direction. In the Atlantic, the ITCZ is almost always north of the equator, and for this reason, hurricanes are never observed in the South Atlantic Ocean.

The *tropical wave* begins as a notchlike irregularity in tropical isobars (Fig. 2-4). Showers and thunderstorms develop on the eastern, or trailing, side of this disturbance. Such easterly waves are common during the summer months, and they usually move from east to west without intensifying. In

certain instances, however, when conditions are favorable, an easterly wave becomes unstable and grows more intense. When one or more isobars become enclosed, indicating that a rotary wind circulation has developed, the wave is called a *tropical depression*. A tropical depression is simply an area of low pressure. Such a disturbance will often continue to strengthen. The central pressure will keep dropping, and the wind speed will increase. Warm air near the center will rise, and the surface winds spiral inward. When the maximum sustained wind reaches 39 miles per hour, the disturbance becomes a *tropical storm*, and receives a name. If intensification continues until the sustained wind reaches 74 miles per hour, the storm qualifies for the title of hurricane.

Hurricanes form just north or south of the equator in many parts of the world (Fig. 2-5). At the equator, there is no Coriolis force, and the whirlwinds cannot develop; the latitude must normally be between 5 and 30 degrees north or south. Hurricanes sometimes mature at latitudes farther north or south than 30 degrees, but that is unusual because the ocean temperature is seldom warm enough so far from the equator. Hurricanes that threaten the eastern United States always mature in the Atlantic Ocean, the Caribbean Sea, or the Gulf of Mexico.

In the northern hemisphere, the hurricane season begins in June and ends in December. In the southern hemisphere, the season is reversed. Hurricanes almost never occur out of season. The greatest frequency of hurricanes in the northern hemisphere is in the months of August and September. This is also the time when a severe storm, such as our hypothetical Hurricane Debby, is most likely to develop.

At the beginning of the Atlantic hurricane season, storms usually mature in the southwestern part of the Caribbean Sea and in the Gulf of Mexico. By late July, the temperature of the Atlantic Ocean water has warmed up sufficiently to allow storms to intensify in that region. By mid-October, the main area of development returns to the southwestern Carribean and the Gulf of Mexico.

In some years, several hurricanes form in the

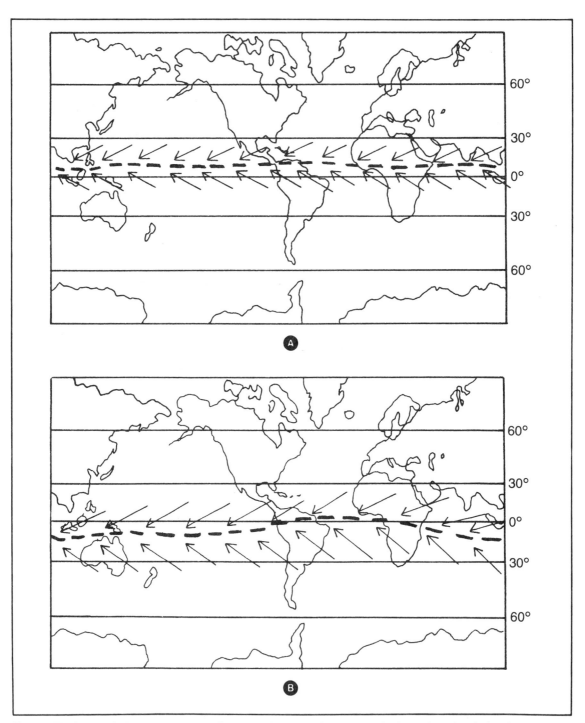

Fig. 2-3. The intertropical convergence zone lies somewhat north of the equator in the northern hemisphere's summer, as shown at A. In the southern hemisphere's summer, the intertropical convergence zone lies mainly south of the equator, except in the Atlantic (B).

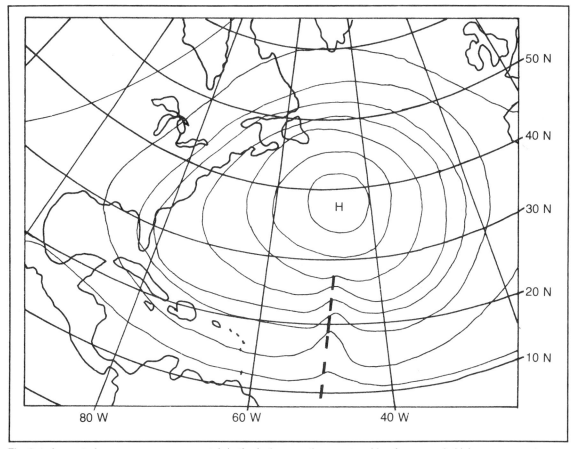

Fig. 2-4. An easterly wave appears as a notch in the isobars on the equator side of an oceanic high-pressure system.

Atlantic. In other years, there may be few or no storms with maximum winds of 74 miles per hour in the Atlantic region. The reason is not fully understood. Dr. Neil Frank, of the National Hurricane Center, has found some correlation between warm ocean temperatures, known as *El Nino*, off the west coast of South America, and a lack of hurricane development in the Atlantic and Caribbean. El Nino is believed to have been responsible for the relatively benign hurricane seasons of 1982 and 1983.

Once a hurricane has formed, it has a natural tendency to move away from the equator. The precise path of a particular storm depends on weather conditions over the continents and the locations of the high and low pressure systems at the higher latitudes. In the Atlantic, hurricanes generally follow the periphery of the Bermuda high in a clockwise direction. This may cause the storms to *recurve*, or swing toward the north and then toward the northeast.

ANATOMY OF A HURRICANE

Although a hurricane is a low-pressure system, it differs from the lows of the temperate latitudes. The hurricane is much more symmetrical than the cyclonic storms familiar to inhabitants of Europe, the interior United States, and other temperate regions. The hurricane, in its tropical stage, does not contain frontal systems. The isobars are almost perfect circles, especially in a well-developed storm (Fig. 2-6). The central pressure is often much lower than that of the extratropical cyclone.

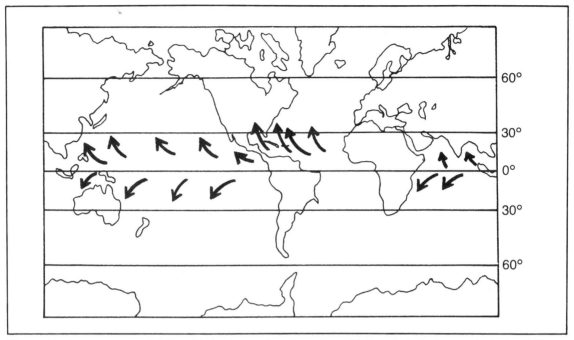

Fig. 2-5. Tracks most commonly followed by hurricanes throughout the world. Note the lack of storms in the South Atlantic Ocean.

At the periphery of a hurricane, cloud circulation becomes noticeable. This is evident in satellite photographs. The winds in this region are relatively moderate. Rain showers occur, but they are not usually severe.

Three cloud decks can be identified in the outer circulation of a hurricane. The lowest layer, consisting of nimbostratus clouds, produces rain. The middle layer consists of altocumulus and altostratus clouds, and the upper cloud layer is composed of cirrus and cirrocumulus. Figure 2-7 is a cross sectional view of Hurricane Debby, our imaginary monster storm.

Nearer the center, thick cloud bands occur in spirals. Heavy rain is produced in these regions which are called *rain bands*. The wind is strong and gusty in these parts of the hurricane circulation, attaining speeds as great as 40 or 50 miles per hour. Tornadoes and frequent lightning are common in the rain bands.

Within about 50 to 100 miles of the center, the circulation picks up rapidly. The *pressure gradient*, or rate of change of barometric pressure, is steepest in the region immediately surrounding the eye of the storm. This is called the *eyewall* or *wall cloud*. At the surface, the eyewall of the storm produces torrential, almost continuous, rains and savage winds. In Debby, the sustained winds are about 200 miles per hour. This is about as powerful as a hurricane ever gets, although in some very rare cases the wind is believed to have reached speeds near 250 miles per hour. An example of such a superhurricane was the storm that struck the Florida Keys on Labor Day, 1935.

At the core of the hurricane, the winds and rains abate. This cylindrical region is called the *eye of the storm*. It may range from about 3 to 75 miles in diameter, but is usually about 20 to 40 miles across. The cloud cover is light, and the weather may be partly clear. During the day, the sun may shine, and at night, the stars or moon might be seen. The barometric pressure is lowest within the eye. The level of this pressure is one basis for determining the intensity of the hurricane. While normal air pressure will support about 30 inches of mercury, the pressure in a hurricane can drop below 28

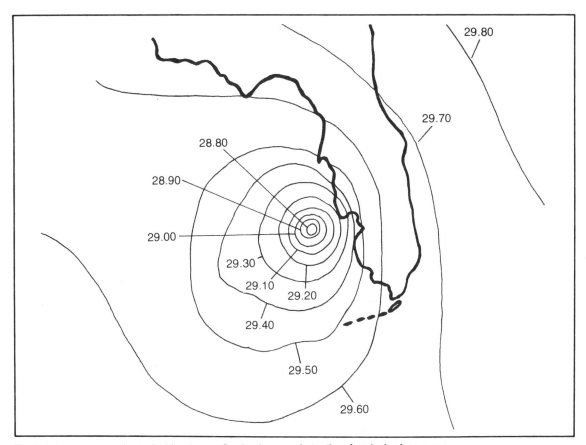

Fig. 2-6. Isobars around a typical hurricane. Graduations are in tenths of an inch of mercury.

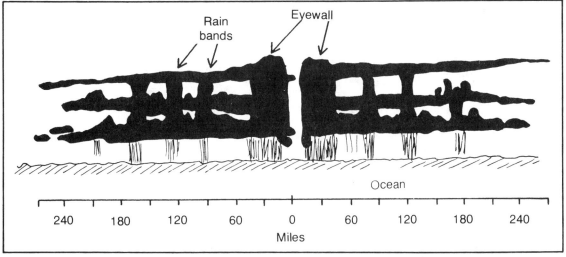

Fig. 2-7. Cross-sectional diagram of the cloud structure of a typical severe hurricane. The highest clouds may extend to altitudes exceeding 8 miles. The eye and wall-cloud diameters may vary considerably.

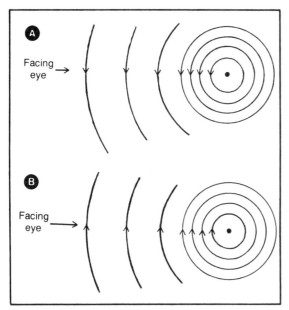

Fig. 2-8. As you face the eye of a hurricane, the winds blow from left to right in the northern hemisphere (A), and from right to left in the southern hemisphere (B).

inches. In Debby, it is 26.9 inches. The Labor Day storm of 1935 produced readings as low as 26.35 inches. By comparison, a low-pressure region in the temperate latitudes rarely produces pressures lower than 29 inches.

The winds of the hurricane spiral inward toward the center. As the air gets closer to the edge of the eye, the angle of inflow gets smaller. In the eyewall, the wind rushes around in an almost perfect circle. As Debby approaches directly from the east, the first strong winds will come from some point between northwest and northeast, and veer toward the north. If you stand at any point and face the eye, the wind blows from left to right in the northern hemisphere and from right to left in the southern hemisphere (Fig. 2-8). This principle of storm circulation is well known to mariners, but it often fools people inexperienced with the storms. Many people think that the hurricane approaches from the same direction as the wind blows. If the eye passes over, they think the storm has "blown itself out." Then, when the winds return with redoubled fury from nearly the opposite direction, such people will say that the storm "came back."

The eye of a hurricane can fool people into thinking the storm is over—but the second, or rear, part of the storm comes with sudden and surprising violence.

THE LIFE STORY OF A HURRICANE

Hurricanes in the North Atlantic Ocean and Caribbean Sea usually begin on an east-to-west or southeast-to-northwest track, following the general direction of the prevailing winds. As the storm moves westward or northward, its direction often changes, and the hurricane turns toward the pole. A hurricane will usually recurve if it enters the westerlies in the temperate latitudes. Recurving storms threaten primarily the eastern coast and the Gulf Coast of the United States. In the southern hemisphere, many hurricanes also recurve. Non-recurving Atlantic, Caribbean, and Gulf storms affect mainly the shores of Texas, Mexico, and Central America.

Some hurricanes recurve harmlessly into the northern part of the Atlantic Ocean. There, the storms may combine with temperate low-pressure systems and lose intensity, but some hurricanes maintain their strong winds, particularly in the right-hand part, well into the temperate zone. Occasionally, such extratropical storms have struck Iceland, the Azores, and even Europe, with devastating results.

A hurricane must eventually face either of two destinies: death by landfall or death by cold water. When a storm strikes land, it rapidly diminishes in intensity because the winds encounter friction on the ground. Satellites show this effect clearly; Fig. 2-9 is an example. When a hurricane moves over cold temperate waters, the supply of heat is cut off, and the storm loses its intensity. In either case, heat is transferred from warmer regions to cooler regions. This is no accident; it is a sort of natural atmospheric safety valve. It is unfortunate that the storms sometimes cause damage and death to mankind.

The shape of the hurricane changes as it crosses a coastline or enters the cool temperate part of the world. The intense, symmetrical circulation gives way to a more elongated and distorted shape.

Fig. 2-9. Satellite photos of Frederic, taken in September, 1979, show the dissipation of a hurricane after the eye moves inland. At A, Frederic is still over the Gulf of Mexico. At B, he has passed inland, and the eye is no longer clearly discernible. (courtesy NOAA/National Environmental Satellite Service.)

51

Frontal zones may develop. When this occurs, the storm is called an *extratropical cyclone*.

When a tropical hurricane crosses a region of land, such as a large island, the storm may lose much of its violence. This happened to Hurricane David in 1979. He raged through the Caribbean Sea, but lost much strength over Haiti and the Dominican Republic before reaching Florida. After he passed over the mountains of Hispaniola, David (like his hypothetical cousin, Debby) weakened. The eye filled in with clouds, and the winds subsided. Once David moved back over the warm sea, he rapidly regained his eye, although he never quite got back his former wind speed—fortunately for the inhabitants of Florida. Debby may or may not cooperate in kind.

STORM-PATH PREDICTION

Upon analysis of past hurricane paths and their relationship to the surrounding weather systems, a correlation can be found between hurricane tracks and the conditions in the temperate zone.

When a large area of low pressure exists to the west of a hurricane, the storm will at first be drawn toward this low-pressure region. Then the hurricane will be steered around the eastern edge of the low, where the winds come from the south. The hurricane moves northward into the belt of prevailing westerlies and finally turns to the northeast. The low-pressure area that causes this recurvature may be a broad tropical wave, a cyclone originating in the temperate zone, or perhaps another hurricane. Figure 2-10 shows this pattern.

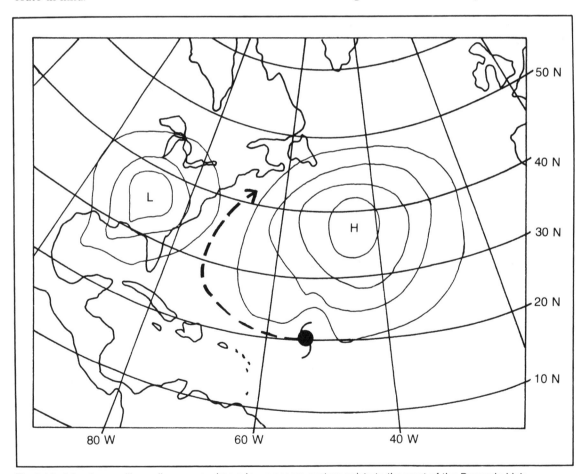

Fig. 2-10. A hurricane will usually recurve when a low-pressure system exists to the west of the Bermuda high.

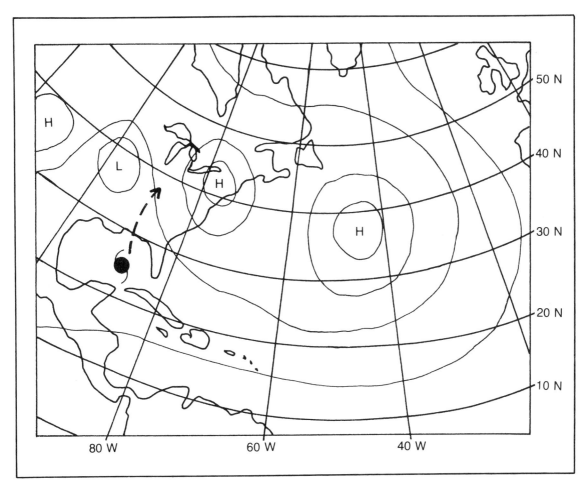

Fig. 2-11. A storm in the Gulf of Mexico will usually recurve when a low is sandwiched between two highs over the continent.

Another weather arrangement that often results in hurricane recurvature is the presence of a low, sandwiched between two high-pressure systems on or near the continent. A hurricane in the Gulf of Mexico, for example, will often turn northward and follow a break between two highs (Fig. 2-11). This brings the storm into the belt of prevailing westerlies, and it turns northeastward as it weakens over the land mass.

Still another possible recurvature situation exists when a break occurs in the Bermuda high. This semipermanent Atlantic ridge sometimes weakens in the middle. It is difficult to predict when such a break will occur, and if it does happen, it may not be well-defined enough to affect the track of a

hurricane, but in many instances, storms have followed such a trough (Fig. 2-12). These conditions are usually responsible for steering hurricanes over Bermuda and the Azores. Under these conditions, an occasional persistent storm may maintain much of its power well into the northerly latitudes, eventually slamming into Europe or even Iceland with surprising violence.

When the Bermuda high is especially large or strong, or is located somewhat to the west of its usual position, hurricanes normally do not recurve. The *easterlies*, or trade winds, push farther north than usual, and this tends to literally expand the tropics. The hurricanes behave accordingly under such circumstances—they tend to follow in almost straight westerly or west-northwesterly path, just as they would in the far-off Atlantic. These non-recurving storms may strike Central America or the Yucatan Peninsula. Occasionally they move into the Gulf and threaten Texas or Mexico. Figure 2-13 shows this type of pattern.

The prevailing westerlies, which constantly fan the North American continent, sometimes slacken or move northward as a result of a massive high over the Great Plains or the southern United States. This kind of situation, like that shown in Fig. 2-13, can prevent hurricanes from recurving.

Hurricane Allen, of 1980, was a nonrecurving storm. He eventually hit the Texas coast in a relatively unpopulated area. It was a minor miracle that Allen caused so little damage. Allen was kept from recurving by high pressure to the north; had he turned and attacked southern Florida or the Keys, he surely would have been among the most memorable hurricanes in American history. Even if he had recurved slightly and blasted Houston, Allen would have been immortalized. Galveston and Houston got a taste from Alicia, in 1983, of what could have been their fate with Allen. Alicia sent panes of glass flying through the air like gigantic razor blades, with maximum sustained winds of barely hurricane force. Allen, a huge and intense tropical maelstrom, packed wind gusts believed to be as great as 215 miles per hour.

Our hypothetical monster, Debby, might well be Allen's twin sister. Will she follow in his footsteps, or will she be a killer?

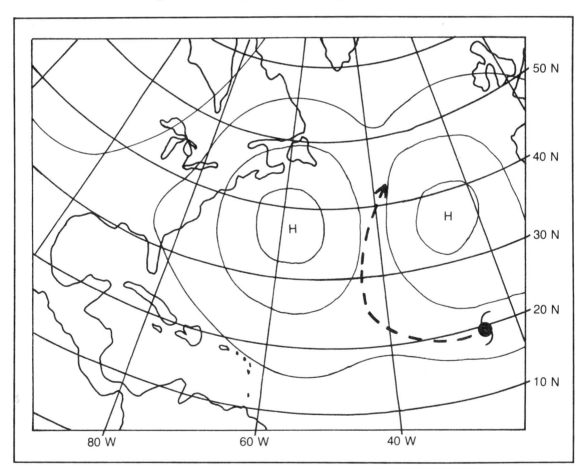

Fig. 2-12. A break in the Bermuda high may result in a hurricane remaining well out at sea.

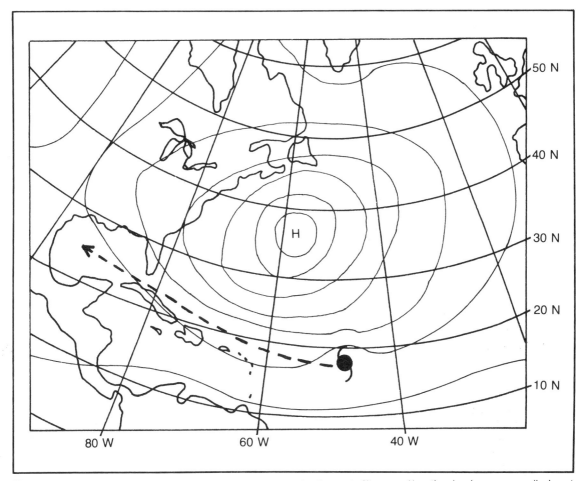

Fig. 2-13. If the Bermuda high is usually strong, large, or centered to the west of its normal location, hurricanes generally do not recurve.

Hurricanes are steered, to a large extent, by the winds in which they are embedded. By locating the isobars over the North Atlantic and the North American continent, forecasters can get a good idea of the future path of a tropical storm. A hurricane usually, but not always, moves parallel, or nearly parallel, to the isobars in its vicinity. A fast-moving storm follows a more predictable path than a stalled or sluggish one.

Tropical cyclones sometimes defy all attempts at path prediction. They may seem to travel against the surrounding winds or across the isobars. A storm may stop, do a complete "loop-the-loop," and turn in an unexpected direction. In 1935, a hur-

ricane in the Atlantic, moving from east to west and apparently bearing down on the Carolina coast, suddenly veered toward the southwest and struck Miami, Florida. Residents called this storm, having come from the northeast, the "Yankee hurricane"—a name that lives to this day. Another example of a hard-to-predict storm was Betsy, of 1965. She took a 360-degree turn before ravaging southern Florida, the Keys, and finally the central Gulf Coast.

Another odd quirk in hurricane paths is the occasional tendency for an intense storm, such as Allen, to behave almost as though it has a distaste for land masses. As Allen churned through the Atlantic and the Caribbean, his central vortex never made a direct hit on any of the major islands. Jamaica got the closest shave, but Allen's eyewall veered slightly away from the island, and Jamaica was spared the brunt of his fury. As Allen bore down on Texas with his fantastic winds, moving at a steady clip of almost 20 miles per hour, catastrophe appeared inevitable. The winds rose to gale force, trees began to blow down, electricity was lost. The residents huddled in their homes, awaiting the onslaught of winds beyond their comprehension and a 25-foot storm surge. Then Allen stopped just short of the coast and spent himself, slowly, over the waters of the Gulf of Mexico. When Allen finally did move inland, he was only a whisper of his former self.

We might almost imagine that Allen was afraid to die. We might console ourselves with the belief that the prayers of the Texas coastal dwellers were responsible for holding Allen off. Perhaps Allen was just a "nice guy!" We can only hope that, if or when she gets to the United States mainland, our hypothetical Debby will be a "nice girl."

In recent years, hurricane forecasters have begun using computers in an effort to improve prediction of storm paths. Since records have been kept, many hurricanes have moved into the United States from the Atlantic and the Gulf of Mexico. Their paths have been accurately recorded. The computer is programmed with all of the available past data. Then, when a hurricane approaches, the coordinates are constantly fed into the computer.

Chances are that several past hurricanes approached along paths nearly identical with that of the storm at hand. The computer, of course, "knows" where all of these past storms went, and it "knows" all of the surrounding weather conditions and how they are likely to affect the path of the hurricane this time. The present conditions, along with past statistics, are processed by the computer. It gives its prediction of the most probable path of the storm for the next 12, 24, or 48 hours. the computer also indicates the degree of uncertainty—in effect, the likelihood that its forecast will be wrong. Watches and warnings are issued, according to this data, for various sections of the coastline.

EFFECTS OF A HURRICANE

The atmosphere normally presses down on the sea with a force of more than a ton per square foot. At the center of a hurricane, this pressure is reduced by as much as 10 percent. The ocean surface, relieved of more than 200 pounds of pressure for every square foot, rises. The rise is greatest in and near the center of the storm, where the barometric pressure is the lowest.

Raz de Marée

In the open sea, the rise of the water is not very great—for each inch the barometer falls, the ocean level rises about a foot. Normally, the barometric pressure is about 30 inches of mercury. Thus, a pressure of 29 inches will cause a 1-foot rise; a pressure of 28 inches will result in a 2-foot rise, and so on. As the center of the hurricane moves into shallow water and approaches a land mass, however, the dome of water encounters friction which exaggerates the rise in the water. The larger the land mass, in general, the more pronounced the effect will be, although it depends, too, on the geography of the coastline and the direction from which the hurricane approaches.

The increased friction of the angry water against the ocean floor causes the water to pile up, exactly as it does when incoming swells form breakers on the beach. The tremendous power of the hurricane winds, its forward motion, and the force of the water being driven ashore combine to produce a tide that can be more than 25 feet above the normal water level. The French have an expression for the resulting catastrophe: *raz de marée* (literal translation: "rise of the sea"). That would seem to be a rather mild way of describing the phenomenon.

The greater the intensity of a hurricane, the higher the tide at the center will be. The right-hand portion of a hurricane produces on-shore winds in the northern hemisphere; in the southern hemisphere it is the left-hand half as a hurricane moves inland. The on-shore winds create a tide by themselves, independent of the fall in the atmospheric pressure. The water is actually pushed up onto the beach. On the opposite side of the storm, where the winds blow offshore, the water level may fall dramatically, grounding ships in harbors and stranding fish in tiny pools hundreds of yards from the usual water line. The most dramatic effect, however, is at the immediate center—the eye—of the whirlwind, where both the wind and the partial vacuum conspire to lift the water.

The *raz de marée* at the center of a hurricane is sometimes a gradual process; the ocean level simply gets higher and higher as the eye approaches. In certain cases, however, the major part of the rise may take place suddenly, in the form of one or more huge waves that smash everything in their path. This sudden rise is the result of *resonance effects* in the water, not unlike the oscillations you can easily set up in your home bathtub.

There are stories of 30-foot waves sweeping in from bays to cause unbelievable destruction within a matter of seconds. Most of the real horror stories come from the Bay of Bengal and the China Sea, where vast populations have settled in low-lying areas adjacent to estuaries and other inlets. A single storm surge in an eighteenth-century hurricane killed 300,000 people in the Ganges River delta area. We cannot blame it on the bad old days; it happened again in 1970. Not all died by simple drowning. A 30-foot wave, carrying timbers, boulders, pieces of glass, and other debris is far deadlier than a 30-foot wave of pure ocean water!

The Gulf Coast of the United States, with its many shoreline irregularities, is particularly vulnerable to the effects of hurricane surges. A storm might move ashore at a certain place and cause very little *raz de marée;* if the eye turns and strikes just a few miles down the coast, there may be a tremendous surge. The importance of accurate landfall prediction is clear. The Tampa-St. Petersburg bay area, on the western coast of Florida, provides a good example. A storm that moves in from the west and strikes land just south of the bay will produce little or no increase in the water level; in fact, water might be pushed out of the bay into the Gulf. If the hurricane makes a direct hit, however, or if the eye comes ashore just to the north of the bay, a *raz de marée* of 25 feet is possible. Many people

have built residences in the Tampa-St. Petersburg area since the last inundation. Should a big storm hit the area again, the people will no doubt be astonished (and terrified) at the resulting saltwater onslaught. Other Gulf Coast cities face the same predicament.

Many have heard of the famous Galveston hurricane of 1900, a storm that killed 6,000 people. Many died because of the surge from the bay. Galveston was rebuilt, a great seawall was erected, and the level of the land generally raised. Galveston is now well equipped to handle all but the worst possible hurricanes. The same cannot be said, unfortunately, for Indianiola, Texas, which was obliterated permanently by a hurricane. Indianiola, too, was located on a bay.

Even if there is no irregularity in the coastline, the *raz de marée* may come with destructive force. The famous Miami hurricane of 1926 produced a storm surge of more than 10 feet in the beach area outside of Biscayne Bay. Water stood waist deep over much of the long, thin island for several hours. The high water weakened the roots of the stately palm trees on Miami Beach, and the sustained 130-mile-per-hour winds toppled them with ease, turning the previously sleepy, beautiful resort into an otherworldly mass of wide-awake ruin (Fig. 2-14).

The *raz de marée* can sometimes lift large vessels completely out of the ocean. This occurred with Camille, in August 1969. Three freighters were washed ashore, and when Camille had departed, the ships were on dry land (Fig. 2-15).

Debby Approaches

In 1926, Miami was a small town compared to its present size. The terrible storm of September 18, 1926, would have caused much greater ruin if it had waited for about 55 years. Debby is not waiting. She's moving along at 15 to 20 miles per hour. She is getting stronger; highest sustained winds have picked up to 150 miles per hour.

September 16, 6:00 A.M. A hurricane watch is posted for the coastline from Fort Myers to Fort Pierce, Florida. Debby is a definite threat, and she might strike within 36 hours. Miami is now a me-

Fig. 2-14. The famous Miami hurricane of September, 1926, caused great destruction as the water flooded the barrier islands, and the wind reached speeds of more than 130 miles per hour. (courtesy NOAA/National Hurricane Center.)

Fig. 2-15. Hurricane Camille of August, 1969, left these ships on dry land after the storm surge receded. (Courtesy NOAA.)

tropolis, facing the sometimes sunny, sometimes stormy Caribbean Sea. Our imaginary Debby is more intense than the storm of 1926. Miamians listen to the advisories concerning Debby.

September 16, 6:00 P.M.. Debby is again strengthening over open water, her eye just to the north of eastern Cuba. The coordinates are given: 22.5 north, 76.4 west. Thousands of pencils each make a little dot on a gridded map of the Caribbean, known as a *hurricane tracking chart* (Fig. 2-16). It appears that southeastern Florida may lie right in Debby's path.

At 6:00 P.M., a hurricane warning is issued for the Florida coast from Fort Myers to Fort Pierce. Landfall may occur within 24 hours.

Storm surges and tides can create new beaches and wash old beaches out to sea. New inlets may be carved through barrier islands, and old inlets closed up. The hurricane cares nothing for whether a park, a home, a condominium complex, or a city might stand in its way. Beach dwellers must pay special attention to hurricane watches and warnings, and evacuate, if necessary, early enough to avoid being cut off from the mainland. Debby threatens to inundate the beach areas with 10 to 15 feet of water. Says an elderly Miami woman who has seen a few bad storms: "There's only one thing to do in a hurricane—leave!"

Some Miamians start to believe, in our hypothetical Debby situation, that leaving might be a good idea. The freeways are slightly crowded on the morning of September 16. By evening, the traffic has become still heavier as the warning is issued. A few people have decided that it might be a good time for a short vacation in Orlando. Others are staying, but they are boarding up their windows. The noises of pounding nails and whining electric saws fill the air.

Some beach dwellers are ignoring the warnings entirely. They smile and say, "A hurricane isn't any big deal. I stayed right here through David in '79, and it was nothing. Nothing at all."

Rainfall

The most destructive force in a hurricane, far deadlier than wind, is the ocean surge, but many hurricanes can produce large amounts of rainfall. In some cases it is welcomed because it relieves a drought, but at other times the rain may cause flash flooding. A typical hurricane might drop 10 inches of rain in one place over a 24-hour period. Hurricanes vary in terms of total rainfall, however, some storms are "dry," while others are "wet." The most intense hurricanes are not always the wettest, and a weak tropical storm is not necessarily a "dry" storm.

In 1981, tropical storm Dennis, not a great threat for his tides or wind, dropped 20 inches of rain in western Dade County, Florida, in a 24-hour period. Although the area had been suffering from a drought, severe flooding occurred. The ground simply could not absorb that much water at one time. Two years earlier, Hurricane David, a far more serious potential threat in terms of the storm surge and wind, hardly wet the sidewalks in much of Miami, in spite of the fact that his eyewall grazed Key Biscayne and Miami Beach.

When a hurricane strikes land, the winds encounter friction against the ground. The result is increased rainfall as the storm spends its energy. If the terrain is irregular, as are many Caribbean islands, the effect is more pronounced than if the land is flat. If a hurricane slows down or stalls over a certain place, there will be much more rain than if the storm sweeps quickly through. If all of the factors—a "wet" storm, mountainous terrain, and a slow forward storm speed—conspire together, the rainfall over several days may be fantastic. For example, in July 1913, certain parts of Taiwan (then called Formosa) received nearly 7 feet of rain from a hurricane.

In a typical hurricane, the total rain accumulation at any single place probably ranges between 5 and 15 inches. The total rainfall is often quite difficult to measure, because the wind interferes with the functioning of the rain gauge. During the periods of heaviest rainfall, the wind may blow the rain horizontally so that only a fraction of the water is caught by the apparatus. Thus, these amounts must be considered approximate at best.

In the United States, the most severe flooding from hurricanes has occurred in the New England

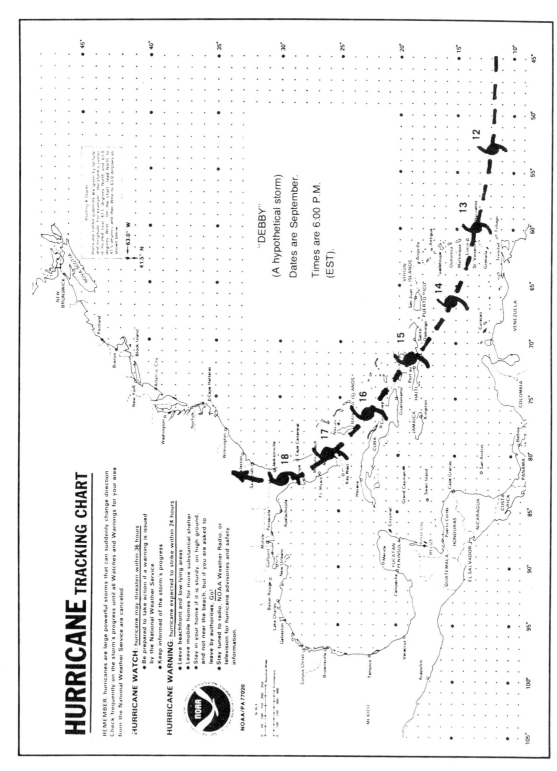

Fig. 2-16. A hurricane tracking chart shows the path of a hypothetical hurricane. The numbers represent dates in September; the time in each case is 6:00 P.M. Eastern Standard Time.

area. A notable example is Diane of 1955, which caused over a billion dollars in damage, mostly from floods. This storm was preceded by several days of heavy rain in Connecticut, Massachusetts, Vermont, and New Hampshire. Finally, when Diane hit the land was saturated and could not handle the runoff. Record 24-hour rainfalls occurred in several places; rivers rose far above flood stage.

Another hurricane that caused great flood damage was Hazel of 1954. Hazel moved inland over the Carolina coast of the United States, causing 150-mile-per-hour winds and unbelievable destruction from beach erosion. As Hazel continued northward, she combined with a low-pressure system from the temperate latitudes and began to drop great amounts of rain in the Great Lakes states. Hazel was an exceptional storm, maintaining considerable wind strength far inland; she caused much wind damage even in Pennsylvania. Hazel moved over Toronto, Ontario on October 15 and 16, 1954. Her rainfall, combined with the autumn rains typical of the Great Lakes area, resulted in over 100 million dollars in damage from flooding in metropolitan Toronto.

Flooding causes terrible loss of property, as anyone who has been affected by a rampaging river will attest, but flooding can threaten lives, as well. This is more true in the less developed countries of the world than in the United States. Flooding can cause contamination of the drinking water and result in widespread sanitation problems and disease, with which the medical community in an underdeveloped nation cannot deal. Even in a major United States city, the water supply may be made unsafe. Flood waters usually carry debris, such as uprooted trees, automobiles, and fragments of washed-out structures, worsening the damage to buildings and causing numerous injuries to people. Fallen utility lines dangling in the water present an electrocution hazard, and many people simply drown.

Ocean Swells

The storm surge and the potentially heavy rains are not the only water-related destructive factors associated with hurricanes. Even if there were no rise of the sea and no rainfall whatsoever,

the wave action would still cause devastation immediately along the unsheltered beachfront.

When wind moves over a water surface, waves are formed. We have all observed sizable waves—perhaps as high as 3 feet or more—on lakes or rivers when the weather is especially windy. In the vast ocean, under the extremely violent conditions of a severe hurricane, the waves can reach heights in excess of 60 feet. In rare instances, the waves immediately surrounding the eyewall may measure as much as 90 feet from crest to trough.

When a hurricane is still far offshore, the swells may be observed on the beachfront. At a distance from the center of the storm, the swells appear to emanate radially outward from the eye (Fig. 2-17). The height of the swell depends on the intensity of the hurricane, the diameter of the eyewall, and the distance of the storm from an observer. For beach dwellers, the earliest sign of an approaching hurricane may be an increase in the size of the breakers, and a corresponding decrease in their frequency. The change can be noticed, in

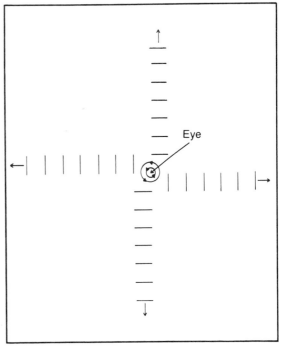

Fig. 2-17. Generation of swells around the eyewall of a hurricane.

some instances, two full days prior to the actual arrival of stormy weather.

The period of a wave train is directly related to the wave height. Under normal conditions, 10 to 12 breakers arrive at the beach every minute. As a hurricane approaches, this frequency drops to perhaps 6 or 8 breakers per minute as the waves become higher and are spaced at larger intervals. As a severe hurricane nears, the frequency may become still lower—perhaps only 4 or 5 breakers per minute. The thundering of the breakers can sometimes be heard for miles inland.

The growing, pounding breakers are accom-panied by a shift in the wind. In the northern hemi-sphere, the wind backs about 90 degrees as the storm nears, so that as you stand directly facing the oncoming breakers, the wind fans the left side of your body. In the southern hemisphere, the wind veers clockwise about 90 degrees; as you look at the oncoming waves, the wind blows from your right. As the waves break, the wind blows the spray laterally through the air.

When a hurricane moves on a track more or less directly toward you, the waves will become continually larger, and their direction will not change significantly. If the storm is moving on a

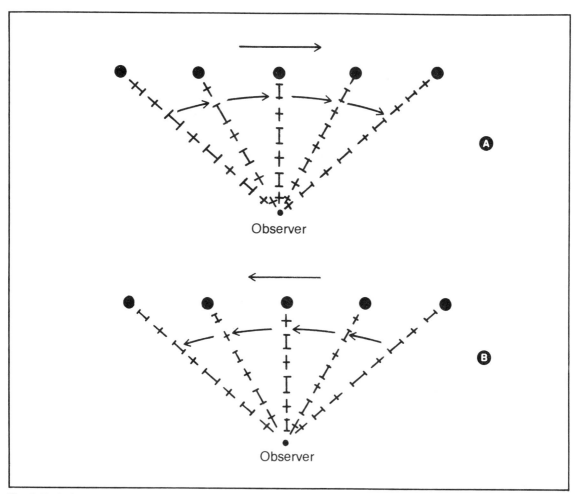

Fig. 2-18. At A, a storm moving laterally toward the right will produce swells that arrive from a clockwise-moving compass direction (veering). At B, a storm moving laterally toward the left will cause swells that arrive from a counterclockwise-moving compass orientation (backing).

lateral path, the wave direction will slowly veer clockwise or back counterclockwise, depending on whether the eye is traveling toward your right or toward your left as you face the sea (Fig. 2-18).

The ocean swells do not always arrive exactly perpendicular to the beachfront. They may come in at a considerable angle, setting up a strong sideways current in the water. (Perhaps you have had the experience of taking a short swim in the ocean and having to walk several blocks on the beach to get back to your point of entry.) If the swells are large, beach erosion occurs. A hurricane need not make a direct hit to cause severe destruction to beachfront property; the swells can wash away much of the shoreline within a day or two. Houses can be washed out to sea, roads undermined, and inlets filled in with sand—all while the sun shines benignly down on the catastrophe.

Tornadoes

The wind damage from a hurricane results mainly from the prolonged, violent "blow" in the eyewall. These winds may reach speeds of more than 200 miles per hour within a few miles of the beach, but they decrease further inland. Few hurricanes retain deadly wind speeds for more than perhaps 50 miles inland, although this depends to a large extent on the terrain, and considerable damage can still result from winds of 75 miles per hour or less.

Hurricanes can produce tornadoes, however, far most frequent in the forward part of the hurricane, especially the right front quadrant, but they can take place anywhere in or around the storm. Winds of the tornado are the most violent known; measuring apparatus never survives a direct hit by a tornado. The tornado strikes with little or no warning and causes almost instantaneous damage. For these reasons, they are dangerous, although tornadoes generally contribute little to the overall destruction from a major hurricane.

The tornadoes associated with a tropical hurricane are not as large, not generally as violent, and do not last as long, as the great midwestern "twisters." Hurricane-spawned tornadoes, however, can still unroof buildings, shatter windows, overturn automobiles, strip trees, and cause other severe damage to property. As the hurricane moves into the temperate latitudes, the tornadoes may become more violent. Hurricane Camille, in August, 1969, caused tornado damage throughout the Gulf Coast and southeastern United States as she moved northeastward past the 30th parallel.

Tornadoes may exist within the eyewall of the storm and pass unnoticed because of the general roar, confusion, and lack of visibility. An exceptionally strong wind gust may, in reality, be a passing tornado. If tornadoes do occur within the eyewall, detection is all but impossible.

In the outer part of the hurricane, where the general weather is not so violent, an approaching tornado can be heard from some distance away. The sound has been most often described as that of a freight train, perhaps accompanied by intermittent banging or popping, like gunshots, as windows are blown out of buildings. As a hurricane approaches, it is wise to listen to the radio for possible tornado reports and warnings, and to stay indoors and away from windows.

Lightning

The amount of electrical activity in a hurricane can vary from practically zero (quiet) to a dazzling, continuous display of lightning. The amount of electrical activity seems to have little to do with the violence of the wind, but is perhaps related to the rainfall in a hurricane.

The mature hurricane may have little or no thunderstorm activity. As Hurricane David passed by Miami, in 1979, no lightning or thunder was observed at my location. Neither was any unusual atmospheric noise present on the radio at any frequency, from the standard AM broadcast band upward through the short waves. Yet tropical storm Dennis of 1981, a much less intense storm, produced lightning so brilliant and continuous that it was possible to read a book by its light during the nighttime. Dennis was less organized, but produced much more rainfall, than David.

Of course, lightning activity is more easily noticed in the less violent part of a hurricane than in the eyewall, and is more readily seen at night than during the daytime. With a 150-mile-per-hour wind, people are not likely to notice (or care about) the lightning and thunder. Heavy rains and limited visibility can make lightning hard to detect.

Immature storms in the first stages of development, and older, decaying hurricanes, appear to produce more lightning than mature storms, but there are exceptions. After the eye of the famous Labor Day hurricane of 1935 passed the Florida Keys, fantastic lightning displays were seen in spite of the high winds and heavy rain. Windblown sand, electrically charged by friction, contributed to the eerie scenario, glowing like billions of fireflies in the night.

THE EXTRATROPICAL HURRICANE

The hurricane of the tropics is a remarkably symmetrical storm, having isobars that form almost perfect circles. The typical hurricane is somewhat more intense and covers a slightly wider area on the side in which the wind blows in the same direction as the storm moves. (In the northern hemisphere, this is the right-hand half of the whirlwind; in the southern hemisphere, it is the left-hand half.) There are no frontal systems associated with the tropical hurricane, however. The forward speed is usually slow—less than 20 miles per hour in most cases. As a hurricane travels farther from the equator, it gets less symmetrical, develops warm and cold fronts, and attains a highter forward speed.

The latitude at which a hurricane changes in character from tropical to extratropical, or the exact moment the transition takes place, varies from storm to storm. It certainly matters whether it is early in the hurricane season, at the height of the season, or late. In the northern hemisphere, the hurricane season begins in June and ends in December; the greatest hurricane frequency is observed between about August 15 and October 15, when ocean temperatures are warmest. Storms that form during that period, such as our Debby, are the most likely to develop into severe hurricanes. Between August 15 and October 15, hurricanes are also most likely to retain their tropical characteristics up to the highest latitudes.

It is, of course, the recurving hurricanes that

eventually become extratropical. Nonrecurving storms stay in the tropics, and eventually strike some land mass, where they spend their fury and disintegrate.

An extratropical hurricane usually has less violent winds than a tropical storm. The winds blow much harder on the side of the extratropical storm in which the forward movement adds to the whirling effect. Some move forward at speeds as great as 50 to 60 miles per hour; this can make quite a difference between the "strong" side and the "weak" side of a storm. In some instances, the winds, cloudiness, and rain are practically nonexistent on the left-hand side of an extratropical hurricane (in the northern hemisphere), while the right-hand side carries torrential rain and winds of 80 miles per hour or more (Fig. 2-19). Such a storm resembles a low-pressure system of polar origin.

Extratropical hurricanes, although weaker than tropical ones in terms of wind, can still cause great devastation. A classic example of this is Hazel, of 1954. Even after moving inland and losing her killer winds and circular structure, Hazel retained winds of considerable force. Hazel caused floods as far inland as Toronto, Ontario. Extratropical hurricanes may strike northern New England, the Canadian maritime provinces, and at times may be felt as far from their hot, humid birthplace as Iceland or even Greenland. A similar situation exists in the other hurricane regions of the world.

Extratropical hurricanes rarely possess identifiable eyes. The pressure gradient is much less pronounced than in the tropical hurricane; the vortex may become greatly elongated, and the center fills up with clouds. Warm fronts occur in the right-hand quadrants (in the northern hemisphere), and cold fronts sweep around from the left-hand side and pass behind the center in a counterclockwise direction. Thunderstorms and squall lines occur along the cold frontal zones. Heavy rain and high winds may be observed hundreds of miles from the actual center of the hurricane. The eyewall loses its identity and its marked violence. If a late-season hurricane penetrates far enough from the tropics, the rain may change to snow in some sections of the storm.

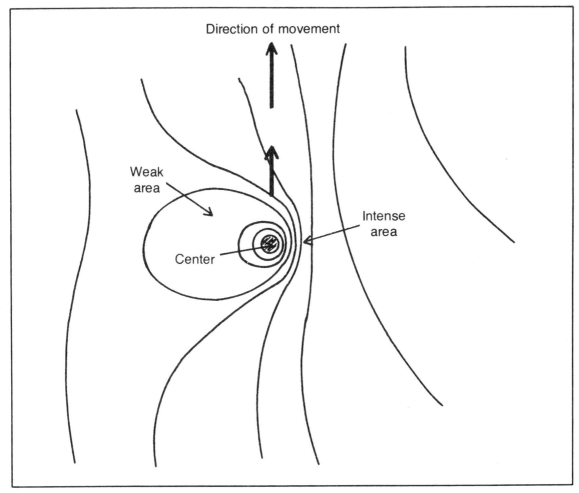

Fig. 2-19. An extratropical cyclone assumes nonsymmetrical characteristics. The isobars are usually most closely spaced on the right-hand side of such a storm in the northern hemisphere.

Although the extratropical hurricane is less intense than the well-defined vortex characteristic of the torrid zone, decaying storms are sometimes much larger, and they often affect far more people. A vigorous extratropical hurricane, passing over the industrialized northeastern United States, is more dangerous and destructive than a small, 200-mile-per-hour whirlwind that moves inland in a place where practically no one lives. New England has, from the arrival of the first settlers, suffered infrequent but terrible strikes. Long Island Sound, for example, is geographically well suited to the occurrence of a devastating *raz de marée,* even in an

extratropical hurricane. Coastal cities are vulnerable to flooding from such surges, and the heavy rains characteristic of extratropical storms compound the problem.

New England is occasionally visited by storms retaining some tropical characteristics. When this happens, the scenario is almost indescribable. Although they are used to bad weather, New Englanders don't expect to be hit with the force of a tropical hurricane. Fortunately, fully developed tropical hurricanes rarely get as far north as the 40th parallel without weakening somewhat, but many New England coastal dwellers have vivid memories of such storms as the "Long Island Express" of 1938, and Carol of 1954. Buildings were unroofed by the hundreds. Trees that had stood for over a century were uprooted or dismembered. Homes were carried away from the angry storm surges. The residents cleared away the debris, salvaged what they could of their stately elms, rebuilt their homes, and hoped that another such strike would not come soon.

NAMING OF TROPICAL STORMS

As the hypothetical Hurricane Debby bears down on Miami, the residents might wonder how this rather benign-sounding name is the code word for such a monstrous storm. Obviously, the name has little to do with the character of the storm. Why do we name hurricanes at all?

During World War II, hurricanes—especially Pacific typhoons—caused trouble for the United States Navy. Often, more than one storm was in progress at a given time, and all of them were constantly moving in various directions. Confusion arose. Which storm was which? There were no weather satellites back then, and it was more difficult to pinpoint the center of a storm. A solution was found: the hurricanes would be named.

At first, the phonets for the alphabet were suggested as possible names for hurricanes. Thus the first storm of a season could be named Able, the second one Baker, the third one Charlie, and so forth. The main problem with this scheme soon became evident: Which ocean was which? There might be three Bakers: one in the Caribbean Sea, one in the Pacific Ocean, and one in the Indian Ocean. While the idea of getting one ocean confused with another may sound silly, such mixups can and do happen. It wouldn't be very funny when a destroyer got caught in a 200-mile-per-hour wind with 70-foot seas!

The naming of hurricanes was not formally considered until after the war. In 1953, the official phonetics were changed, and a two-year plan for giving hurricanes phonetic names was dropped. It was decided that women's names would be used instead. Different lists of names would be used for different oceans to eliminate the possibility of the sort of confusion just described.

In the next year, 1954, hurricanes Carol, Edna, and Hazel demonstrated their appreciation for the new practice by raking New England, the middle Atlantic states, the Ohio Valley, and the Great Lakes region.

In 1978, it was decided that hurricanes should receive men's names as well as women's names. The letters Q, U, X, Y, and Z are not used, because there are so few names that begin with those letters. The new lists provide for up to 21 storms in any given year.

David of 1979 immediately showed his enthusiasm for receiving a boy's name by hammering the Caribbean islands and giving South Floridians a scare that they hadn't felt for 14 years.

Developing tropical storms are not named until they attain a certain intensity. Before then, the systems are simply called tropical disturbances or depressions. A tropical disturbance has little or no rotary circulation at the surface. A well-defined easterly wave is an example of a tropical disturbance. A tropical depression has at least one closed isobar, thereby showing rotation around a central point. If the depression strengthens so that the maximun sustained winds are at least 39 miles per hour, the system is classified as a tropical storm, and it receives an official name (for example, Debby). If the storm intensifies further, and its maximum sustained winds reach 74 miles per hour or more, it is called a hurricane—a "devil wind."

If a hurricane or tropical storm loses its intensity and returns to tropical depression or disturbance status, it loses its name as well. If it regains strength, the storm gets its old name back. Such occurrences are not especially frequent, but this sort of thing did happen with Dennis in 1981. After becoming a tropical storm, he decayed to a mere easterly wave south of Cuba. Dennis was all but dismissed as a threat to Florida. Then, suddenly, the weather over southern Florida became squally. Forecasters said, "Tropical Storm Dennis is affecting our weather." Dennis lumbered up from the south and stalled over the state, drenching some sections with more than 20 inches of rain and fanning the coasts with gale-force winds. Finally,

Dennis moved off into the North Atlantic, and for a day or two, he attained hurricane strength.

PREPARING FOR A HURRICANE

For those who live in hurricane-prone regions, it is wise to begin preparations for a possible storm at the beginning of each hurricane season. In North America, the season officially starts on June 1. Nonperishable foods, tape, flashlight cells, and other storable items should be obtained well ahead of time. When warnings are issued, there will be immediate shortages.

It is especially important that an adequate water supply be maintained. After the hurricane, municipal water may be contaminated and unsafe; there may be saltwater intrusion as a result of the storm surge.

The best way to store water is simply to fill every available container before the storm hits. The 1-gallon plastic bottles in which milk is sold are ideal for this purpose. All sinks and bathtubs should be thoroughly cleaned, sterilized with chlorine bleach, and the drains made completely watertight using some kind of nonwatersoluble sealant. Then they should be filled with water.

A substantial store of nonperishable food might include a wide variety of canned meats, vegetables, juices, fruits, nuts, and canned or evaporated milk. Such foods should be purchased before the start of the hurricane season (June 1) and can be used up slowly after the end of the season (about November 30). If it appears possible that a storm might strike within several days, certain foods can be purchased that will keep for several weeks in the refrigerator and a few days in a closed refrigerator without electricity. Examples of such foods include certain processed cheeses, fresh fruits and vegetables, bread, and hard-boiled eggs. You can be inventive!

It is best to get foods that can be eaten without cooking. If it is necessary to cook foods, and you happen to have a gas stove and/or oven with your own independent gas tank, be sure the tank is filled well before the storm approaches. (Don't try to call the gas man after the warning has been issued!) During the storm, the tank valve should be closed,

and no attempt should be made to cook anything. Wait until the hurricane has passed.

Charcoal should never be used indoors, since the fumes are dangerous in a confined area. Portable burners are available for camp use, however; most of these are all right to use indoors, but be careful with fire.

Fill the gas tanks of all your vehicles. After the hurricane, electricity may not be restored for days, and gas station pumps use electric motors.

If you have a boat, it should be moved away from the ocean or bay. Don't wait until the storm is almost upon you; get it to safety a day or two in advance of the hurricane. If there is no safe place to put a boat, it can be anchored and sunk. Boats on trailers should be kept indoors if possible. If that is not possible, the boat and the trailer should be anchored down with aircraft cable. A hurricane can pick up a boat bodily and carry it for blocks or even miles.

If time is available, it is a good idea to prune down trees and shrubbery to protect them against destruction by the hurricane winds, and to reduce the danger of damage from flying limbs. Actually, pruning should be done, and kept up to date, on a routine basis. Even a minimal hurricane can uproot large trees. Take the cut branches to the dump; do not leave them lying around. If you have coconut trees, take the coconuts off; a hurricane wind can propel them like cannon balls.

The winds of a hurricane can easily shatter windows. Although flying debris is partially responsible for breaking windows, the force of the moving air alone is sufficient to break larger windows at 80 to 100 miles per hour, and virtually all windows at 120 to 130 miles per hour. Windows should preferably be either boarded up or protected by steel or aluminum shutters. If this is not feasible, masking tape should be placed in an X-pattern over the inside and outside of every window pane. Of course, once the storm strikes, you should stay as far as possible from windows.

As the storm bears down, windows on the lee side of the house or building (the side facing away from the wind) should be opened. This will help to equalize the pressure difference between the inside and the outside of the structure and reduce the chance that windows will explode inward or outward.

Loose objects can become lethal missiles in a hurricane wind. Trash cans, radio antennas, bicycles, tools, lawn mowers, and other objects can be hurled for blocks at high speed. Such objects must either be stored indoors or tied down, preferably with strong wire.

False rumors will probably be circulating during the days and hours before a hurricane strikes. It is important to get the facts. The Weather Bureau and the National Hurricane Center will disseminate the information via local radio and television statons.

If you live near the beach or bay shore, and you are advised to evacuate to higher ground, do it!

As the eyewall of the storm moves inland, electricity will probably be lost. A battery-powered radio, with two or three sets of spare batteries (that have been checked and found good), should be available for use during the blackout. A good flashlight, with several sets of spare batteries and one or two spare bulbs, is a great convenience. The lantern-type light, with the large battery, is the best, since the battery life is roughly proportional to battery size. Candles and matches can be used, but they can create a fire hazard. Candles in glass jars are least likely to be tipped over.

When power is lost, switch off all lamps and appliances to protect them against a possible voltage surge when power is restored. Shut off the main switch or switches at the distribution box.

The hours immediately before the arrival of the eyewall may be deceptively calm. The rain and wind may diminish to little more than a drizzly breeze, but when the vortex moves over you, there will be no doubt about it. It is important to remain calm and not to panic. Children and elderly people will need reassurance, because the confusion and the sound of the wind and pelting rain can be especially upsetting to them.

A HURRICANE STRIKES

As the warning is issued, the broadcasts are the only directly visible evidence of what is coming.

The sky has a few high cirrus clouds, with scattered cumulus at lower levels. The sun sets with the reddish glow familiar to Floridians. The barometer has dropped slightly, but not yet to an unusual extent. The large ocean swells, thrown out in advance of the storm, do not get to the beaches because of the reefs offshore. Just one day away, however, one of the most violent hurricanes in memory is churning up the ocean waters.

Experienced mariners might suspect the hurricane because of the backing of the wind into the northeast and because of the peculiar gustiness of the breeze. The few cumulus clouds seem to move a little more quickly across the sky than usual, and as the sun sets, they assume a dusky gray appearance. The fishermen of the keys know, almost instinctively, that Debby is coming. The radio and television broadcasts leave no question.

In terms of diameter, Debby is not a particularly large hurricane, and she is still about 450 miles away, approaching at a little less than 20 miles per hour.

September 16, 9:00 P.M.. Debby appears headed straight for greater Miami, with maximum sustained winds of 160 miles per hour and gusts estimated at over 200 miles per hour. Personnel of the National Hurricane Center try to describe the fury of Debby to the residents. A radar picture, obtained from a reconnaissance aircraft near the eyewall, is shown on television (Fig. 2-20). The eye of the storm shows up clearly, as do the spiral rain bands ahead of, and to the right of, the eyewall.

Preparations for the arrival of Debby continue throughout the night. Most of the people are taking the storm warning seriously; they are busy boarding up windows, securing loose objects, and taking other emergency measures. Hardware and grocery stores remain open until all their supplies are gone. Gas stations, too, remain open.

At 2:00 A.M. on September 17, the bright, full moon is suddenly obscured by the cumulonimbus clouds of the outermost rain band of the hurricane. The wind gusts fitfully, constantly blowing from the northeast with little or no variability. The shower is over within a few minutes, and the moon reappears dimly behind layers of fast-moving clouds. Every

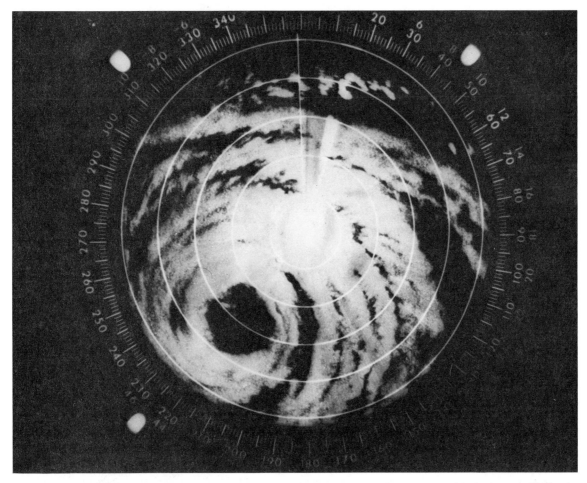

Fig. 2-20. A radar photograph of a hurricane. Although it is described in the text as Debby (our hypothetical storm), this view is actually of Betsy, a storm that passed near Miami in 1965. (courtesy NOAA/National Hurricane Center.)

few moments a ragged fractocumulus or "scud" cloud temporarily blocks the moon; then the silvery disk reappears, yet more dim.

The full moon means that the normal gravitational tides will be at their highest, and if the hurricane tide strikes along with the occurrence of normal high tide, the flooding will be phenomenal. This, say the forecasters, is all the more reason for the coastal dwellers to evacuate inland. Most heed the warnings; a few do not.

The next rain squalls move into Miami at about 4:30. The smattering of rain against boarded-up windows awakens the residents that have managed to fall asleep despite the growing general tension and apprehension. A glance out the door reveals slanting rain, swaying trees, and a still more rapidly moving rack of gray clouds, illuminated by the lights of the city. The showers again pass, but the weather grows darker and windier by the hour.

Dawn arrives dim and gray. "It's all fuzzed up now," remarks one man with a deep southern twang, as he and his family sit on their screened-in patio, watching the breeze and eating a hearty, hot breakfast of sausage and pancakes. "Won't see much of the sun till tomorrow." Within 12 hours the patio, furniture and all, will be completely gone. Tomorrow, this family will be eating crackers and canned sardines for breakfast.

Rain showers and thunderstorms continue intermittently throughout the morning hours, but none are especially violent, and some people are getting the idea that Debby might be an overrated storm. The forecasters warn, however, that Debby is an unusually fast mover. Most hurricanes at this latitude move at speeds of 15 miles per hour or less. Debby has speeded up to an even 20-mile clip. This means that the destructive eyewall will strike with greater than usual rapidity. It also means, fortunately, that the storm duration will be shorter than that of the average hurricane—if Debby doesn't stall or slow down. The eyewall is rather small, having contracted to an outside diameter of only about 60 miles. If Debby makes a direct hit, she will get her work done in a hurry.

Just after noon, the sky lightens a little, and for a few minutes the animated trees cast their shadows on the damp ground. The wind along the beaches has picked up to a 50-mile northeasterly gale (Fig. 2-21). Inland, it could be a typical, squally, windy day in September. The barometer reads 29.50. A sharp tap jolts the needle down to 29.40. It's falling fast.

Coral Gables, a southwestern suburb of Miami, is graced with green, lush foliage and beautiful homes. Although the residents don't yet know it (nor can the forecasters precisely predict it at this point), Coral Gables lies squarely in the path of the oncoming whirlwind. Tree limbs begin to break off and litter the streets at about 3:00 P.M. as the innermost rain band passes through the area, accompanied by two tornadoes, driving rains, lightning, thunder, and wind gusts to 70 miles per hour. The power goes out. Broken utility lines flap and spark in the gale. There is one last, brief letup in the rain. Then, at 3:45, a milky green, sideways-moving wall of rain and debris swallows up the landscape from the southeast.

Whirlwind

As the edge of the wall cloud approaches, the

Fig. 2-21. A hurricane approaches the coastline, driving salt spray into the air and buffeting palm trees. Although it is described in the text as Debby, this photograph is of Frederic, 1979. (Courtesy NOAA.)

sound is not unlike that of an airplane taking off overhead. In fact, some people dismiss the rising roar as just that for a moment.

The air becomes filled with flying debris—tree limbs and whole palm tree tops, unsecured bicycles, lawn mowers, boats, roofing shingles, and pieces of broken glass and bent sheet metal. Automobiles are overturned, and some smaller cars are actually rolled until they come to an obstruction. Coconuts smash against the outside walls of the houses, the thudding sounds hardly audible above the bansheelike screaming and wailing of the wind. The rain lashes with the force of a firehose spray. Corrosive salt spray from Biscayne Bay, blown for miles inland, mixes with the rain. Visibility is about 50 feet.

Atop the building containing the National Hurricane Center, the anemometer is destroyed shortly after the recorded wind speed exceeds 100 miles per hour. The true wind speed will never be measured. We can only guess at it.

Inside their homes, the residents huddle in broom closets, under kitchen and dining room tables, or any place they feel relatively safe. For a short time, some radio stations, equipped with emergency generators, continue to operate, giving the latest radar information and other data. It is difficult to hear what they are saying; the noise of the wind, rain, and flying debris almost drowns out the feeble voices that come from battery-powered transistor radios. One by one, the broadcast stations go off the air as their towers collapse in the wind.

The blow continues unabated. Along the bayfront and beach, the on-shore winds push the thrashing salt water higher and higher. As the edge of the eyewall moves up the coast, the few people who have remained on the waterfront discover why they were advised to evacuate. The sea seems to be about to carry them and their homes away. The wind tide around the northern periphery of the eyewall reaches 14 feet above normal, washing sand and silt into the lower stories of the buildings. Some houses and condominiums collapse as 8-foot waves literally batter them to pieces or wash the foundations out from underneath. We might try to imagine what goes through the minds of people as they watch their homes being demolished by an angry sea, and as they feel their very lives imperiled!

Miami Beach and Key Biscayne become part of the ocean floor for two long hours. When the violent water finally subsides, most of the causeways will be gone; the only transportation to the mainland will be by boat. The beach will have been rearranged; sand will be knee deep on Collins Avenue.

Finally, at about 5:00 P.M., some of the coastal dwellers notice that the shriek of wind is beginning to get lower in pitch. Is the hurricane letting up? Yes, a break is coming. The visibility improves, and the sky lightens. The rain slackens, and then stops altogether. The edge of Debby's eye is moving ashore.

The eye of this storm is relatively small—only about 8 miles in diameter—but it is extremely well defined. The small size of the eye, combined with the fact that Debby is moving at 20 miles per hour, means that the calm will be short-lived. Those who lie precisely in the path of the storm will have about 24 minutes of relief before the second half of the hurricane strikes. In many places, the calm will last for a much shorter time. Most of the residents will not see the eye at all, but will notice a rapid shift in wind direction, veering in the right-hand half of the storm and backing in the left-hand portion.

While some people are cautiously peering out of their battered homes at the eerie landscape around them, taking advantage of the momentary letup in the wind and rain, others, only a few miles away, are still experiencing the full fury of the hurricane.

The clouds in the eye are thin and broken. The blue sky is visible in patches. The slanting, late-afternoon sun illuminates the towering banks of cloud surrounding the eye; the strange shadow of the western wall cloud falls on the eastern cumulonimbus, as if the eye of Debby were a huge white well 8 miles across and 8 miles deep. All of the clouds are continually in motion. The roar of the wind can be heard in the distance, like hundreds of jet aircraft circling around, never stopping.

The air in the eye seems unusually warm. A

hasty, nervous trip is made out to the back yard; we know that the storm may return at any moment. Where is the thermometer that used to be outside the kitchen window? It has blown away, but the air is definitely warm, and seems quite dry despite the heavy rains that have fallen.

The air within the eye of a hurricane is, in fact, usually warmer than the air surrounding the eye. A hurricane is a warm low-pressure system, and the humidity is often observed to fall in the core of a storm.

In a badly battered grapefruit tree, a strange tropical bird roosts. It is certainly not a local bird; it must have come all the way from the Caribbean. Birds can be carried for thousands of miles in the comparatively serene eye of a hurricane. Tropical birds have been seen in the northeastern states following hurricanes from the Caribbean. Birds have been know to alight, exhausted, in great numbers as a storm center passes over a ship or over land.

There is no time to sit and watch this bird; we must return to shelter as soon as possible, for the rear part of the hurricane is moving steadily closer.

The barometer still hangs on the wall in the living room. What does it show? The house is dark, because all the windows have been boarded up. In the dim light, the needle seems to be pointing almost straight down. Normally, the needle points upward. A flashlight facilitates close observation. Yes, it is way off: it shows 27.05 inches.

Normal atmospheric pressure will support about 30 inches of mercury. Thus, the pressure within the eye of Debby is only 90 percent of normal. Instead of the usual 14.7 pounds of pressure per square inch, the air in the eye of this hurricane produces only about 13.2 pounds of pressure per square inch. This difference of 1.5 pounds per square inch is spread over a region of about 50 square miles, or 200 billion square inches. No wonder the storm is so violent, as the air rushes in to fill this void.

Structural damage is extensive. A few brave (and perhaps foolhardy) people venture outside to survey the ruins of their neighborhood. Tree branches are everywhere; some trees, still par-

tially intact, have been carved into odd and ugly configurations. A boat leans up against a badly damaged house (Fig. 2-22). Some houses have been twisted as if by the hand of a giant (Fig. 2-23).

The sky begins to darken toward the south and east; the wind has shifted to the southwest. Rain begins to fall again. Then, the rear half of the storm moves in, and the noise, confusion, and terror returns. After the period of light winds and absence of rain, the storm seems even more violent than it was before the arrival of the eye. In many hurricanes, the second half is actually more violent than the first. Houses vibrate and shake with the force of the blast; the noise and pressure are painful to the ears.

A few people get caught outside as the storm returns; they have waited too long. Some of them are killed by flying debris. A few manage to crawl back to the doors of their houses. One lone man struggles and slides on the wet concrete of his driveway. His wife throws him a piece of clothesline and pulls him in.

During the ensuring 90 minutes, what little is left of the foliage in Coral Gables is stripped of almost every leaf. Some of the stronger pine trees remain standing; others lean as if they have been pushed down by a great bulldozer. Houses and apartment buildings are unroofed, and the rain comes rushing in.

By 7:00, the storm has abated somewhat. Nightfall arrives with a deepening gray. There will be little sleep this night. Although the worst of the hurricane is over, many comfortable homes are now little more than drenched hovels.

Aftermath of a Killer

The full extent of the damage from Debby will not be realized for some time. All telephone service has been wiped out. There is no electricity. Most broadcast stations are off the air because of antenna damage. The sun rises in a clear, bright, breezy sky, and shines benignly down on piles of rubble that once were buildings (Fig. 2-24).

Along the beachfront, many buildings have been completely washed away. Only the foundations, some obscured by tons of sand, remain. Fish are strewn everywhere. Seaweed hangs from the

Fig. 2-22. The effects of the winds of a severe hurricane. Although it is described as Debby in the text, this photograph was taken after Camille struck the Mississippi coast in August, 1969. (courtesy NOAA).

Fig. 2-23. A house is twisted and blown from its foundation. The doorsteps remain intact. Although it is described as Debby in the text, this photograph was taken after Camille, 1969. (courtesy NOAA.)

tops of telephone poles. Streets and highways have been undermined (Fig. 2-25).

Hurricane Debby has moved into the Florida peninsula, and her violence has decreased somewhat. Orlando is buffeted by a salvo of tornadoes, violent squalls, and heavy rains. The storm drenches the swamplands to the west of Jacksonville, and moves on into southern Georgia. Savannah gets 26 inches of rain, Brunswick 23 inches. As Debby passes into South Carolina, she combines with a low-pressure trough and drops 29 inches of rain on Charleston. Over the hills of Virginia, even more rain occurs; Richmond gets an unbelievable total of 38 inches in 2 days. Then Debby moves into the Atlantic as an extratropical cyclone. New En-

gland escapes all but the fringe effects.

Meanwhile, the people of Miami dig through the piles of broken trees, rooftops, and other debris. Most of those who heeded the warnings have come through the experience with their lives, but some have been injured as their houses folded up around them. Some of the waterfront residents who chose to stay and ride the storm out have not been as lucky. The death toll stands in the hundreds.

Certain precautions must be observed following a hurricane. While electricity may be off for an extended period of time, some fallen wires will probably still be live. Utility lines carry hundreds or even thousands of volts. If live wires are dangling or lying in a puddle of water, the whole vicinity can

Fig. 2-24. Some buildings are completely demolished by the forces of wind and water in a hurricane. Although it is described as Debby in the text, this photograph was taken after Camille, 1969. (courtesy NOAA.)

Fig. 2-25. After the angry water recedes, many coastal roads, such as this highway, are left without support because of erosion. Although it is described as Debby in the text, this photograph was taken after Camille, 1969. (courtesy NOAA.)

become hazardous. Stay away from standing water and downed power lines.

The drinking water, if not totally shut off, may not be safe for human consumption. As radio broadcasting stations return to the air, advisories will probably be given concerning the safety of the water supply. Do not use the water until you are certain it is safe.

If your telephone still works, don't try to use it except in an emergency. The switching networks will probably be working at only part of their normal capacity.

Do not attempt to drive your car until most of the debris has been cleared. After a storm such as our hypothetical Debby, you wouldn't be able to get far, anyway.

When using portable cooking apparatus, be extremely careful to avoid the possibility of fire. The same applies to candles and other flame-type lighting apparatus. Firefighters may not be able to reach you quickly. The water pressure will probably be very low or nonexistent, making it still more difficult to deal with fires.

I have illustrated, by the make-believe hurricane Debby, a worst-case scenario. Hurricanes of such intensity do not occur often, but every few years, a hurricane of this magnitude does develop, and such storms have hit the United States coastline. A memorable example is Camille of August, 1969. Figures 2-15 and 2-22 through 2-25 are actual photographs of some of the damage caused by this hurricane. They show what can happen when a major storm strikes a populated region.

Many coastal areas have experienced tremendous population growth since the last great hurricane. Most of the residents of these places have no idea what could happen if a Camille or Debby were to visit them. Many of these people will never have to live through a severe hurricane, but some are destined for an experience that old-timers can still vividly remember. They will, someday, ride out a devil wind of the sea, and, as did their predecessors, they will survive and rebuild.

Chapter 3

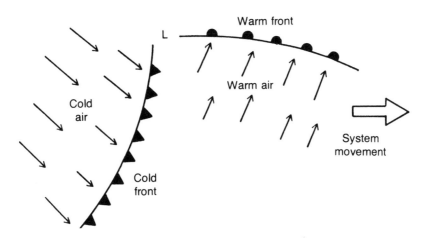

Showers,
Thunderstorms, and Squall Lines

Showers, thundershowers, and heavy thunderstorms occur throughout the world in the temperate and tropical latitudes. Usually, such occurrences cause no problems for human beings; in fact, the rainfall they produce is beneficial. In some cases, however, rain showers continue to intensify and grow, developing into storms that can ruin crops, damage buildings, and, in their most severe forms, kill people.

As a cumulonimbus cloud begins to form, what determines its behavior over the next few hours? Why, in two seemingly identical situations, will one cloud develop into a gentle summer shower while another turn into a violent storm? How can we tell when conditions favor the development of heavy thunderstorms?

A CUMULONIMBUS CLOUD FORMS

Thunderstorms are always associated with cumulonimbus clouds. The word *cumulonimbus* means "puffy maker of rain." Cumulonimbus clouds can form all by themselves, or they can form in groups of two or more. When several thunderstorms band together and move as a unit, the combination is called a *squall line*. The most extensive squall lines are found in hurricanes, but squall lines often form near fronts in temperate low-pressure systems.

In the early stages of formation, a cumulonimbus cloud appears as an oversized cumulus cloud. The top is rounded, and little or no rain falls. Warm ground-level air ascends, pushing into the cooler air above and resulting in the formation of water droplets, making the cloud visible. As the warm air rises through the center of the cloud, additional warm air flows inward at the cloud base, supplying new energy to the system. The cloud rapidly grows, in breadth as well as in height. It is often possible to observe a cumulonimbus cloud expand in its early stages, just by watching for a few seconds. A rapidly developing cumulonimbus cloud is shown in Fig. 3-1.

The cumulonimbus cloud gets larger as strong updrafts push its top higher. More warm, moist,

Fig. 3-1. A developing cumulonimbus cloud. In the background, the high cirrostratus anvil top of a more distant, mature thundershower, is visible.

low-level air is pulled into the circulation from all sides, and the cloud continues to expand outward. Eventually, precipitation begins. The cloud may continue to increase in size until its top reaches an altitude of 40,000 feet or more, and its rain area covers dozens or even hundreds of square miles. Some cumulonimbus clouds can build up until they tower to 65,000 feet, or 12.3 miles—higher than any commercial airliner ever flies. The cloud edge contrasts starkly with the surrounding sky (Fig. 3-2).

Finally, the top of the cumulonimbus cloud encounters the high speed winds in the upper troposphere and lower stratosphere, and the top of the cloud is sheared off. This results in the well-known anvil shape, the signature of a fully developed thunderhead.

THUNDERSHOWERS IN THE TROPICS

In the torrid zone of our planet, between the Tropic of Cancer and the Tropic of Capricorn, cumulonimbus clouds form on an almost daily basis. This is particularly true in the rain forests near the equator. During the midmorning hours, the sun, rising high in the sky, heats the ground. This heat is conducted to the air at low levels, and the warm, moist air rises. By early afternoon, large cumulus clouds have formed. These clouds continue to grow, and rain begins to fall. The rain may become quite heavy, and it is not unusual for gusty winds, lightning, and perhaps small hail to accompany the shower. This type of storm is not entirely unique to the rain forests; such cumulonimbus formation is common in the subtropics during the summer months. It is also well known to residents of the southeastern United States, especially Florida and the Gulf Coast region.

There is no frontal system associated with the development of the tropical thundershower. The clouds show little or no movement. The effect is local; it may be raining furiously in one place, while the sun shines just a few miles away. Such showers are relatively short lived; once their rains have cooled the earth beneath, the source of heat energy is spent, and the showers dissipate. By early evening, the sky may clear sufficiently so that the sunset can be seen. The following day, the cycle will be repeated.

Sometimes, a cold front will push southward into the subtropics, intensifying the daily thermal showers. This situation occurs frequently in the spring, resulting in fast-moving, severe thunderstorms. Damaging winds are common in such storms; speeds can reach 80 to 90 miles per hour in peak gusts. Small tornadoes are not unusual. Such storms are similar to the violent squall lines that rake the midwest in the summer. Although severe storms of this variety are most likely to take place during the afternoon hours, they sometimes occur in the late morning. The storms can develop with great rapidity and strike with very little warning. A fair sky can turn frighteningly dark within a few minutes (Fig. 3-3).

THE WILD WESTERLIES

Tropical thundershowers occasionally get violent, but their ferocity can seldom match that of the tremendous squall lines of the temperate latitudes. The effects of a fast-moving cold front are well known to residents of the Midwestern states, from the Rockies to the mid-Atlantic region, and from Canada to Texas.

In west-central Minnesota, the town of

Fig. 3-2. A well-developed thundershower, with its high cloud tops contrasting against the blue sky. This is an isolated tropical rainstorm,

A

B

Fig. 3-3. Tropical thundershowers may develop into fast-moving and sometimes sinister-looking squall lines. At A, sunlight creates vivid contrast between the landscape and an approaching heavy thunderstorm. At B, a severe thunderstorm bears down as the sun shines through from behind.

82

Alexandria is well known for its fine lake resorts. Thousands of vacationers flock to the area every summer to enjoy the fishing, swimming, boating, and mild, sunny weather. The weather in Minnesota during June, July, and August is hard to beat—most of the time.

In August, 1962, vacationers awoke one morning at about 4:30, jolted from their sleep by the sounds of thrashing tree branches and pounding rain. A squall line bore down from the west-northwest. For nearly an hour the winds shrieked through attics, uprooted and dismembered trees, and caused general structural damage. As the sun rose, it shone on streets that were carpeted with green foliage. A motel had lost most of its roof. The winds had been clocked at 96 miles per hour. Similar storms have occurred several times since.

In July, 1983, an especially intense squall line passed through the vacationland, causing damage to buildings, ripping trees apart, and even flipping small aircraft (Fig. 3-4). Top winds were measured at 100 knots (115 miles per hour) at the Alexandria airport—the highest speed the anemometer could record. The actual peak gust speeds may have been considerably greater. Such winds are comparable to those in a typical hurricane.

A Midwestern summer storm can cause severe flooding. Rochester, Minnesota, had a wet spring and early summer in 1978. Then, in July, a line of severe thunderstorms produced several inches of rain within a 24-hour period. The Zumbro River could not handle the runoff, and a flash flood ensued. Many homes were severely damaged; a large part of the city was underwater.

In addition to wind and rain, the Midwest receives frequent severe hailstorms. These storms cause damage to farm crops, kill livestock (and sometimes people), wreck automobiles, and shat-

Fig. 3-4. A squall line, accompanied by wind gusts of more than 115 miles per hour, overturned this small aircraft near Alexandria, Minnesota, in July, 1983. (courtesy Alexandria Newspapers, Inc.)

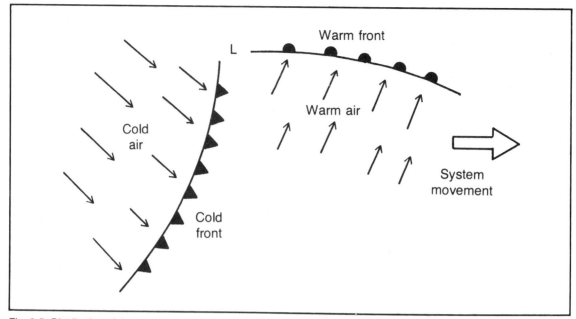

Fig. 3-5. Distribution of the warm front and the cold front in a typical northern-hemisphere low-pressure system.

ter windows. Sometimes a hailstorm even brings out the snow plows. One June day brought more than 12 inches of hail to the area of Wabasha, Minnesota. In some places, deciduous trees were stripped of every leaf, and hurricane-force winds piled the hailstones into drifts that did not disappear for two days. People were treated to a winter wonderland in the middle of June.

The thunderstorms and squall lines of the Midwest also produce lightning. Although the tropics and subtropics are more noteworthy for lightning frequency, the central states get their share of damage from lightning strikes. Lightning can cause fires in homes and forests. It often damages electrical wiring, and it kills more people each year than tornadoes.

The most frightening aspect of the midwestern thunderstorm is its ability to generate large, destructive tornadoes. These rotating storms sometimes grow to a mile in diameter, with winds of such force that they have never been measured. We will look at the tornado in more detail in Chapter 4.

What causes storms to attain such destructive characteristics? Certain weather conditions favor the development of severe thunderstorms and

squall lines. Most heavy summer storms are associated with rapidly moving cold fronts. Severe storms also occasionally develop along a stationary, occluded, or warm front.

FRONTAL SYSTEMS

Low-pressure systems in the temperate latitudes almost always contain frontal zones. A *front* is the boundary between two air masses having much different temperatures.

In the northern hemisphere, warm air flows from south to north along the leading side of a low-pressure system, and cool or cold air streams from the north and west on the trailing, or right-hand, side of the system. This results in a pattern similar to that shown by the hypothetical weather map of Fig. 3-5. In the southern hemisphere, warm air moves southward along the leading side of a clockwise-rotating low-pressure system; cold air moves toward the northeast or east along the trailing, or left-hand, side.

The poleward-moving warm air produces clouds and showers along its frontal boundary. The cold front is characterized by a well-defined band of clouds ahead of the frontal boundary and little or no cloudiness behind producing a characteristic comma shape in the satellite photographs.

The cold front almost always moves much faster than the warm front in a temperate low. Because of this, the cold front may catch up with the warm front and overrun it. A front of this type is called an *occluded front.*

Sometimes a cold front trailing a low-pressure system may lose its forward momentum and stall over one area producing prolonged cloudiness and rain. The bad weather may persist for several days. Warm fronts may also stall in this manner. Such a nonmoving front is called a *stationary front.*

All types of frontal systems—warm, cold, occluded, and stationary—can cause severe weather.

THE ANATOMY OF A TEMPERATE LOW

Figures 3-6 and 3-7 are satellite views of an early fall Midwestern low-pressure system centered over Nebraska. The view in Fig. 3-6 is in visible light; that in Fig. 3-7 is in infrared light. Although the system appears similar at both the visible and infrared wavelengths, there are some differences. Meterologists make extensive use of infrared views to determine the cloud structure within the frontal regions. This allows storm areas to be located.

In this low-pressure system, the cold front has caught the warm front, forming an occlusion. The system is mature. The occluded front can be seen clearly in both pictures, extending toward the east from Nebraska, across central Iowa, and into Illinois. Farther from the storm center, the cold front has not yet caught up with the warm front to the northeast.

In Iowa, the circulation is toward the north, and in Illinois it is toward the northeast. South of Illinois, a strong cold front pushes eastward across western Kentucky and Tennessee, and southwestward into extreme northwestern Mississippi and Louisiana. The front disappears over eastern Texas.

The counterclockwise circulation of the system is very apparent; so is its immensity. At the moment these photographs were taken, this cyclonic system was affecting the weather from the Great Lakes and the Ohio Valley to the shores of the Gulf of Mexico.

The differences between the visible light photograph and the infrared photograph are subtle. Cloud types are easier to identify in the infrared, however. The brightness of a cloud in visible light depends mostly on its thickness: low, dense cumulus or stratus clouds, for example, reflect light better than high-altitude cirrus clouds, which are comparatively thin and transparent. In infrared, the high clouds, such as cirrus and cirrostratus, appear bright, while the lower-level clouds appear darker. This is because the brightness in the infrared depends directly on the temperature—the colder an object, the brighter it looks—and clouds get colder with increasing altitude. This fact allows us to make some deductions concerning cloud types. In many

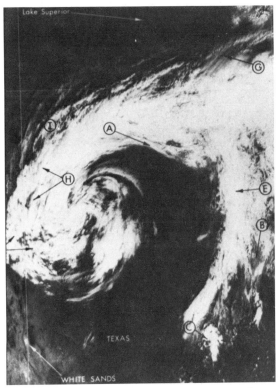

Fig. 3-6. An early fall low-pressure system, centered over Nebraska, as seen in visible light from the NOAA-2 satellite on September 29, 1973. (courtesy U.S. Department of Commerce, NOAA.)

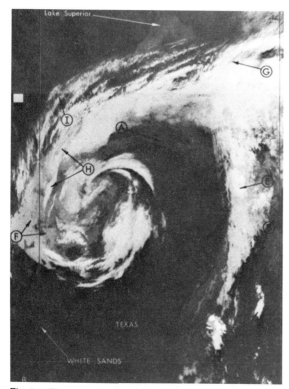

Fig. 3-7. The same system as at Fig. 3-6, but in infrared light. (courtesy U.S. Department of Commerce, NOAA.)

Isolated thundershowers (C, D) appear bright in both the visible and the infrared photographs because the cumulonimbus clouds are dense, and they also extend to high altitudes. These storms are in the vicinity of the Mississippi River delta. A more concentrated band of showers (E) brings heavy rains and possible squall lines to west-central Kentucky.

Middle- and high-level clouds move into the system from the north and west (F, G, H, I). These clouds always appear bright in the infrared. Severe storms are not likely to occur in these areas, although rain may fall over southern Minnesota, southeastern South Dakota, and much of Nebraska and Kansas. For them, the chilly and wet weather brings a clear message: summer is over.

THE BATTLE OF WARM AND COLD

It has been said that warm and cold air are constantly at war. When asked, "What makes severe thunderstorms?" almost anyone in the midwestern or eastern United States will reply, "Storms happen when cold and warm air meet." In general, this is true, but cold and warm air can meet in many different ways. One air mass battlefield may be much different from another.

Normally, the temperature of the atmosphere decreases as altitude increases. The drop in temperature is uniform, amounting to about 5.4 degrees Fahrenheit for every 1,000 feet. This holds true for several miles upward. Frontal systems upset the uniformity, and this is partly responsible for the formation of rain clouds.

Suppose we get into a balloon and take a ride up into the atmosphere. At the ground, our thermometer might read 70 degrees. At an altitude of 1,000 feet, it is down to a little less than 65 degrees. As we ascend past the 1 mile point, we feel a definite chill; the temperature has dropped to about 40 degrees. Soon, our hands and feet begin to grow numb, as the temperature plummets below freezing.

In any frontal system, warm air overlies cold air, forming a temperature *inversion*. In the vicinity of a frontal system, the temperature drops at first with increasing altitude, but when the boundary

instances, it would be very hard, if not impossible, to determine cloud types from only the visible light view.

Along the edge of the occluded front, low stratocumulus clouds (A) can be seen. They appear bright in visible light, but dark in the infrared, so we know that these clouds are comparatively warm, and thus they are confined to lower altitudes. Light rain or drizzle may fall from these clouds, but storms are very unlikely to occur in this part of the system.

Well in advance of the cold front (B), you can see more warm clouds. These are fair weather cumulus. Storms will not be found in this part of the system, although the circulation will bring heavier clouds, with possible stormy weather, to this area within a few hours.

Heavy thundershowers are likely to occur in the areas near the eastward moving cold front.

between air masses is reached, the temperature increases. This increase may be abrupt and large. Then, as you ascend still higher, the normal pattern resumes. In our balloon, we would notice a sudden (and welcome) rise in the temperature. We would also probably get quite wet, since it is likely that clouds, and perhaps rain, would be present.

Figure 3-8 is a side view of a typical warm front. The inversion is shown by the dotted line. The warm air, because it is lighter than the cold air, tends to rise. As the front advances, the warm air flows over the top of the cold air mass, resulting in an inversion at various altitudes, depending on the horizontal distance from the front itself (the point at which the warm air meets the ground).

The inversion in advance of a warm front may extend for hundreds of miles. Because a warm front usually moves at a sluggish pace—a few miles per hour—cloudiness and rain may last for two or three days at any one place. Warm fronts are fairly stable in most cases, and they do not ordinarily produce severe weather. There are a few exceptions, however. A particularly fast moving or intense warm front can cause heavy thundershowers.

A warm front may slow down almost to a standstill, sometimes resulting in large accumulations of rainfall. Such a stalled front is called a *stationary front.* This is the type of weather system that seems to be most common on Saturdays and Sundays!

A cold front is a major producer of severe thunderstorms. Figure 3-9 illustrates a typical cold front. The cold air, because it is denser than the warm air, pushes underneath the warm air mass. The leading edge of a cold front is well defined, and it advances rapidly along the surface of the earth. The temperature difference may be as much as 30 to 40 degrees at ground level at points separated by only a few miles. It is not unusual for the temperature at one location to drop from 85 to 55 degrees

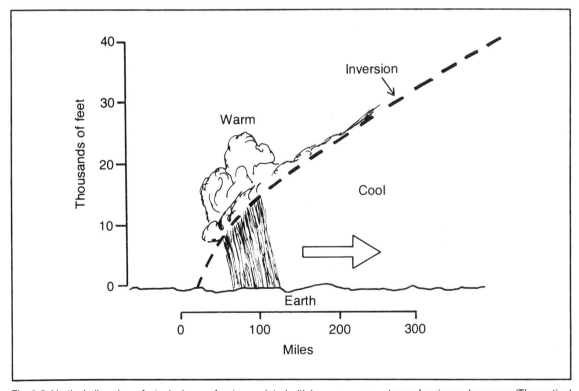

Fig. 3-8. Vertical-slice view of a typical warm front associated with low-pressure systems of spring and summer. (The vertical scale is greatly exaggerated.)

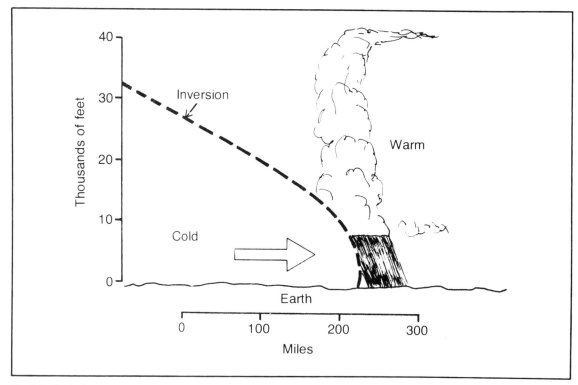

Fig. 3-9. Vertical-slice representation of a typical cold front associated with low-pressure systems of spring and summer. (The vertical scale is greatly exaggerated.)

Fahrenheit within a few minutes as the front passes, accompanied by high winds, heavy rains, and perhaps hail and tornadoes.

If a cold front encounters irregular terrain, or if the front is moving extremely fast, the leading edge of the cold air mass may literally fall over itself because the air moves a little faster at an altitude of a few thousand feet than it does immediately at the surface. If this happens, warm air pockets will be trapped under the leading part of the cold air mass, creating great instability. It is believed that such trapped warm, moist, air "bubbles," with cold, dry air overlying them, are likely to produce hail, damaging winds, and tornadoes.

The surface winds ahead of a cold front do not blow straight away from the advancing cold air mass, but at an angle instead. Sometimes this angle is very sharp, so that the winds blow almost parallel to the front. An example of such a situation is shown in Fig. 3-10. This is a visible light satellite view of the eastern United Sates and the western Atlantic Ocean, showing two midsummer storm systems in progress. One low is centered over the northeastern United States, and a second, smaller low is drifting eastward across the Atlantic, centered at about 43 degrees north latitude and 55 degrees west longitude.

An advancing cold front is moving off the coasts of the Carolinas and Georgia. Ahead of the cold front, surface winds are as high as 55 knots, or about 63 miles per hour. Although the cold front is moving toward the east and southeast, the winds are predominantly from the southwest. Wind speed and direction, at various points on the surface, are shown by the indicators. (Single short barbs indicate 5 knots, long barbs 10 knots, and pennants 50 knots. The barbed ends of the indicator lines point in the direction from which the wind blows.)

Another system of stormy weather is visible at the right of Fig. 3-10. High winds are also present here, at speeds of up to 45 knots (about 52 miles per hour) from the southwest. Further south, an area of showers and cloudiness can be seen, with breezy northwest winds. This system is probably an easterly wave or developing tropical depression, and is unrelated to the more northerly low-pressure area.

If a low-pressure system develops an occluded front (Fig. 3-11), severe weather is somewhat less likely to develop in the vicinity of the occlusion, although it is still possible. The advancing cold air mass behind the occluded front has a lower temperature than the air ahead of the occlusion, but the difference is not as large as it is when a cold front pushes rapidly into a mass of warm, moist air.

WATCHES AND WARNINGS

It is a hot, muggy, sunny July afternoon in Minnesota. Such days are common in the summer throughout most of the United States and other countries at similar latitudes. We are in the warm southeastern sector of a large, rather intense low-pressure system.

The recent passage of a warm front has moistened the ground, and as the bright sun strikes the soil and vegetation, the humidity rises higher. Tropical air, streaming up from the Gulf of Mexico and the southeastern states, presents the ideal scenario for severe thunderstorm development, in conjunction with a fast-moving, intense cold front.

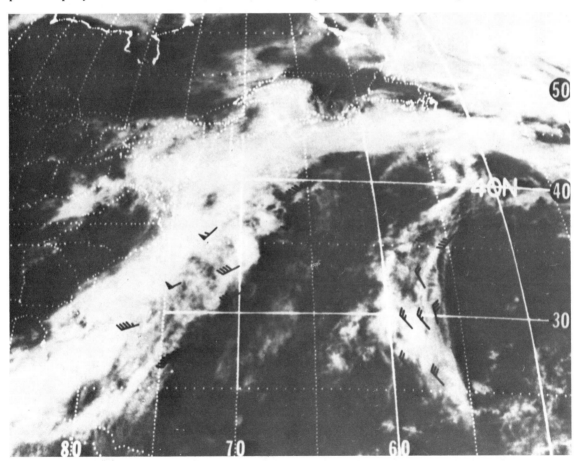

Fig. 3-10. Two summertime low-pressure systems and associated regions of heavy rain and high winds. While the cold fronts move in a generally easterly or southeasterly direction, the winds come mostly from the southwest. (Courtesy U.S. Department of Commerce, NOAA.)

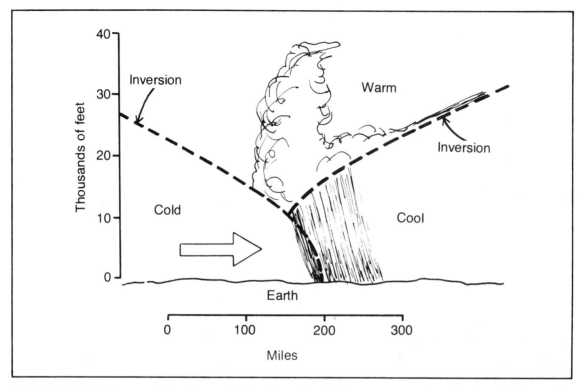

Fig. 3-11. Vertical-slice representation of an occluded front associated with low-pressure systems of spring and summer. (The vertical scale is greatly exaggerated.)

While temperatures in southern Minnesota are in excess of 90 degrees, some parts of the Dakotas are already in the 50s and 60s.

A severe thunderstorm watch is issued; this means that conditions are favorable for heavy storms. A tornado watch is also disseminated. Severe thunderstorms and tornado watches are often given together, because severe thunderstorms are likely to contain tornadoes.

Severe weather watch areas are generally rectangular in shape because heavy thunderstorms usually develop only within the most intense part of a cold front. Sometimes, several widely separated regions will receive severe thunderstorm watches at about the same time. The long span of the rectangle is parallel to the direction in which the storms are expected to move.

The weather announcement reads: "Severe thunderstorms, possibly containing large hail and damaging winds, are likely until 9:00 P.M. Central Daylight Time. The greatest probability of severe thunderstorms and tornadoes is in areas along, and 60 miles either side of, a line from 25 miles north of Sioux Falls, South Dakota, to 40 miles southwest of Hayward, Wisconsin." This precisely denotes the boundaries of the rectangle. The watch area covers about 32,000 square miles.

Of course, severe storms will almost certainly not be present everywhere within the rectangle at the same time. In fact, most people living within the watch rectangle will not see a severe thunderstorm at all; some will have a mostly sunny, hot day and a pleasant evening. The following day will be much cooler throughout the region, after the passage of the cold front.

The first reports of severe weather come from the western and southern portions of the watch rectangle at 4:00 P.M. Worthington, Minnesota, gets 2 inches of rain in ½ hour, along with marble-sized hail in some locations and wind gusts to 65 miles per hour. The storm quickly passes, leaving a cool, gray late afternoon.

In Minneapolis, we keep the radio on constantly, because we are in the watch area. There is no particular cause for alarm; severe thunderstorm watches are not unusual at this time of year, and the storm at Worthington, although quite heavy, is far from life threatening for those who stay indoors, away from windows (which can be broken by high winds) and electrical applicances, showers, and antenna installations (which are hazardous because of lightning).

At 5:00 P.M., we hear the announcement that all of Hennepin and Ramsey Counties are under a severe thunderstorm warning. "A line of heavy thunderstorms has been sighted. Movement is toward the east-northeast at 30 miles per hour." A group of thunderstorms, called a *multicell storm*, is approaching. The warning is effective until 6:30 for Hennepin County, and 7:00 for Ramsey County.

There may be other warning areas, scattered throughout the watch rectangle, at the same time as this warning is in effect; in fact, there probably are. Severe thunderstorm warnings are typically issued for much smaller areas than that of the weather watch. Of course, it is possible that severe thunderstorm warnings may have to be issued for localities not within the original watch rectangle. A damaging thunderstorm may occur, for example, in Alexandria, Minnesota, or in Hayward, Wisconsin. Both of these towns are slightly outside the watch area in this hypothetical situation.

The sun is still shining, bright and hot, over the Twin Cities. The haze obscures the towering cumulonimbus thunderheads off to the south and west.

Diagnosis: Severe or Not?

Thunderstorms may develop in isolated form, in which case they are called *single-cell storms*. Groups of two or three thunderstorms are called *multicell storms*; this is the type of system now bearing down on us.

The heaviest thunderstorms characteristically develop a *double-vortex* structure. Deep within the towering cloud, a clockwise, or anticyclonic, vortex

forms in the left-hand portion of the storm, and a counterclockwise, or cyclonic, vortex forms in the right-hand half, as we view the storm from the rear. In the center of the thunderstorm, air movement is upward and opposite to the direction of storm movement. This structure is illustrated in Fig. 3-12. The effect is not unlike the formation of double eddies as you pull a canoe paddle through the water.

The double-vortex nature of severe thunderstorms was discovered fairly recently by means of a modern, sophisticated form of radar, called *dual-Doppler radar*. The dual-Doppler radar shows not only the location of rain masses within showers and thunderstorms, but also indicates their speed and direction of movement. With the aid of computer graphics, severe thunderstorms, monitored by dual-Doppler radar, can be diagrammed in three dimensions.

As a thunderstorm moves toward the east, the clockwise vortex occurs in the northern half of the system, and the counterclockwise vortex is in the southern half.

When a thunderstorm has developed the double vortex structure, severe weather is likely. Tornadoes are a particular risk in such cases; we will look at this in Chapter 4.

A double vortex thunderstorm may split into two separate cells after it has traveled some distance. The clockwise spinning vortex tends to turn toward the left as the thunderstorm moves forward, and the counterclockwise vortex often veers toward the right. After the two vortices have separated sufficiently, they each develop a counter-vortex, or mate that spins in the opposite direction: the cell divides. If the process is repeated a number of times over a period of several hours, a single storm can become a multicell complex, and a group of thunderstorms can become a squall line.

The typical thundershower lasts for about 2 to 4 hours. Severe storms may last much longer, perhaps 6 to 8 hours, and in exceptional cases, half a day. The multicell and squall-line types of severe thunderstorms generally persist for a greater length of time and are more likely to become severe than the single-cell storm. This is because a group of storms exhibits a synergistic effect: the constituent cells keep each other going. It's a sort of community effort.

Thundershowers are frequently observed to form, mature, and dissipate at about the same time in different parts of a severe weather system. In Fig. 3-13, a group of midsummer thundershowers is shown as it develops and matures while moving through the New England region.

The satellite view at A shows a band of cloudiness moving into upper New York and Vermont at 7:30 A.M., Eastern time, on June 26, 1983. This is a developing frontal system, with low pressure toward the east and high pressure to the south and west. The remnants of a cold front, trailing a low now situated far off in the Atlantic, can be seen near

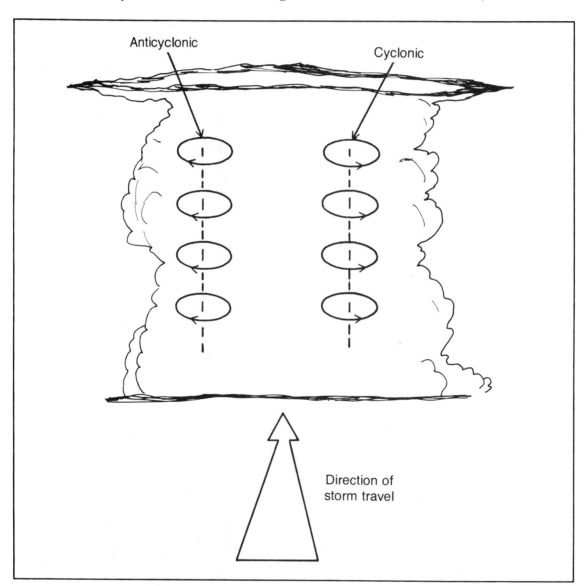

Fig. 3-12. In the double-vortex thunderstorm, viewed from slightly above as it moves away, the air in the left-hand part of the cell spirals clockwise and downward, while the air in the right-hand portion spirals counterclockwise and upward.

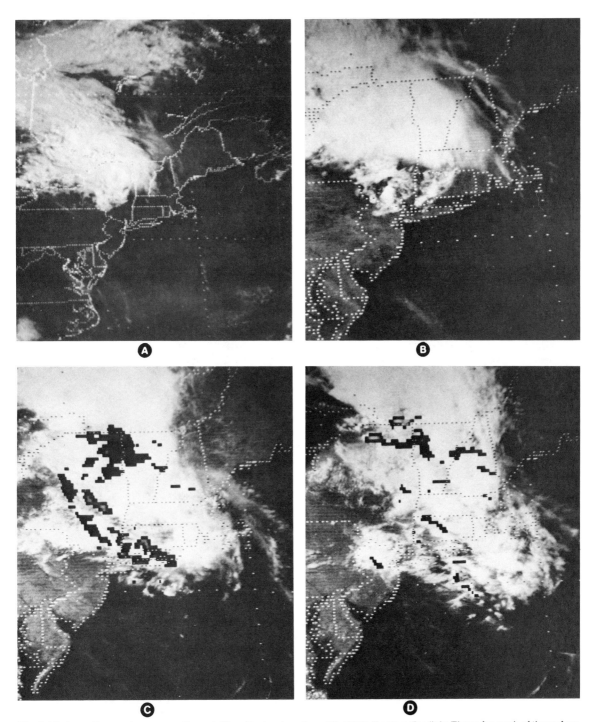

Fig. 3-13. A weather system moves through New England on June 26, 1983. Eastern Daylight Times for each of these four satellite photos are: A, 7:30 A.M.; B, 9:30 A.M.; C, 1:00 P.M.; D, 3:00 P.M. Showers and thunderstorms are indicated at C and D by black rectangles. (courtesy U.S. Department of Commerce, NOAA.)

the bottom of this photograph.

By 9:30 A.M. local time (B), the cloudiness has largely covered New York state and is moving into Connecticut and Massachusetts. No thundershowers, have yet begun. At 1:00 P.M., numerous showers and thunderstorms, shown by black rectangles, are in progress over eastern New York, northwestern Vermont, and southern Connecticut (C). By 3:00 P.M., the showers have mostly dissipated (D) as the system progresses eastward into the ocean. Although the thundershowers occur over a fairly large geographic area, they all develop and dissipate at about the same time.

Showers and thunderstorms form more often during the afternoon and evening hours than at other times of day. This can be explained by the fact that the most thermal energy (heat) is present during the afternoon and evening. The sun heats up the ground, and the warm earth imparts heat to the lower atmosphere, intensifying the contrast between the air temperatures on either side of a moving cold front. The showers of Fig. 3-13 were triggered largely by this effect. The showers did not last long over New England on June 26, 1983, suggesting that they were not especially intense.

Severe thunderstorms show more variability with respect to time of day, because they last much longer than light showers. The line of destructive storms that occurred in August, 1962, raking Alexandria, Minnesota, with 96-mile-per-hour winds, occurred in the predawn hours. Although it is rather uncommon for storms to remain severe through an entire night, an especially intense squall line can strike at any time.

In our hypothetical Minneapolis scenario, all of the factors for the formation of a severe storm are present, including a hot, sunny afternoon with plenty of ground heating. By 5:30 P.M., the sun is obscured by the tops of the cumulonimbus cloud bank, which reaches to almost 60,000 feet. Reports of large hail and damaging winds begin to arrive at the office of the National Weather Service from residents of the outlying southwestern and western suburbs.

WHAT, WHERE, AND HOW MUCH?

The severe effects of an intense thunderstorm—heavy rain, hail, damaging winds, and tornadoes—take place in different parts of a single cell. A particular place is seldom subjected to all of the wrath of a single storm. In multicell storms or squall lines, however, the chances of getting heavy rain, hail, high winds, and even a tornado are greater, since two or more different storms may affect the same area over a period of time.

Rain

The heaviest rains usually occur toward the left front part of a thunderstorm. This is usually the northeast or northern half, beneath the clockwise vortex. The upper-level winds tend to blow water droplets from southwest to northeast. In the northern and northeastern parts of the cell, the clockwise spinning vortex develops a downdraft, which pulls the rain toward the ground. The result can be a blinding torrent, reducing visibility to near zero. Less rain falls near the center of the thunderstorm, and still less in the right-hand, southern, areas.

Hail

In the center of a severe thunderstorm, powerful updrafts carry water droplets to great altitude. The cold high-level air causes the raindrops to freeze. The ice pellets fall back as they are scattered out of the updraft zone by high-altitude winds. Some of the ice pellets melt in the warmer, low-level air and fall to the ground as rain. Others are pulled back into the central updraft before they get a chance to melt. Water droplets condense on these pellets, and then freeze to enlarge the pellets' size as they are tossed upward again to high altitudes. A single pellet may be carried up and down many times in this way until it grows to such a size that, once it finally does defeat the updrafts and get to the ground, it arrives still frozen; this is *hail*.

Most of the hail in a severe thunderstorm falls near the center of the cell, where the updrafts are strong, and there is a fair amount of rain. Hail is uncommon around the periphery of a thunderstorm. The size of the hailstones depends on the strength of the updrafts in the storm; the more powerful the air currents, the more times a hailstone can be carried upward to acquire another coating of ice. Hail is usually about the size of peas or marbles. Occasionally, golf ball-sized hail forms. In rare instances, hail stones may become as large as baseballs or even grapefruit. Such large chunks of ice, falling from an altitude of several miles, cause horrible damage to farm crops, livestock, and property. A person caught outside under a barrage of large hail can be seriously injured.

The amount of hail that falls, and the size of the stones, varies greatly within a single storm. Baseball-sized hail may fall in one part of a moderately large town, while little or no hail is reported in other places. Hail can sometimes accumulate to a depth of several inches, and if high winds are present, drifting may occur. Plants may be defoliated by a prolonged onslaught of hail. In extreme cases, hail drifts may not melt for two or three days, in spite of the fact that the storm takes place in mid-summer.

Hailstorms are most frequently observed during the months of April through September, with a peak around June and July. Winter hail almost never occurs, and in those rare cases where hail does fall in winter, the stones are usually so small that it is hard to tell whether it is really hail, or merely sleet.

Wind

Damaging straight-line (nontornadic) winds in a severe thunderstorm can occur for three different reasons.

The heavy rain in the left-hand part of a storm and the accompanying downdraft from the anticyclone produce a rush of cool air ahead of the storm. You have probably observed this effect quite often; it occurs even in ordinary showers. This is known as a *gust front*, and the wind speed may reach 50 to 60 miles per hour near a very heavy storm. As the rain begins, the wind speed decreases, and conditions may become nearly calm.

Within a severe storm, high winds can result from the two vortices. These winds can attain speeds of hurricane force, perhaps as much as 100 miles per hour in an extremely large and severe thunderstorm. Near the left-hand periphery of a double vortex storm, the clockwise twisting of the air acts in conjunction with the forward movement of the cell to produce the strong winds. The same thing occurs in the right-hand part of the thunderstorm. Since the cyclonic vortex is usually the stronger of the two, the most damaging winds of this type are almost always observed in the right-hand half of a storm.

The third possible cause of high straight-line winds, the least understood but potentially the most destructive, is known as a *downburst*. The downburst, so called because it is believed that the jet stream dips down to the ground, can produce straight-line winds of such violence that cars are flipped over and thrown about like toys, huge trees snapped off like matchsticks, and houses knocked from their foundations. The Alexandria storm of July, 1983, was probably of this type. A 1977 storm in and around Sawyer county, Wisconsin, produced winds that were unofficially clocked at 157 miles per hour.

As we watch our hypothetical thunderstorm approach Minneapolis, the calm, sultry air is suddenly disturbed by a refreshing, cool, westerly breeze. The breeze rapidly increases to a gale, and loose papers and other light objects are picked up and carried along. The trees come alive with motion. It is a good idea to get inside: the sky is dark and threatening.

Lightning

The most dangerous aspect of a thunderstorm, from the standpoint of risk to human life, is not the hail, the high winds, or even the tornadoes. It is lightning. On the average, lightning kills more people in the United States each year than tornadoes, hurricanes, or floods.

Lightning can occur anywhere within a thunderstorm, but is somewhat more common around the periphery of the cloud than near the center. Some thunderstorms contain much more lightning than others. The amount of lightning in a thunderstorm is correlated with the severity. A severe thunderstorm can be expected to contain more lightning than a mild shower; a storm with a lot of lightning is more likely to be severe than one with very little lightning, but this rule does not always hold.

We will take a closer look at the way lightning works, and how we can protect ourselves, a little later in this chapter.

Tornadoes

Tornadoes rank just behind lightning in terms of deadly effects. The tornado is certainly one of Nature's most spectacular phenomena and also one of the most frightening. Winds in tornadoes may blow more than 300 miles per hour. The destruction is almost complete; very few structures can withstand the pressure of such winds.

Tornadoes occur in the cyclonic, or counterclockwise rotating, part of a thunderstorm in the northern hemisphere. This is almost always the southern or southwestern part of the cell. Tornadoes are often observed to "follow" a severe thunderstorm. After the heavy rains, hail, or wind have subsided, the tornado can be seen.

In Chapter 4, we will see how and why tornadoes form, what they can do, and what we can do to protect ourselves and our property from them.

A SEVERE THUNDERSTORM STRIKES

Just as we enter the house, the rising wind slams the door back against the siding. It is not easy to pull a door—even a light screen door—shut against this gale, but finally it is latched, and we push the solid inner door closed behind it. It's a good thing we're inside. A large tree branch comes tumbling down into the yard. Then, branches of all sizes, from mere twigs to halves of trees, begin to litter the streets.

The rain begins. At first, it is a sprinkle, but it quickly turns to a blinding, sideways-moving sheet of water. It pounds with alarming fury against the north and west windows of the house. We'd better get to the basement!

As we hurry down the steps to the cellar, the lights wink out. That's not surprising.

For 30 minutes the winds rage. A small transistor radio tells of widespread wind damage. In the extreme southern suburbs, a tornado has been sighted, but it has not touched down. Closer to the downtown area, hail has been unofficially reported, some the size of golf balls. From our vantage point near downtown, it is apparent that we may well be experiencing a downburst in the northern part of a thunderstorm cell.

The meteorologist checks his radar at the airport station. The display shows that the storm system, now over us, has matured into a squall line and that the Twin Cities are near the middle of it (Fig. 3-14).

The sounds of the wind and rain slowly subside, and we return from the cellar to survey the damage. Many trees have been uprooted or snapped at the trunk. The tree damage is by far the most awesome of the wind effects. Our house, and those in the neighborhood, appear unscathed. No, the tar paper from our garage roof is lying in the middle of the street.

The meteorologist at the airport is on the radio. He says that they have clocked winds of 85 miles per hour. The Minneapolis-St. Paul International Airport is located in the southern suburbs. The areas nearer downtown, including our neighborhood, have received a more severe blow.

Hail in some sections have completely covered the grass, streets, and sidewalks.

The tornado, fortunately, has stayed above ground, and no damage is reported from it. The only fatality from the storm was perhaps indirect. A man was hit by a falling tree in his backyard. (An autopsy will reveal, however, that he had been drinking. The storm must share the blame).

Power outages are widespread. Live wires dangle in puddles and hang, sparking, from utility poles. It is extremely unwise to go wandering around after a severe thunderstorm to gape at the damage. Electrical shock is a great hazard, especially when wires, carrying thousands of volts, lie in puddles of muddy water.

The thermometer reads 53 degrees Fahrenheit as the western sky begins to clear. The cold front has passed. The sun sets, bathed in fiery red, briefly illuminating the last of the clouds from underneath. Tomorrow will be a fine day, and the cleanup will begin.

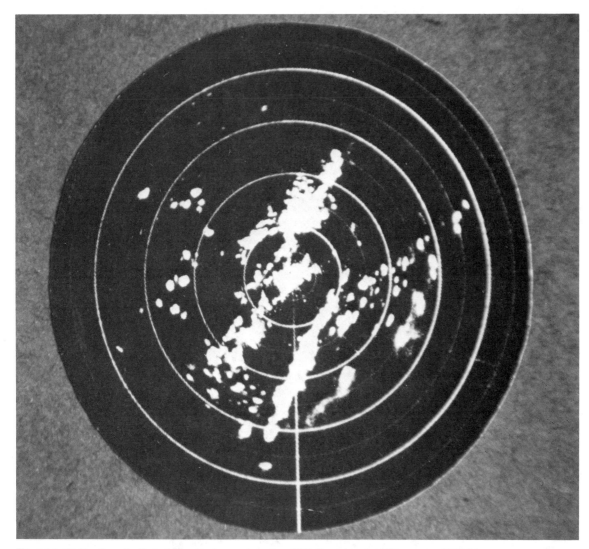

Fig. 3-14. Radar view of a line of thunderstorms. (courtesy U.S. Department of Commerce, NOAA.)

PROTECTING LIFE AND PROPERTY

Severe thunderstorms, although sometimes violent, need not be especially life threatening. Property damage may be impossible to completely avoid, but reasonable precautions can keep it to a minimum.

When a severe thunderstorm watch is issued for your area, tune the radio to a station that you like, and keep it playing in the background, continuously if possible. If you cannot listen continuously, then monitor the news broadcasts, usually given on the hour and sometimes also on the half-hour.

If time permits, get your car or other motor vehicle to a sheltered place to protect it against possible damage from hail or flying debris. Pick up loose yard tools, garbage cans, and other objects that could be thrown by high winds.

If you have a boat on a trailer, put it in a sheltered place if possible. Otherwise tie it down with aircraft cable. (This is a good routine practice, anyway.) Stay at home unless you absolutely must travel.

If your county or municipality is placed under a severe thunderstorm warning, it means that you can expect heavy rain, possibly hail, high winds, and perhaps a tornado within the warning period. Your immediate neighborhood might escape severe weather altogether, or it may be extremely hard hit. There is no way to know, precisely, where, or if, damage will occur. Certain precautions will help minimize personal or property damage if your neighborhood is hit.

Most severe thunderstorms in the temperate latitudes approach from a direction between southwest and northwest. The warning will tell you the direction in which the storm is moving, and also the speed of its progress. Open the windows on the side of the house or building away from the approaching storm. (This is usually the east side. The most violent thunderstorms in the temperate latitudes typically bring winds from a direction between southwest and northwest.) The open windows will help to equalize the pressure differential that can build up when hurricane-force winds are present. Don't open the windows too wide, though, or rain may spray in and soak curtains and carpets.

Sometimes a storm will come from an unusual direction, such as the north or south. (In the temperate zone, severe thunderstorms almost never arrive from the east. The warnings will tell you if this is the case.) You should then open the windows on the side of the house most nearly opposite the bearing of the approaching storm.

People sometimes laugh at the little old ladies who run around unplugging appliances before a storm, but this is not a bad idea. Lightning can ruin electrical appliances if it strikes the power lines nearby. If you have any kind of radio or television apparatus that is connected to an outdoor antenna, disconnect the antenna feed line at the equipment well before lightning begins.

When the storm strikes, it may be with surprising rapidity. The wind may rise from an almost complete calm to hurricane force within a matter of seconds. The best place to go is the basement if you have one. Stay in the corner away from the wind. Avoid windows: they can break from the force of the wind or because of flying debris. Also stay away from electrical appliances, and avoid any kind of radio or television equipment.

In some areas, heavy rains can produce basement and general flash flooding. If a flash flood is imminent, you will be informed by local authorities. If they recommend that you evacuate, you should do so immediately.

If the electricity goes out, it is a good idea to switch off as many lamps and appliances as possible, especially those that draw large amounts of current or that may be damaged by a voltage surge when power is restored. Air conditioners, radios, and television sets should be shut off or unplugged. Better yet, open the main and branch circuits at the central fuse or breaker box, and leave them open until electricity has been restored to your area.

Following a severe thunderstorm, there may be considerable damage to trees, buildings, and utility lines. Fallen trees may block roads, and standing water can accumulate to depths of several feet. Do not drive around in your car to survey the damage; stay at home. Downed power lines are especially hazardous, because they can cause electrocution via conduction through puddles of water.

Fires may occur as a result of lightning, or sometimes because of wind damage to fuel tanks. Report any fires immediately to your local fire department. If there are any injuries to people, take appropriate first aid action and, if necessary, call an ambulance. Do not make unnecessary telephone calls, however, since the switchboards will probably be overloaded already.

LIGHTNING STRIKES

Severe thunderstorms, and sometimes even ordinary thundershowers, can produce dangerous and frequent lightning. A direct hit on your house can be a terrifying experience. You sit in your living room, reading a book, listening to the sound of rain on the roof, and enjoying the relief the shower has brought from the afternoon heat. Suddenly, you hear a crackling sound, like someone crushing a piece of cellophane. An instant later, a deafening crash makes you jump from your chair. The lamp beside you has gone out (as have all the rest of the lights in the house), smoke rises from the bulb

Fig. 3-15. Lightning illuminates the nighttime sky. (courtesy U.S. Department of Commerce, NOAA.)

socket. Your wife screams from the other room that the television set has literally blown up, and fragments of the picture tube lie scattered all over the floor of the den.

Lightning is one of the most interesting, as well as dangerous, natural phenomena (Fig. 3-15). In the United States alone, lightning kills many people every year. Not all of the victims are playing golf or flying kites during thundershowers. Some of them are talking on the telephone when they are hit; some are operating amateur or CB radio equipment; some are watching television, or ironing, or taking a shower, and some are just sitting in a chair in the living room, reading a book.

What causes lightning? How can we protect ourselves and our property from it?

The Atmospheric Capacitor

The earth is a fairly good conductor of electricity; so is the upper part of the atmosphere known as the ionosphere. The air between these two conducting regions, in the troposphere (where most weather occurs) and in the stratosphere, is a poor conductor of electric current. When a poor conductor is sandwiched in between two layers having better conductivity, the result is a *capacitor.*

A capacitor has the ability to store an electric *charge*, or potential difference. The amount of charge that a capacitor can hold is proportional to the surface area of the two conducting plates. The earth-ionosphere capacitor is spherical and is about 8,000 miles in diameter, resulting in a surface area of about 200 million square miles. Such a capacitor can store a tremendous electric charge.

The atmosphere of the earth is a good insulating material, but it is not perfect. Air currents and regions of high moisture content can cause "channels" of higher conductivity than would be present without them. Cumulonimbus clouds, which sometimes reach to the top of the troposphere, present paths of better ground-to-ionosphere conductivity than stable, dry air. The average effective resistance between the ground and the ionosphere is about 200 ohms, about the same resistance as a 75-watt bulb has in a 120-volt household circuit. In cumulonimbus towers, the resistance is considerably less than this average value. Thus, these clouds present an attractive environment for discharges to take place. Some discharge occurs slowly, but a fast discharge—a spark—happens frequently. This is lightning. Numerous thunderstorms are in progress on our planet at any given moment, helping to limit the charge between the ground and the upper atmosphere.

The atmospheric capacitor maintains a constant charge of about 300,000 volts: a very high voltage. You have observed a potential difference of this magnitude if you have ever seen a Van de Graaff generator in operation. The average current that flows across the atmospheric capacitor is about 1500 amperes. Hence our atmosphere is constantly dissipating about 450 megawatts of power—the equivalent of a fairly large city.

Most of the current flow between the upper and lower atmosphere takes place within thundershower cells. These cells concentrate the charge, increasing the local voltage. Thundershowers also reduce the space between opposite electric poles in the atmospheric capacitor, creating a particularly attractive place for discharge. A typical thundershower discharges about 2 amperes of current on the average. At any given moment, there are 700 or 800 thundershowers in progress on our planet.

A current of just 2 amperes per thunderstorm may seem rather small. (A 250-watt light bulb consumes about 2 amperes.) Remember, however, that this current does not flow continuously, but occurs in brief moments. A single lightning discharge lasts just a few thousandths of a second. Therefore, the peak current is extremely large and can cause damage.

Frequency of Lightning

The probability of a lightning strike in any given place depends on many things. Lightning almost always occurs in or near thundershowers. Occasionally, a "bolt from the blue," which seems to strike from out of nowhere, is seen, but this is rare. The area of a cumulonimbus cloud base, the height of the cloud base above the ground, the intensity of the thundershower, the presence of tall objects, and the conductivity of the soil all affect the chances that lightning will strike at a particular time.

There is some evidence that a large solar flare is followed by a period of increased lightning activity on the earth. Evidently, a solar flare causes a temporary increase in the amount of charge in the atmospheric capacitor. Solar flares are most likely during peaks in the 11-year sunspot cycle. The last peak took place about 1980. Solar flares are known to cause aurora displays and disturbances in radio communications, but further research must still be done before a definite correlation between solar flares and lightning can be established.

Experiments have shown that lightning is most likely to occur between the hours of 1500 and 1800 Coordinated Universal Time (UTC). Lightning creates radio waves called *sferics*, or *static*. The sferics propagate all over the world at the very low radio frequencies. Scientists can listen to the sferics with a special receiver and determine how much lightning activity is occurring.

The hours 1500 and 1800 UTC correspond approximately to midday in North America. In Minneapolis, for example, these hours correspond to the period 10:00 A.M. to 1:00 P.M. local daylight time. This is not the peak time for thunderstorms in the Minneapolis area, nor in North America in general, but it represents the middle and late afternoon—the best time for storms to develop—in the vast rain forests of Africa and South America, where tropical thundershowers occur almost every day. Africa and South America have by far the greatest equatorial land mass, presenting the most favorable conditions for thundershower development in the world.

In the United States, thunderstorms occur most frequently in west central Florida. Many thunderstorms also take place in the Rocky Mountain states and in the Midwest. Somewhat fewer lightning strikes are observed in the Northeast. Very few strikes occur in the northwestern states, in spite of the fact that much of this part of the country receives abundant rainfall.

Warmth and moisture are both very important to the formation of thundershowers. Most of the charge concentration in the atmosphere takes place in the lower latitudes, particularly in the tropics. The least charge concentration is seen near the poles. Radio communications enthusiasts, such as ham operators, are quite familiar with this fact. The wet tropical and subtropical areas are, not surprisingly, stricken the most often by lightning.

The Electric Charge in a Cloud

Lightning almost always occurs in, or near, cumulonimbus clouds. For a sufficient amount of electric charge to build up, it is necessary for air movement to be present. The best conditions for a large electric charge occur within certain temperature and humidity ranges. This is why we do not normally see lightning in the winter or in dry weather.

In a thundershower, the temperature decreases rapidly with increasing altitude. There are strong updrafts and downdrafts present in such a system, and this can generate a large separation of electric charge as well as severe weather such as hail, strong winds, heavy rains, and tornadoes. Positive charge accumulates near the top of a cumulonimbus thundershower. Negative charge accumulates near the base of the cloud. The resulting pair of charge centers is called a *cell*. This is why the meteorologist sometimes calls a thundershower a cell: it actually is an electric cell, with a potential difference amounting to millions or billions of volts. Figure 3-16 illustrates a typical thundershower with its separation of charge.

In some cases, a negative charge may accumulate at the top of a tall cumulonimbus tower, above the positive layer. This forms a second cell, at a higher altitude than the first. There may also be differences in charge in a horizontal direction. One part of a cloud, at a given height, may have a different voltage than another part of the same cloud at the same height. A single thundershower can have several cells within itself, and thus several possibilities for lightning discharges. Lightning within a single shower, or between nearby clouds, is the

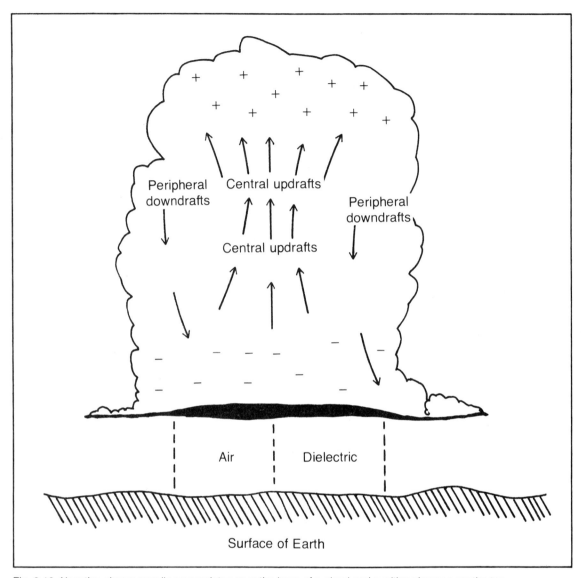

Fig. 3-16. Negative charge usually accumulates near the base of a cloud and positive charge near the top.

most frequent type of lightning. Cloud-to-cloud lightning never hits the ground, although we may see the flash and hear the thunder. At night, we may see cloud-to-cloud lightning from more than 100 miles away.

Cloud to Ground

The most common kind of lightning discharge between a cloud and the earth occurs as a flow of electrons from the base of a thundershower to the ground. The base of the cloud carries a negative charge, inducing a localized positive voltage on the surface beneath. The charge concentration on the ground can get so great in some locations that people's hair stands on end. (Perhaps you have had this experience.) The electrons eventually jump through the air to equalize the potential difference.

Many people experience mood swings just

102

before, during, and after thundershowers. The large positive charge concentration creates positive ions in the air. These ions are believed to cause restlessness and irritability in animals and people. You may get into a fight with your spouse, the dog might run and hide under the sofa. As the storm passes, and the positive charge diminishes and finally vanishes altogether, moods brighten along with the skies.

Atmospheric downdrafts, which take place near the periphery of the thundershower, reduce the effective resistance of the air. Updrafts, which take place near the center of a shower, increase this effective resistance. This is why we see the most lightning near the edge of a storm, especially bordering the area of heaviest rainfall (Fig. 3-17). As a thundershower passes overhead, the most lightning occurs before and after the heavy rain.

Let us see what happens in the fraction of a second during which a cloud-to-ground lightning

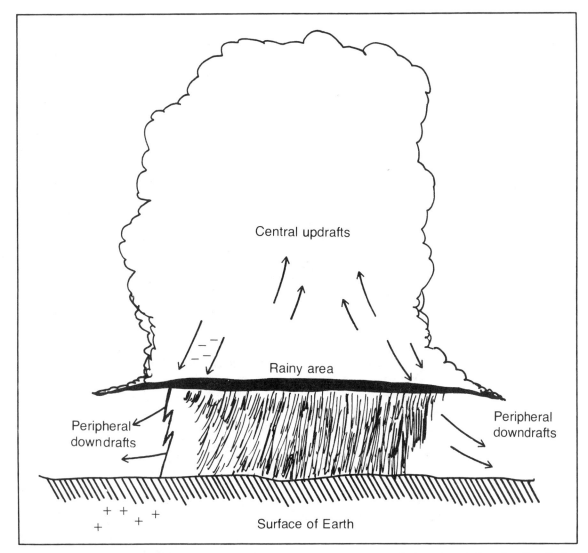

Fig. 3-17. Lightning is most likely to occur near the periphery of a cumulonimbus cloud, where downdrafts reduce the effective resistance between the ground and the cloud base.

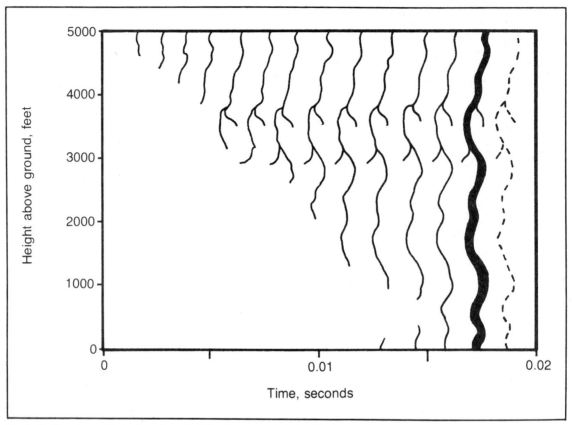

Fig. 3-18. Time lapse illustration of a typical cloud-to-ground stroke. The leader is shown by the light solid line and the return stroke by the heavy solid line. The air near the stroke path remains ionized for a moment after the return stroke, as shown by the dotted line.

strikes takes place.

When the voltage builds up sufficiently and the air can no longer maintain effective insulation, a streamer of electrons, carrying negative charge, begins to probe outward and downward from the base of the cloud. The electrons literally "try" to find the path of lowest resistance to the ground, in the same way that a river finds the path of lowest resistance from a mountain to the sea. There are many dead-end paths that have good conductivity for a short distance but then terminate. Finally, the *leader* reaches the ground, having found the path of lowest resistance.

The leader moves quite fast, at about 50 to 100 miles per second. This is an average speed, because the leader actually moves in jumps or steps. The leader takes 0.01 to 0.02 second to get from the cloud base to the ground. If you happen to be very near the point about to be stricken, you may actually be able to hear the accumulating charge. It makes a crackling noise, like someone crumpling a piece of cellophane.

As the leader approaches the area of positive charge at the surface, the air *dielectric* breaks down completely. When the leader is about 400 to 800 feet from the ground or the object about to be stricken, a *flashover* of positive charge takes place. The flashover meets the downward moving leader a short distance above the ground. This point is called the *point of strike* (Fig. 3-18).

The circuit is complete. The leader has generated an ionized, highly conductive path from the cloud base to the ground. A massive discharge occurs, beginning at the ground and progressing upward to the cloud. (Although the individual electrons travel downward, the discharge as a whole is in an upward direction.) This is the main lightning discharge, known as the *return stroke*. It is responsible for the flash that we see, and it causes the thunder that we hear.

The diameter of a typical return stroke is just a few inches, but it is as hot as the surface of the sun. Fires can be started within the few milliseconds during which the current flows. A stricken animal or person may be severely burned, besides badly shocked. Some people have been hit by lightning and survived. Most are knocked unconscious instantly and do not even realize what has happened until later.

After the return stroke, another leader may move downward from the cloud base. Since an ionized, conducting path has already been established by the first stroke, this leader moves much faster than the original leader. As the second leader reaches the point of strike, there is another massive discharge. A third leader may follow. The whole process might be repeated several times. The complete lightning stroke lasts about 0.02 second if there is only one return stroke. The flash may last as long as 0.5 second if 10 or 15 return strokes occur.

The greater the number of return strokes, the brighter the flash we will see, and the louder the thunder we will hear. A multiple stroke presents a much greater fire hazard and is also more deadly to stricken animals or people than a single stroke.

Sometimes a strong wind is present in the vicinity of a lightning stroke. The wind blows the conducting path sideways. A 60-mile-per-hour wind, for example, moves the air 9 feet in 0.1 second. As several return strokes occur in rapid succession, they appear to blur together as we watch. This gives the lightning a ribbonlike appearance, or makes it look thick, even though the actual diameter is just a few inches. In a time exposure photograph, the multiple strokes can be seen, side by side.

Other Types of Discharge

Cloud-to-cloud lightning is the second most common type of lightning. Intercloud and intracloud discharges occur more often. A single cumulonimbus thundercloud may contain several different cells. In a group of thundershowers, or in a squall line, the areas of maximum positive and negative charge sometimes exist at different altitudes, creating a multiplicity of possible discharge paths. When lightning occurs inside a distant cloud at night, the whole towering storm may be illuminated in an eerie and spectacular way. This so-called cloud-to-cloud lightning does not damage objects on the ground, except perhaps indirectly as a result of the electromagnetic field that all lightning bolts generate. (I will have more to say about the electromagnetic pulse shortly.) Cloud-to-cloud lightning sometimes strikes airplanes. In a few cases, airliners have been brought down by cloud-to-cloud discharges because of damage to the electrical systems or engines.

Although the base of a cloud usually develops a negative charge, and the ground beneath a cloud accumulates localized positive charge, the situation is sometimes reversed. This causes a form of lightning called a *ground-to-cloud discharge*—the electrons flow upward rather than downward. Ground-to-cloud lightning takes place in exactly the same way as a cloud-to-ground discharge, but upside down. The leader starts from the ground or the object to be stricken and advances upward until it nears the center of positive charge in the cloud (Fig. 3-19). The positive leader meets the negative leader at a distance of about 800 to 1200 feet from the center of positive charge; this is the point of strike. The return streamer transfers the positive charge downward (although the electrons actually flow upward). Ground-to-cloud lightning is usually less destructive to a stricken object than cloud-to-ground lightning.

In some situations, there exists a large potential difference between two points, but it is not enough to produce a full discharge. The leader will then fail to complete the circuit and simply die out. This is called an *air discharge*. The air discharge causes very little thunder, and generally there is no damage to objects on the ground.

The most intense form of lightning discharge

takes place when the positive voltage at the top of a cloud builds up to such magnitude that a flashover occurs all the way from the ground (Fig. 3-20). This is known as a *superbolt*, because it carries much more current than the ordinary cloud-to-ground, cloud-to-cloud, or ground-to-cloud stroke. A superbolt may strike the gound at a considerable distance from a thundershower, suprising people who call it a "bolt from the blue." A superbolt causes an extremely loud clap of thunder, and can cause extensive damage because of the large amount of electric current that flows.

Some odd forms of lightning are sometimes seen. *Ball lightning* is one such strange phenomenon. People have reported seeing spheres of fire that persist for several seconds. The spheres range in diameter from less than an inch to several feet. A ball of fire may roll down the hall from the living room to the kitchen, and then disappear in a puff of smoke. Ball lightning seems to enter buildings via electrical appliances or telephones.

A slow form of lightning discharge, generally not damaging but often fascinating or terrifying, is known as *Saint Elmo's fire.* When a thundershower is nearby or overhead, metal objects such as radio antennas, lightning rods, and sailboat masts may acquire an eerie, supernatural glow. Saint Elmo's fire is often observed on airplane wingtips. Some airplanes have pointed rods on the wingtips and tail structure to facilitate electrical discharge via Saint Elmo's fire.

Thunder

In ancient times, people believed that thunder

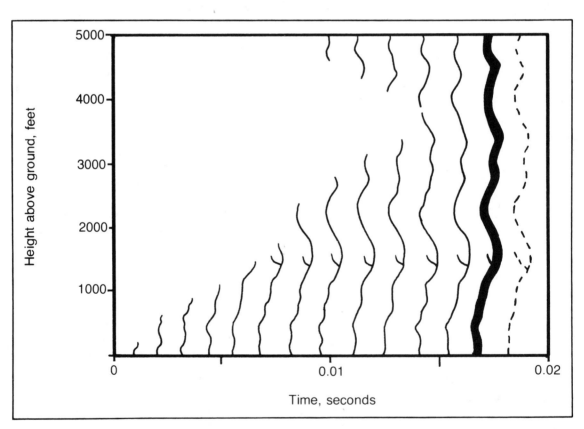

Fig. 3-19. Time lapse illustration of a typical ground-to-cloud stroke. The leader is shown by the light solid line and the return stroke by the heavy solid line. The air near the stroke path remains ionized for a moment after the return stroke, as shown by the dotted line.

Fig. 3-20. A superbolt is a tremendous lightning flash that sometimes occurs between the ground and the top of a thundercloud. (courtesy U.S. Department of Commerce, NOAA.)

resulted from the anger of the gods. Today we know better, but thunder can still scare us half to death. When the return streamer occurs, the air is heated almost instantaneously to a temperature of several thousand degrees Fahrenheit. The heating causes the air to expand with great force, generating a shock wave that we hear as thunder. The same thing happens on a small scale when you shuffle across a carpet and then touch an electrically grounded object. The small spark makes a snapping sound: miniature thunder.

Thunder can be heard for varying distances, depending on the wind direction and speed, the presence or absence of favorable sound propagation conditions, and the amount of background noise. Usually, thunder is audible up to about 5 miles from the point of strike. If the lightning flash can be seen, the thunder will be heard somewhat later. Sound travels through air at a speed of approximately 1 mile per 5 seconds, or 1 kilometer per 3 seconds. . You can determine the distance to a lightning flash

by counting the number of seconds it takes for the thunder to arrive. Divide by 5 to get the distance in miles, or by 3 to get the distance in kilometers.

The rumbling, or booming, noise of thunder puzzles some people. A lightning flash has very short duration, but thunder seems to last for several seconds. This occurs for two basic reasons: echoes and *propagation delays*. Thunder is, in reality, an extremely loud bang and is generated within a few milliseconds. (If you have ever been just a few steps away from a lightning-stricken object, you already know this!)

In hilly or mountainous terrain, or in cities with many tall buildings, the shock wave from a lightning stroke gets a chance to bounce around. We hear not only the orginal thunder, but its echoes. This creates a prolonged rumble. In flat, open country, or on a lake or at sea, there are no objects to cause the echoes, and the rumbling is much less pronounced.

Propagation delays also contribute to the

rumbling effect. Suppose you stand 1 mile from a stricken object, and the lightning flash occurs vertically from a cloud base 1 mile high (Fig. 3-21). You are closer to the bottom of the lightning bolt than

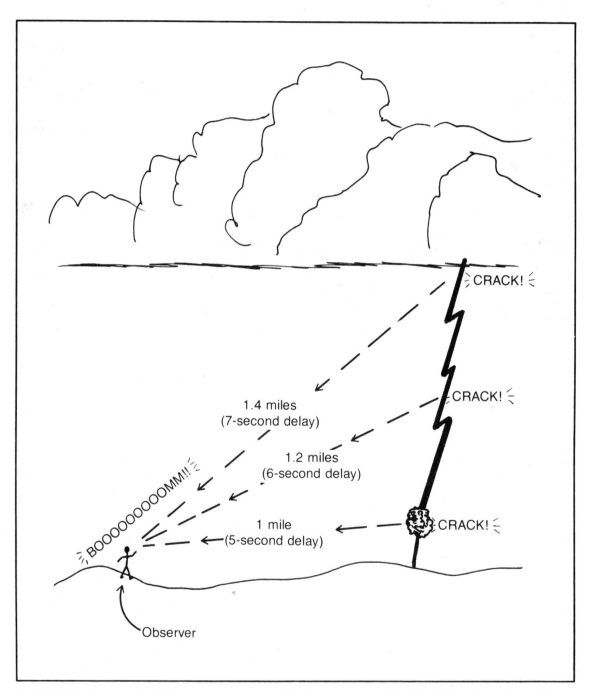

Fig. 3-21. Sound-propagation delays are one reason why thunder seems to rumble, rather than make a sharp report.

you are to the top, and the sound therefore requires less time to get to you from the bottom of the flash than from the top of the flash. The closer you get to the stricken object, the greater the time difference, and the longer the rumble will seem to be. If you were to stand just a few steps away from the tree in a situation such as that shown in Fig. 3-21, you would hear an almost deafening explosion, followed by a 5-second rumble as the thunder reached you from progressively more and more distant parts of the return stroke.

The Electromagnetic Pulse

In any lightning stroke, electrons are rapidly accelerated as they jump the gap between poles of opposite charge. Whenever electrons are accelerated, radio waves are produced. This is how a broadcast transmitter works: electrons are made to accelerate back and forth in a metal conductor, at a precise and constant frequency. In a bolt of lightning, electrons are accelerated in a haphazard way and this produces radio noise at all frequencies. The radio "signals" from thunderstorms are known as static or sferics.

Sferics travel great distances at low frequencies and progressively shorter distances as the frequency becomes higher. A fairly distant group of thundershowers can cause interference to low-frequency radio communications. Low-frequency direction-finding apparatus is sometimes used to locate regions of intense thunderstorm activity. When a severe thunderstorm watch is issued, you may hear static on the radio even as you sit in the sun and listen to the announcement. You know, then, that some thundershowers are already in progress.

As thundershowers approach, the static becomes more frequent and intense and is observed at increasingly higher frequencies. A general coverage shortwave radio receiver can be used to demonstrate this effect. At first, static is heard only on vacant channels near the bottom of the standard AM broadcast band. Then the static becomes discernible even on occupied channels. Finally, the sferics occur almost continuously at frequencies up to several megahertz, and an occasional burst of noise punctuates the airwaves even at television frequencies.

A thundershower can generate radio waves of much greater intensity than any radio transmitter that man has ever devised. The bursts of electromagnetic radiation within a storm can induce dangerous voltages in utility wires, telephone lines, radio antennas, fences, and other metallic objects. These voltages can be lethal to people and can cause damage to electrical and electronic devices. This is why you should never use electric appliances, telephones, or radio equipment during a thunderstorm.

Lightning Protection

Lightning is dangerous. It kills more people than any other form of severe weather. Lightning also causes millions of dollars' worth of property damage every year. Fortunately, there are certain precautions you can take to minimize the hazard, both to yourself and to your property.

If you have ever taken a drive through the country, you have no doubt seen lightning rods. A lightning rod is simply a metal conductor, usually copper or steel, erected vertically on top of a building or house. The lightning rod is electrically connected to an earth ground via a heavy wire.

Until recently, it was thought that a pointed lightning rod would serve best to protect an object. The idea was that, because a pointed metal rod allows charge transfer to occur more easily than a blunt rod, the pointed rod might prevent the charge accumulation from becoming large enough to cause lightning. Lately, this idea has been challenged. It seems that nothing can prevent the charge accumulation that results in a lightning stroke. Pointed lightning rods are often severely damaged when they are hit. A rod with a spherical tip, on the other hand, is seldom damaged by lightning. We may see, in future years, more lightning rods with spherical tips.

When a lightning rod is installed, the conductor running to the ground should be as heavy as possible. Copper wire, measuring ¼ inch in diameter, is an excellent choice. Copper tubing is also good. The conductor should follow the most

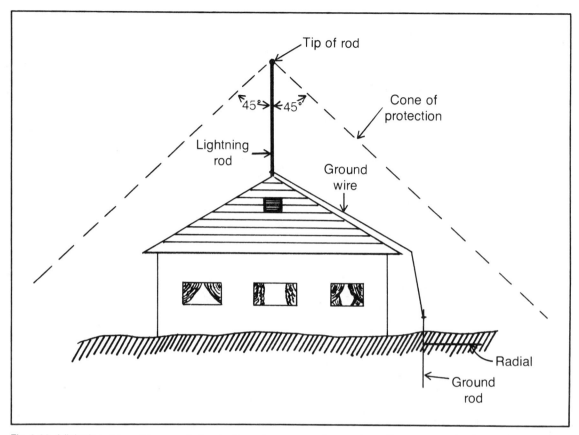

Fig. 3-22. A lightning rod provides a conical protection zone, or cone of protection, with an apex angle of about 45 degrees.

direct possible path to ground along the outside of the building or house. The conductor should never be run inside the structure, or anywhere near flammable materials.

The ground connection should be made to a ground rod, preferably at least 8 feet long, driven into the earth several feet away from the foundation of the house. An enhanced ground connection can be obtained by using several ground rods, or by installing buried radial wires a few inches under the ground. A complete lightning rod installation is shown at Fig. 3-22.

A lightning rod will theoretically provide a "cone of protection" that has a height equal to the height of the tip of the rod, and an apex angle of 45 degrees (Fig. 3-22). It is not likely that lightning will strike any object inside the "cone of protection," but it is still possible. You can easily calculate

how high the rod must be to provide protection for your house or building. A good rule is as follows: measure the largest diameter (corner to corner) of the building roof, divide by 2, and this will give you the height above the center of the roof that the top of the lightning rod should be.

Once you have installed one or more lightning rods, do not become overconfident. If lightning strikes the rod, the resulting electromagnetic field may cause severe damage to electrical applicances and radio equipment in the vicinity. The chances of damage can be reduced by unplugging electrical appliances before a thunderstorm. Obviously, there is a limit to how much of this can be done before you run out of physical energy and patience. It is a good idea, however, to unplug home computers, amateur and CB radios, and other electronic devices that contain solid-state components. Of course, all radios and television sets should be disconnected from outdoor antennas.

Stay away from windows during a thunderstorm, because it can cause a thunderclap that shatters windows. Lightning may also enter a house or building through a window, causing burns or electrocution. If lightning strikes near a window, tree branches or other debris can be thrown through the glass.

Hopefully, you will never be caught outdoors in an electrical storm, with no way of getting to shelter. If this does happen, you should move to a low place, away from tall structures that might attract lightning, and crouch down with your feet close together and your face toward the ground. A car or truck will provide excellent personal protection from lightning, if you can get into one.

If you are caught in a boat during a heavy electrical storm, your situation is quite dangerous. If it is a sailboat with a mast, a lightning strike is a definite possibility. You should crouch in a position facing away from the mast, with your face down and your feet close together. (You might also want to cover your ears.) If the boat has an enclosed space, you should get inside it and stay away from metal objects.

Although lightning kills more people in the United States than any other single severe weather phenomenon, it need not be especially life threatening if reasonable precautions are taken. Some lightning deaths are probably inevitable, but most are the result of carelessness, or occur in avoidable situations.

Lightning is not all bad. It generates beneficial nitrogen compounds that aid in the fertilization of the soil. Lightning limits the charge in the atmospheric capacitor; the bolts that we experience during heavy thundershowers are mere sparks compared to the discharge that would ultimately take place if the earth-ionosphere voltage were to rise to a high enough value. Lightning may even be responsible for life on our planet. Some scientists believe that the first organic substances, the amino acids, were formed from inorganic compounds as a result of chemical reactions requiring electrical discharge. We may be the descendants of molecules that formed long ago in a prehistoric sea, in the few moments following a single bolt of lightning.

Chapter 4

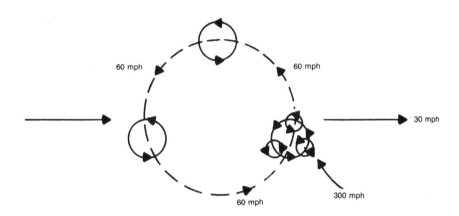

Tornadoes: Marauders of the Land

Spring fever—we all know what that means. After a dismal winter you thought would never end, the weather brightens and brings warm, clear, breezy days that make you want to play "hooky" from work or school. The last of the snow disappears. One day you notice that the grass is no longer brown, but vivid green; then the trees start to come alive. The sun climbs high in the midday sky, and the twilight lingers into the evening. You set your clocks an hour ahead of the true astronomical time, a symbolic attempt to make each day last a little longer.

Spring brings gentler weather, as a whole, than the icy months of December, January, and February. The tropical air returns from its long vacation. The large, strong cyclones of winter give way to smaller, less intense low-pressure systems, but their character, as well as their size and overall power, changes. The spring brings more tornadoes than all of the other seasons. A day that begins like a pleasant dream can end like a nightmare.

May 6, 1975, was such a day for people living in a major Midwestern city. The residents of Omaha, Nebraska, saw nature's wrath, as well as

her gentleness, on that grim Tuesday. Countless other similar stories can be told.

TORNADOES ARE BORN

The winter of 1974-1975 was, as all winters inevitably are, long and gloomy throughout the Midwest. May 6, 1975, dawned with the infectious promise of balmy weather and fair skies. Residents of large cities, smaller towns, and the green countryside were restless with spring fever. The atmosphere, too, was affected. The metropolitan area of Omaha, Nebraska, was right in the middle of it all.

Far to the north, following the retreating jet stream, a powerful low-pressure system was swirling, bringing cool arctic air from the northwest across the Rockies and eastward into the wide-open Great Plains. A thousand miles to the southeast, a benign springtime high-pressure system was pushing tropical air far into the continent, to be drawn in by the northern low (Fig. 4-1). The arctic air mass advanced like an army across the

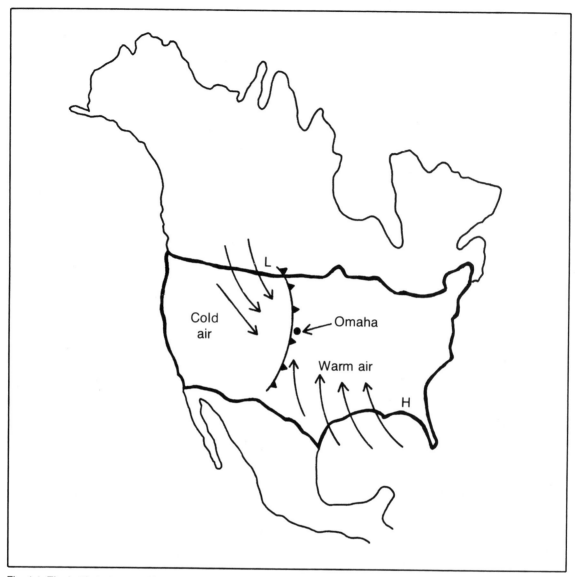

Fig. 4-1. The battle between cold air from Canada and warm air from the Gulf of Mexico resulted in the devastating Omaha tornado of May 6, 1975.

Dakotas, Nebraska, and Kansas. Ahead of the front, thunderstorms and squall lines developed. The flat prairies offered no resistance to their progress.

The skies darkened over the Nebraska farm towns. The wind suddenly shifted to the west, kicking up dust and whistling through utility wires and tree branches. People ran for cover to avoid getting drenched as the rains came. The tempera-

ture plummeted as the storms moved on toward the east, and the sun returned. Western Nebraska was spared most of the wrath of the thunderstorms.

The sun continued to shine on the black, plowed fields in the eastern part of the state. The already warm tropical air, heated still more by the early afternoon sun, rose to fantastic heights. The thunderheads reached the top of the troposphere and merged together to form squall lines. The spring rains became torrential, and hail pounded the earth. Deep inside the darkening clouds, the air, water, and ice began to swirl.

Large thunderstorms commonly develop a double-vortex inner structure. In a northern hemisphere thunderstorm, descending air twists clockwise in the left-hand half of the cell, and rising air spins counterclockwise in the right-hand half. The counterclockwise-spinning vortex is called cyclonic, and it appears in the southern or southwestern part of a thunderstorm moving toward the east or northeast. The cyclonic vortex has a tendency to grow stronger and tighter, because the pressure drops at its center. On May 6, 1975, this phenomenon occurred in numerous thunderstorms over Nebraska and Kansas.

As the pressure continues to fall within the cyclonic vortex of a large thunderstorm, the air spins faster and faster. This leads to a further drop

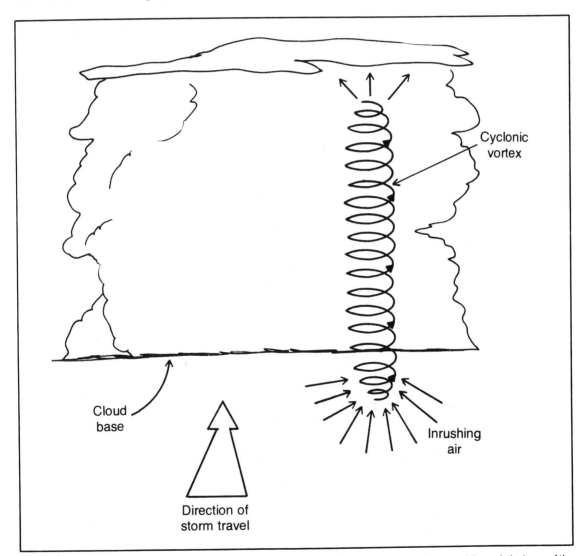

Fig. 4-2. The cyclonic vortex in a large thunderstorm becomes a funnel cloud as it extends downward through the base of the cloud.

Fig. 4-3. A tornado throws up dirt and debris at Denver, Colorado (courtesy NOAA).

in pressure, which causes the air to speed up still more. The effects then become visible to observers on the ground: the clouds rotate. Air near the ground is drawn upward to feed the vortex (Fig. 4-2). A vertical cloud, shaped like a funnel, rope, or tube, appears at the base of the larger cumulonimbus "mother cloud." The twisting vortex gradually works its way downward to the earth. If the funnel cloud finally extends all the way to the ground, we call it a tornado. As soon as the vortex reaches the earth, it makes a roaring sound louder than a dozen jumbo jets.

Once a funnel cloud has touched down, it kicks up clouds of dirt and debris. This gives a tornado a characteristic black appearance (Fig. 4-3). The cloud moves along the ground, sometimes hopping back up into the "mother cloud" for a few moments and then touching the earth again. Sometimes the vortex becomes thicker and more fierce looking; sometimes it gets almost threadlike. The diameter of a tornado may be as great as a mile or as small as 100 feet.

As the tornado moves across the countryside, it often follows an erratic path. Sometimes a tornado loops around after it has passed a place and hammers it for a second time. The funnel cloud may swing back and forth like the trunk of an elephant, or it may drill along in a constant, straight line. After a period of a few minutes, most tornadoes begin to dissipate (Fig. 4-4), although they sometimes last an hour or more. Depending on the population density of the stricken area, the damage can range from inconsequential to utterly catastrophic.

TORNADO PREDICTIONS

The conditions on May 6, 1975, were ideal for the development of tornadoes. Meteorologists recognize these conditions, and when it seems as if there is a good chance for tornadoes to form, a watch is issued. You can recognize some of these conditions yourself.

Tornado Watch

Tornadoes are most common in the spring. A warm, muggy day in October is far less likely to bring a tornado than a warm, muggy day in May.

Most tornadoes take place in March and April in the extreme southern United States. In the middle of the country, April and May are the most common months, and in the northern plains, May and June bring most of the tornadoes.

Tornadoes are rare west of the Rockies. They are also unusual in New England. The "breadbasket" states are most subject to tornadoes, but tornadoes can strike anywhere in the 48 continental states. Damaging tornadoes have occurred in such places as Windsor Locks, Connecticut, and Los Angeles, California.

Assuming that you live in a tornado susceptible region, and it is a spring or early summer day, you should be familiar with the type of weather that is associated with tornadoes. How can you tell if the conditions are favorable for tornadoes? Some signs are a falling barometer, a southerly or southeasterly wind, and humid air. A crisp, dry, clear day with a northwesterly breeze does not generally portend tornadoes. Tornadoes always occur in conjunction with thundershowers, especially heavy thundershowers.

If you suspect that conditions are right for tornadoes, listen to the weather forecasts on local radio stations. The National Weather Service will issue a tornado watch if it appears that tornadoes are likely to form. Tornado watches are often issued in conjunction with severe thunderstorm watches. A typical tornado watch statement might read: "The possibility of a tornado exists until 6:00 P.M. along, and 60 miles either side of, a line from 40 miles southwest of Omaha, Nebraska, to 20 miles north of Sioux Falls, South Dakota." (Specific counties and towns are usually mentioned, since not everyone has a map, a ruler, and a pencil handy.) When the watch period expires, a new watch may be issued for a different area, the watch period may be extended, or the watch might be cancelled altogether.

A tornado watch does not mean that a tornado has actually been sighted. Many, if not most, of the places in a tornado watch area will not see severe weather at all. Quite frequently, not a single tornado occurs anywhere within the watch area, but experience has shown that more tornadoes form per

A

B

Fig. 4-4. At A, a funnel cloud forms and touches ground at Enid, Oklahoma. At B and C, the tornado grows in size as dirt spirals upward around its perimeter. At D, the vortex begins to die out (courtesy NOAA).

square mile in watch areas as compared with non-watch areas. In other words, meteorologists know what they are talking about when they issue a tornado watch!

Tornado Warning

When conditions are favorable for tornadoes, no one can tell precisely where—or if—tornadoes will develop. Tornado forecasting is imprecise because tornadoes behave in strange ways. Meteorologists try to provide as much warning as possible, but tornadoes frequently strike with almost no notice. If a tornado warning is issued for a certain area, there isn't much time to do anything except run for shelter.

A tornado warning means that there is an immediate threat of a tornado in a particular area. A tornado warning is usually issued for a much smaller region than a tornado watch. Tornado warnings are given whenever a funnel cloud is actually sighted, or whenever a hook-shaped echo is observed on weather radar.

A tornado does not actually show up on a radar screen, but the cyclonic vortex, deep within a heavy thunderstorm, produces a characteristic pattern (Fig. 4-5). The raindrops, spiraling upward with the whirling air, create the echo. The development of a strong cyclonic vortex, visible as a hook-shaped echo, almost always precedes a tornado. Radar can provide up to several minutes of warning prior to the formation of a funnel cloud.

In cities equipped with civil defense sirens, a tornado warning is announced by a continuous tone. The sirens are blown for 3 to 5 minutes, but the sirens are not within earshot of everyone. If there is heavy rain, a high wind, or hail in progress, the majority of people will not hear the sirens blowing. If the tornado warning is issued in the middle of the night, many people will sleep right through the faint wailing of distant sirens. Some municipalities have overcome these problems by installing more sirens, but in other places, and especially in the open country, a radio is the only medium by which a tornado warning can be made known.

Special storm warning radios are available that stay silent until a tornado warning is issued. Then, an actuating signal, transmitted by the weather bureau in the vicinity, causes the radios to emit a loud tone. Anyone who lives in a tornado-prone region without adequate civil defense sirens should have one of these units. They are available from various electronics stores at a modest price.

As soon as a tornado warning is issued, a secure shelter should be found until the all-clear is broadcast over local radio and television stations. In some towns, the civil defense sirens are blown a second time to indicate that the warning period is over.

Recognizing a Tornado

Not every ominous-looking cloud presents the danger of a tornado. People often mistake quite ordinary clouds for funnel clouds. High winds or moderate turbulence near a cloud base can make the bottom of a cloud irregular, and some of the ragged edges might look a little like a funnel cloud. The true tornado is, however, accompanied by easily recognized signs.

The first thing to look for is rotation at the base of a cloud. One part of a cloud may be moving toward the northeast, while another part drifts toward the southwest. The rotation is not necessarily very rapid. It is always counterclockwise (as viewed on the next page).

Another sign of a developing tornado is the appearance of obvious violent updrafts or downdrafts near the base of a cloud. Pieces of the cloud are rapidly torn off, and the fragments descend toward the ground, or rise upward from the ground into the main body of the cumulonimbus.

If a funnel cloud actually forms, it usually appears smooth and well defined. There may be more than one funnel cloud at the same time (Fig. 4-6). The funnel or funnels may seem to appear out of nowhere and disappear for no apparent reason. If a funnel cloud touches down, a cloud of dirt will appear at its base.

Some tornadoes are hidden within masses of low cloud. This type of tornado appears as a low, wide, boiling mass of darkness, with no apparent shape. As it moves along, it seems to swallow up everything in its path.

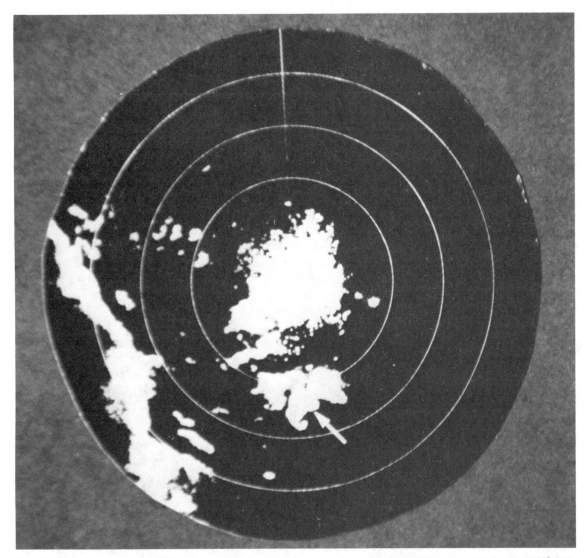

Fig. 4-5. The cyclonic vortex within a severe thunderstorm shows up as a hook-shaped echo on radar (courtesy NOAA).

So far, I have made the tacit assumption that observations can actually be made. Of course, direct visual observation is not always possible. It might be nighttime, and a funnel cloud can't be seen in the dark. There might be a strong wind with heavy rain, which can sometimes reduce visibility to near zero.

Once a funnel cloud touches the ground, it produces a loud, continuous noise. The roar has been described as resembling "a hundred freight trains," or "a great horde of bees," or "a jet plane circling overhead." In the open country, the sound of a tornado can sometimes be heard from several miles away and can provide warning when visual observation fails.

Radio and Television Tests

The interior of a funnel cloud contains almost continuous lightning. Lightning produces a familiar crackling sound on radio receivers. Lightning also causes a darkened television screen to light up momentarily. A radio receiver, or better, a television set, can be used in some instances to detect a nearby funnel cloud.

An ordinary, portable AM transistor radio can be tuned to a frequency on which no station is broadcasting. Normally, a moderate hiss or roar will come from the speaker when the volume is turned up. In the vicinity of a thunderstorm, the hiss is accompanied by frequent popping and crackling because of numerous lightning strokes, but a funnel cloud, with its continuous discharges, creates an uninterrupted noise on the radio. The normal background hiss becomes much louder and sometimes has a buzzing or whining quality.

The television test requires that the set be connected to an antenna, not to a cable network. The antenna can be either indoors or outdoors, but it is best to use an indoor antenna because of the lightning hazard in and near a severe thunderstorm. For the test to work, channel 2 must be free of broadcasting stations, so that there will be no interference.

The television test is conducted as follows:

The set should be switched to the highest empty channel and the brightness control adjusted so that the screen is dark except for an occasional spot of "snow." The contrast control need not be adjusted. The selector should be set to channel 2.

Under normal conditions, the screen will stay dark, except for momentary bright flashes caused by lightning discharges. If a funnel cloud exists within a few miles, however, the screen will brighten up continuously.

Although it is possible to detect a tornado by listening for its characteristic roar, or by using a radio or television set as just described, the best way to keep informed is to listen to weather an-

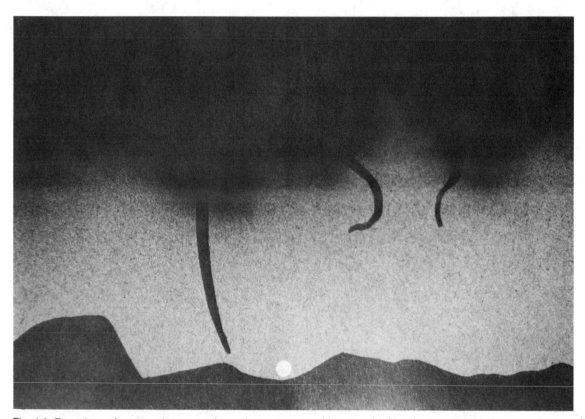

Fig. 4-6. Tornadoes often occur in groups of two, three, or more, with one major funnel.

nouncements on local radio or television stations. The meteorologist has radar with which hook-shaped echoes can be detected. The police, high-way troopers, and other officials will report funnel cloud sightings. Tornado warnings will then be disseminated through the commercial broadcast stations.

Movement

After a funnel cloud touches down, it is practically impossible to tell exactly how it will progress. The average forward speed is about the same as that of the thunderstorm that produces the tornado, normally 20 to 40 miles per hour. As the funnel snakes along, however, it may speed momentarily up to 60 miles per hour or more, or come to a complete halt. Some tornadoes have been known to backtrack for a short distance.

Single tornadoes usually describe either a straight path (Fig. 4-7A) or a looping path (Fig. 4-7B). The looping tornado is especially dangerous, because it passes over certain points twice. The second strike is from a different direction than the first strike. People climbing out of their basements (or what is left of them) may be greeted by the opaque wall of the funnel, bearing down on them again.

A multiple-vortex storm generates funnel clouds that move in curved paths and then dissipate. New funnels continually form near the trailing part of the cyclonic vortex and move around to the front of the circulation, near the center of the thunderstorm, before dying out (Fig. 4-7C). The average speed of this type of tornado is a little greater than the speed of the "mother cloud." The multiple-funnel tornado is, like the looping type, particularly dangerous, because some places may be hit by two, three, or more different vortices in rapid succession.

Many people believe that tornadoes always come from the southwest. This is not necessarily so. The average movement of a tornado is in the same direction as the movement of the "mother cloud," and most thunderstorms move from the southwest toward the northeast. A looping or multiple-vortex tornado can come from any point of the compass, however.

If the looping tornado of Fig. 4-7B is contained in a storm moving from the southwest toward the northeast, the funnel will, on the average, move in the same direction as the storm. It is easy to see, however, that the funnel will hit some places from the south, from the east, or even from the north. Similarly, multiple-vortex tornadoes (Fig. 4-7C) can strike from almost any direction.

If a tornado or funnel cloud can be seen, its movement is sometimes obvious. A straight-path funnel cloud, several miles away and retreating, presents little danger. Often, if not usually, however, the progress of a tornado is hard to observe. Tornadoes can move in ways that we don't understand. If you see a funnel cloud, the best thing to do is take shelter until the threat is entirely over.

LIFE CYCLE OF A TORNADO

Most tornadoes get their work done in a hurry. The average funnel cloud lasts for less than an hour and stays on the ground for only a few minutes. The average tornado path is only a few miles long, but if that path cuts through a heavily populated area, the damage done in those few minutes can cost millions of dollars.

As the funnel cloud first begins to reach toward the earth, it is usually very thin, almost threadlike. Many funnel clouds dissipate before they ever touch down to become tornadoes. Of the funnel clouds that do reach the earth, most never attain diameters of more than a few hundred feet. Occasionally, however, a "maxi tornado" develops. The cloud gets low and wide, bloating to a mile or more across. These large tornadoes last for the longest time, contain the most violent winds and the lowest internal pressures, and do the greatest damage of any tornado. Some maxi tornadoes travel hundreds of miles in an uninterrupted path. The most famous of the maxi tornadoes was the tri-state storm of 1925, which killed over 600 people in a rampage lasting several hours. Fortunately, such massive and long-lived tornadoes do not occur very often.

Once a tornado has reached the ground, the funnel picks up all sorts of things. The dirt, grass,

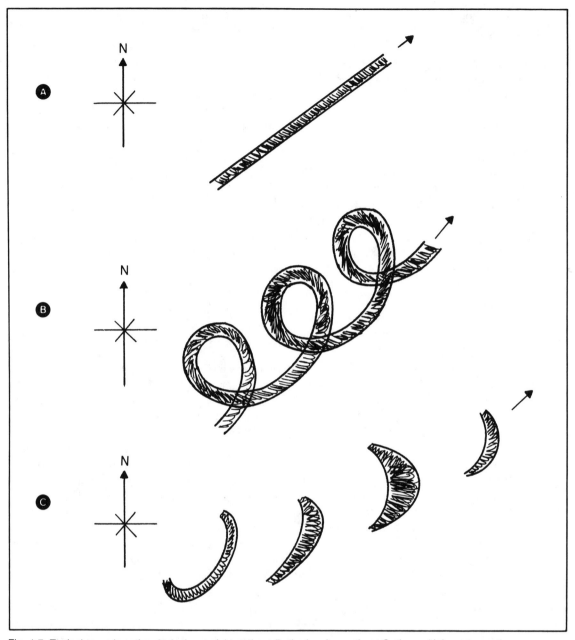

Fig. 4-7. Typical tornado paths. At A, the straight path; at B, the looping path; at C, the multiple-vortex path.

and leaves color the clouds, giving them a strange and ominous appearance. Plumes of dust sometimes rise up and surround the funnel, making it look bigger than it actually is.

As the vortex begins to dissipate, it may rise partially back into the mother cloud, its path of destruction narrowing and the damage becoming less complete. Smaller tornadoes sometimes disappear abruptly. The base of the mother cloud swirls more slowly, until finally the rotational motion is no longer evident. The ragged cloud base, darkened by dirt sucked up earlier, still presents a threatening spectacle, but the danger has passed.

Once a thunderstorm has stopped producing funnel clouds, it normally weakens and dissipates over an hour or two. Some thunderstorms generate tornadoes for a while, weaken temporarily, and then strengthen again and spawn more funnel clouds. This is most likely to happen in a multiple-cell thunderstorm or in a squall line.

STRANGE EFFECTS

Tornadoes are known for their awesome, and sometimes unearthly, methods of destruction. Pine needles are driven into wooden planks, timbers hurled through cinder block concrete walls, and cars wrapped around tree trunks. Even people have been airborne in tornadoes, some inside cars, trucks, or houses, and others all by themselves. Whole houses have been moved off their foundations without other structural damage.

A tornado might reduce a house to a pile of rubble, while the shade trees in the yard don't lose a single branch. A tornado once pulled a curtain through a closed window around the edge, without breaking the glass. In another instance, a wooden beam passed through a piece of glass, punching a hole in the glass but not shattering it.

If a tornado passes over colored soil and sucks up a lot of dirt, the funnel and the whole cloud base acquire the tint. This is responsible for the eerie light that often precedes or accompanies a tornado. Ordinary soil produces a greenish or yellowish hue. Some types of soil or sand make the sky look pink, brown, red, or even purple.

If a tornado passes over a lake, stream, or swamp, the vortex picks up fish and frogs. The hapless creatures are carried by the updrafts within the mother cloud and later fall back to the earth with the rain and hail beneath the downward-spinning anticyclonic vortex. If the storm passes over a populated area, the streets will be littered with fish and frogs.

Tornadoes have been known to strip chickens and other birds of their feathers. Most of the birds are killed as they are flung about by the storm winds, but some survive. Chickens are denuded so routinely, in fact, that a scientist has seriously put forth the idea that the intensity of a tornado could be inferred from the proportion of feathers remaining on the birds following the passage of the vortex.

WINDS IN THE FUNNEL

Within the vortex of a funnel cloud or tornado, the winds blow with almost incredible violence. In cases where tornadoes strike weather stations, the anemometers are invariably wrecked before the speed of the winds can be determined. Indirect methods must be used to ascertain how hard the winds blow in a tornado.

It was once believed that tornadoes packed winds in excess of 500 miles per hour, perhaps even exceeding the speed of sound. It was theorized that the roar of the vortex was caused by air breaking the sound barrier as it whirled around. Analysis of the structural damage caused by tornadoes, however, indicates that the wind speeds are less than was previously thought. It is doubtful that the winds ever exceed 350 miles per hour, but that is fast enough to cause almost complete destruction.

When the wind blows against an object, the force is proportional to the square of the wind speed. Most of us have seen winds of 75 miles per hour and know how much damage can be done by air moving at this speed. In a tornado with 150-mile winds, the damage is four times that bad. A 300-mile wind causes 16 times as much damage as a 75-mile wind. It is difficult to imagine a wind with that much force, but it is easy to understand why the effects are so catastrophic (Fig. 4-8).

A tornado researcher, T. Fujita, of the University of Chicago, has formulated a scale of tornado intensity, based on observation of the effects of hundreds of the storms. The wind speeds range from less than hurricane force to more than 300 miles per hour. There are six categories, designated F0 through F5, in order of increasing violence. The *Fujita tornado intensity scale*, as it is called, is outlined in Table 4-1. The relative force of the winds is illustrated in the graph in Fig. 4-9.

The Omaha tornado of May 6, 1975, caused damage characteristic of an F5 storm. There have

A

Fig. 4-8A. Examples of tornado damage. At A, the remnants of the high school gymnasium at Pleasant Hill, Missouri, after a tornado on May 4, 1977 (courtesy NOAA).

Fig. 4-8B. The wake of a violent tornado that occurred in Monticello, Indiana, in April 1974 (courtesy Army National Guard).

Table 4-1. The Fujita Tornado Intensity Scale.

Classification	Wind Speed	Damage
F0	< 72 MPH	Light
F1	73-112 MPH	Moderate
F2	113-157 MPH	Considerable
F3	158-206 MPH	Severe
F4	207-260 MPH	Devastating
F5	> 260 MPH	Unbelievable

been other famous F5 tornadoes that have struck populated areas and caused great destruction. The tri-state tornado of 1925, and several tornadoes on April 3 and 4, 1974, are noteworthy examples.

The winds of a tornado, like those in a hurricane, blow fastest in the right-hand part of the vortex, where the forward movement of the funnel adds to the rotational motion of the air. If the winds whirl at 150 miles per hour, for example, and the funnel cloud travels at 30 miles per hour, then the right-hand side will pack 180-mile winds while the left-hand side will contain winds of 120 miles per hour (Fig. 4-10A). This might not sound like much of a difference, but it represents a ratio of more than 2 to 1 in terms of destructive power. The faster the tornado moves, the greater the difference will be.

The "add-on" velocity effect is more pronounced in multiple-vortex tornadoes. The vortices

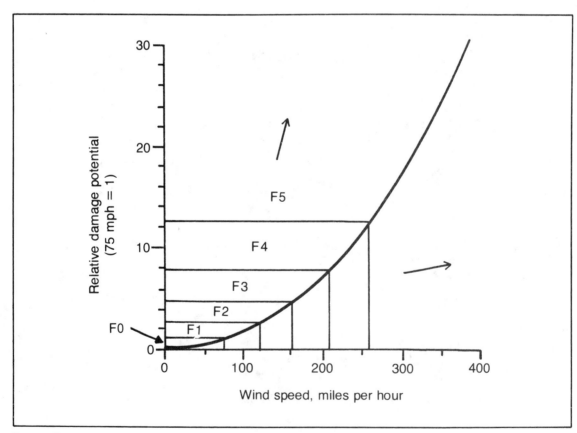

Fig. 4-9. Relative damage scale for tornadoes of Fujita intensity F0 through F5.

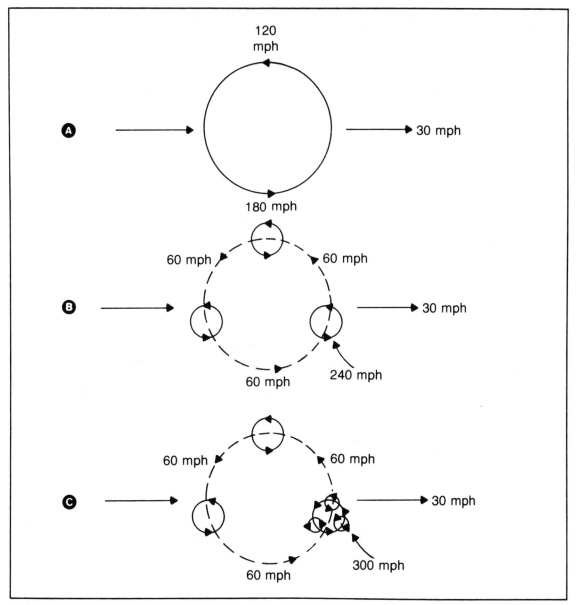

Fig. 4-10. The movement of a tornado and the whirling of its vortex, act concomitantly to produce extreme wind speeds. At A, illustration of effects of forward motion; at B and C, effects of multiple and suction vortices.

all rotate around a common center. While the center moves at 30 miles per hour, the vortices revolve at speeds of up to 60 miles per hour. Thus, the actual speed of the whirling wind in each vortex may be increased by as much as 90 miles per hour in some parts of the complex (Fig. 4-10B). If the winds actually whirl at 150 miles per hour, the maximum speed in such a multiple-vortex storm would be 240 miles per hour.

Within any tornado funnel, small eddies form. These eddies are known as *suction vortices,* and they revolve around the center of the funnel in a counterclockwise direction. The suction vortices contain the most violent winds known. The combined effects of the movement and whirling of the main funnel, along with the tightly spiraling winds of a suction vortex, produce winds characteristic of an F5 storm (Fig. 4-10C). A suction vortex can rip a building to pieces while leaving adjacent structures unscathed. This explains how your next door neighbor's house can be destroyed, but yours spared—or vice versa.

PRESSURE IN THE FUNNEL

In many ways, a tornado is like a miniature hurricane. The barometric pressure inside the funnel cloud is lower than the normal atmospheric pressure. As the air is pulled inward, it spins because of the Coriolis effect. The intensity of a tornado is correlated with the internal pressure.

It is almost impossible to measure the exact barometric pressure inside a tornado. When one strikes, most people do not rush to a barometer and take a look. We know that the inside of a tornado funnel is far from a perfect vacuum, because people have been at the centers of tornadoes and survived. One man who had been through several tornadoes noted that the rapid drop in pressure caused his ears to "pop," as they would while driving up a mountain or ascending in an airplane. Some people who have been through tornadoes have noted that they had no difficulty in breathing, even while they were in the very center of the funnel. The pressure probably does not fall by more than a few inches of mercury.

The barometric pressure does not have to drop very much, however, for a tremendous pressure gradient to build up. Consider the example of a closed house in the center of a tornado in which the barometric pressure drops to 90 percent of normal (supporting 27 inches of mercury). This will produce a pressure change of over 200 pounds per square foot—more than enough to break windows, and perhaps sufficient to knock down the walls or lift the roof.

For years, it was believed that the primary destructive power of a tornado comes from the pressure change as the funnel passes by. It was theorized that buildings literally explode because of the expanding air inside. Today, it is generally thought that the winds, not the air pressure itself, are mainly responsible for the damage that a tornado inflicts on buildings. The suction vortices cause the most damage because of their twisting nature and their extreme violence. Once a building has been torn to pieces, the debris is scattered by winds in and around the funnel cloud.

The notion that damage is caused by the wind, and not the pressure inside the tornado, is supported by analysis of the damage. If the pressure actually caused buildings to explode, we would expect most of the debris to be carried along with the storm and fall in the leeward (usually northeast) corner of the foundation, but this is not what happens. The windward side is where most of the wreckage lands.

TAKING COVER

The safest place to be, should a tornado directly strike in your vicinity, is several feet underground in an old-fashioned storm cellar. This type of shelter is completely separate from the house and has an entrance like a trap door, made from heavy steel or reinforced hardwood. Another excellent refuge is a fallout shelter. These heavy structures are practically immune to demolition from anything less than a direct hit in a nuclear holocaust. Because the storm cellar is completely autonomous, people inside are totally safe from flying debris. Most homes built today, unfortunately, have neither a storm cellar nor a fallout shelter. Some dwellings don't even have a basement.

From studying the damage done by tornadoes, scientists have found that the windward side of a structure is the least safe, and the leeward side is the most safe. *This is directly contrary to the earlier, and still more widely believed, idea that "the southwest corner of the basement" is the best place to take cover. The windward side is con-

---

* This is discussed in detail in the book *Severe and Unusual Weather*, by Joe R. Eagleman (Van Nostrand Reinhold Co., 1983).

sidered to be the wall or corner that faces in the direction from which the tornado is approaching: usually the south and west. The leeward sides most often face toward the north and east, but there are occasional exceptions. For example, a storm in June 1971, that struck near Rochester, Minnesota, moved from north to south. In that tornado, the southern parts of buildings would have been the safest. (Fortunately, the funnel clouds did not touch down in the city.) It is therefore important that you know the general direction from which a tornado is approaching.

The reason why the windward part of a building is the most dangerous is simply because the greatest wind speeds are found in the part of the tornado in which the forward movement adds to the whirling effect (Fig. 4-10). In a tornado approaching from the southwest, the highest winds will blow from the southwest. Most of the debris will approach from that direction and will be hurled at the highest speeds. The windward walls of a building, if not torn down outright, are likely to be heavily damaged by flying objects. Even in the basement of a house, the windward corner can be dangerous. The whole house might be picked up and moved a few feet, with the windward side or corner dropping into the basement.

Of course, if you can get to a basement, you are better off than if you must stay on a floor that is above ground level. If there is no basement, you should go to the first floor on the leeward side or in the center of the building and get under something heavy, like a bed, desk, or table. If you are in a large building, you should go to the basement if possible, and get inside a closed room. If there is no basement, you should go to a room with no windows, such as a closet, storage area, or lavatory. Never take shelter in a subway or hallway, because high winds and flying debris are likely to injure you or even blow you away.

No two tornadoes are exactly alike, and the storms behave in strange and sometimes totally unexpected ways. We can only look at statistics, based on a large number of cases, to make meaningful conclusions. With the exception of a storm cellar, there is no place that is entirely immune to the effects of flying or falling debris. If this all sounds scary, you can take comfort in one fact: even if a tornado makes a direct hit, your chances of survival are more than 99 percent, provided you are in a sheltered part of a house or building.

The worst place to be in a tornado is outdoors or in a car. You might try to outrun or dodge a tornado if you are driving a vehicle, but it is difficult to predict exactly how the storm will travel. If you are unlucky enough to get caught outdoors as a tornado approaches and there is no way for you to get to a shelter, you should lie face down in a ditch or ravine, with your feet pointing in the direction from which the tornado is coming, and pray.

IN THE CENTER

Tornadoes seldom pass over meteorological installations, and this makes it difficult to probe inside the whirling storms. Little is known about conditions within a funnel cloud. There are few eyewitness accounts by people who have been through a tornado and seen the strange, cylindrical chamber within the opaque wall of cloud. Those who have had the experience have told of oppressive silence, black, smokelike, dust-and-debris-filled clouds moving with incredible swiftness from right to left, bizarre lightning flashes, and sometimes a gassy smell.

One person who watched a tornado pass directly overhead described the interior of the funnel as a long, hollow tube of cloud with zigzagging lightning flashes, surrounded by thin, hissing, writhing suction vortices. Another inside witness watched as the rear wall of a funnel cloud swallowed up his neighbor's house, tearing it apart in an imperceptibly brief fraction of a second. As he looked upward into the hollow, rotating mass of cloud, he could see the cylindrical chamber undulating as if it were somehow alive.

There can be little doubt that conditions inside a tornado are weird, but the scientist needs meaningful, quantitative data. If humans want to probe inside a tornado, the instruments must be brought to it. The National Oceanic and Atmospheric Administration (NOAA) has recently built a portable device for measuring extreme wind speeds and atmospheric pressures. It is known as the totable tornado observatory, or TOTO.

The TOTO instrument contains a wind vane for determining wind direction, a pressure sensitive wind speed detector, an electric charge sensor, a barometer, and a thermometer. The instruments are designed to withstand the winds in all but the most violent tornadoes. The TOTO device is shaped somewhat like a cylinder or barrel, and is weighted so that it will not be blown away by tornadic winds. All of the instrument readings are plotted against time, so they can be evaluated when TOTO is recovered.

Putting TOTO in place is a dangerous business. When a tornado is sighted, two scientists drive toward its path in a truck, along with TOTO. An educated guess must be made concerning the exact route the funnel will take. The closer the scientists can get to the tornado as it approaches, the better the chances of its passing over TOTO. Once the position has been chosen, the scientists stop the truck, wheel the 400-pound instrument box out and set it down, get back in the truck, and speed away. If the scientists are lucky, TOTO will be hit, and they will not.

INJURIES AND FATALITIES

While tornadoes are extremely dangerous, they cause fewer injuries and deaths, on the average, than lightning. This is mainly because tornadoes batter only a tiny percentage of the land area of the world. Lightning strikes many more places. In addition, tornadoes are much more terrifying. People are more likely to run for shelter as a black, funnel-shaped twister bears down, than they are when there is a little lightning and thunder. People are extremely safety conscious about tornadoes, and the violent whirlwinds deserve the respect they receive.

Some parts of the United States get more tornadoes than other regions. The largest number of tornadoes strike in the Midwest and South. The Great Plains states are particularly hard hit, but interestingly, the greatest number of people are killed in the South, especially in Louisiana, Mississippi, and Georgia, and not in the Midwest.

There are two factors that are believed to be responsible for the greater number of tornado-related deaths in the South as compared with the Midwest, in spite of the fact that the Midwest gets more tornadoes.

In the South, many houses lack basements, either because of low-lying ground and a high water table, or because basements are not traditional in that region. Because a basement offers superior protection in a tornado, a house without a basement is much more dangerous than a house with a basement. Flying debris tends to be propelled horizontally in straight paths. A depression, such as a basement, offers protection for this reason. Also, a house with no basement can be swept completely away by the winds of a tornado—occupants and all.

The other reason tornado deaths occur in the South is a comparative lack of warning systems and storm awareness. The tornado warning system in the Midwest is sophisticated because of the more frequent "maxi twisters" that occur there. In the rural South, warning systems are almost nonexistent.

The principal life-threatening aspect of a tornado is the flying and falling debris. A temporary drop in pressure is not likely to injure a person; the wind, all by itself, is not necessarily dangerous. The chances of getting hurt or killed in a tornado can be minimized by avoiding places where objects are likely to fall or be hurled through the air.

TROPICAL AND
SUBTROPICAL TORNADOES

Tornadoes do not take place in the tropics and subtropics as often as they occur at temperate latitudes for two reasons. First, there is less Coriolis acceleration in the tropics and subtropics, so there is less twisting action. Second, the battles between air masses, so necessary for the formation of tornadoes, are not common in the tropics and subtropics. The atmosphere is comparatively free of frontal cyclones at low latitudes.

At times, however, tornadoes do occur in the tropics and subtropics. In the extreme southern United States, especially Florida, there are occasional tornadoes in conjunction with heavy thundershowers. In the winter, cold fronts from the continent repeatedly move down the state, triggering thundershowers and squall lines, which may contain tornadoes. In the summer, cumulonimbus clouds build up almost every day as the sun shines practically straight down on the land and heats the moisture-laden air. In the center of the state, the thundershowers generate so much lightning that the region has acquired the nickname "the lightning belt." Torrential rains, gale-force winds, and small hail are common in these thundershowers. Tornadoes are frequently observed.

The island continent of Australia lies largely in the subtropics. Tornadoes are observed fairly often in Australia; they arise from basically the same causes as the tornadoes in Florida. Much of Asia, as well, lies in the subtropics, and the wetter regions sometimes get tornadoes. In general, tornadoes of the subtropics are smaller, less violent, and have shorter life spans and path lengths, compared with twisters in the temperate zone.

Tornadoes have been observed in the outer rain bands of tropical storms and hurricanes. These tornadoes, like other ones in the subtropics, are usually quite small, and do less damage than the big Midwestern storms. Nevertheless, near a hurricane, tornadoes present a definite hazard. They can strike virtually without warning and do considerable damage. Funnel clouds are most likely to develop in the forward semicircle of a tropical storm, especially the right front quadrant in the northern hemisphere. If you are in a hurricane warning region, you should listen to local broadcast stations for possible tornado warnings.

TORNADOES OVER WATER

Not all tornadoes whirl over land; sometimes they form or pass over bodies of water. A violent twister may move over several lakes during its trek across the countryside. Then, for a short time, it becomes a *waterspout*. The funnel cloud changes color as the available debris becomes liquid instead of solid. The storm can suck up anything on, or near, the surface, including fish, boats, and people.

Marine waterspouts form over the warm waters of tropical and subtropical oceans. They are also observed during the warmest months in the temperate latitudes. Whirlwinds are very common over the Gulf Stream off the east coast of the United States, especially in the summer. Waterspouts often acquire a snowy white appearance, contrasting with the blue-gray clouds of a marine thundershower. There are sometimes two or more separate funnel clouds. Where the vortex meets the water, a cloud of spray is thrown up (Fig. 4-11).

Ocean waterspouts, and the thundershowers that breed them, are not usually as vicious as their land-born cousins, but small craft can be damaged or even capsized by a waterspout. For this reason, the pleasure boat owner should be aware of the potential for danger when waterspouts threaten.

Large vessels are not usually affected much by waterspouts. The water twisters present little more than an inconvenience to the captain of an ocean liner or destroyer. Winds in a waterspout probably do not reach speeds of much more than 75 miles per hour. A military ship was once struck directly by a waterspout and received nothing more than a gale-force buffeting. Personnel at the front of the ship noted gale winds at starboard (from the right), while personnel aft reported gale winds at port (from the left). Sailors amidships reported sharply shifting gale winds. There was, however, no damage or injury.

VARIATIONS ON A VIOLENT THEME

Smaller, less violent whirlwinds occur very often in all parts of the world as a natural result of wind shear, heat effect, and Coriolis acceleration. You have probably seen little vortices form and dissipate on hot, windy days. The dust begins to stir, and within a few seconds the rotating nature of the "mini storm" is apparent. Leaves, loose papers, and other light objects are picked up and carried along. If the whirlwind strikes you directly, you get dust in your eyes. Wind speeds are perhaps 40 miles per hour at the most.

In desert regions, a somewhat more violent "mini storm" can form. This type of vortex is most likely to occur on especially hot days. The weather is usually clear or partly cloudly. The development of this "mini storm," known as a *dust devil,* is caused

Fig. 4-11. A group of marine waterspouts that developed near the Grand Bahama Island, in the path of the Gulf Stream (courtesy NOAA).

by rising, heated air. Coriolis force gives the air a spinning motion. Sand and dust are picked up and carried aloft.

The dust devil looks very much like a tornado, except that the diameter is much smaller—usually only a few feet. Dust devils rarely do much damage to property, but a few have produced winds sufficient to uproot small trees and shrubs. Although dust devils are not notorious for causing destruction or injury, it is not a good idea to walk into one; the blowing sand can hurt your eyes and sting your skin. Wind speeds may reach hurricane force in extreme dust devils, but rarely exceed 40 or 50 miles per hour. The life of a dust devil is just a few minutes.

Whirlwinds similar to the dust devil sometimes result from the intense heat generated by massive fires. In the Hiroshima holocaust of 1945, several violent twisters developed as the fierce heat from the bomb explosion caused the air to expand and rise. A nuclear burst of several megatons might, in fact, generate one or more tornadoes of greater violence than the black Midwestern killers. Forest fires have been known to produce tornadolike whirlwinds with destructive effects. Artificial fires have been used by scientists to generate "mini tornadoes" for research purposes.

Small tornadoes can also be produced by *orographic lifting*. As the wind blows against a hill or mountain, the air is forced upward because it has no place else to go. The rising air may begin to twist, especially if the hill or mountain has irregularities that produce wind shear. The vortex tightens until

134

it resembles a dust devil. A similar thing happens when air is forced down a slope.

Most of us are familiar with the effects of buildings in a city. It is a bright, clear day with balmy breezes; you walk out of a tall building and are buffeted by gusts that seem to be of hurricane force. It is more than just your imagination. If it is a windy day, the funneling effect of adjacent tall buildings can produce winds strong enough to blow people off balance and even roll them like tumbleweeds. Such a thing happened to a woman in New York, in January 1982. The whirling winds

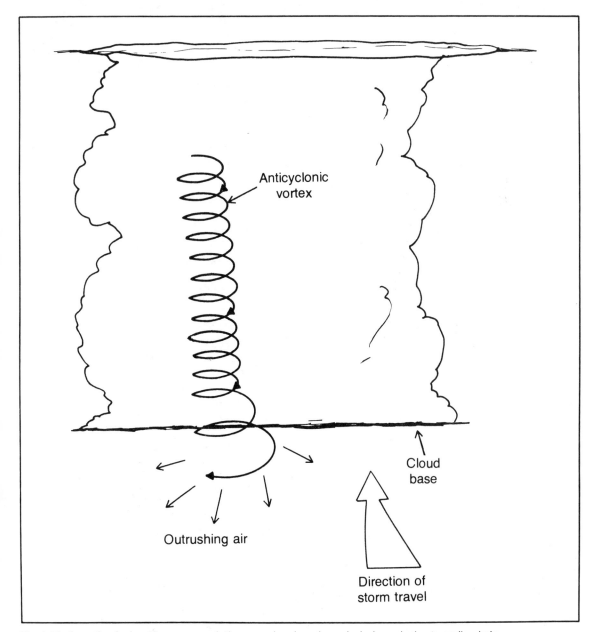

Fig. 4-12. An anticyclonic vortex may reach the ground and produce clockwise-spinning tornadic winds.

threw her down and broke her shoulder. During a thunderstorm already packing high winds, the effects of buildings can produce gusts and updrafts characteristic of small tornadoes.

Although the Coriolis effect dictates that a tornado should always rotate counterclockwise in the northern hemisphere and clockwise in the southern, there are some puzzling exceptions. As one man in Kansas watched a tornado pass directly overhead, he noticed that some of the peripheral suction vortices appeared to be spinning clockwise, although the main funnel twisted counterclockwise. Waterspouts have been known to spin in either direction. In some cases, an examination of tornado damage has indicated that the winds must have been spinning clockwise, contrary to the Coriolis force.

Although scientists are not certain why some tornadoes seem to disobey the laws of physics, T. Fujita has one theory: a few tornadoes occur along with downdrafts instead of updrafts. Such whirlwinds would have internal pressure higher than that of the surrounding air, and the winds would therefore spiral clockwise, outward, and downward. Such vortices might develop in the anticyclonic part of a thunderstorm, in connection with an especially intense downburst (Fig. 4-12). A tornado of this type would be especially dangerous, because it would be almost impossible to predict. Also, the anticyclonic downburst part of a thunderstorm usually contains heavy rains, which would conceal the funnel cloud—if there even was a cloud formation associated with the whirlwind. Fujita's idea might explain why some severe thunderstorms have produced such extreme wind gusts: more than 115 miles per hour, for example, in Alexandria, Minnesota, in July 1983, and an unofficial 157 miles per hour in a 1977 summer storm in northwestern Wisconsin.

ARTIFICIAL TORNADOES

Real tornadoes are inconvenient, as well as dangerous, to study while they are in progress. For this reason, meteorologists have devised various ways of making "micro tornadoes" in the laboratory.

Two basic ingredients are needed to create a tornadic vortex: updrafts and wind *shear*, or rotation. The updraft can be produced by something hot, such as a boiling pan of water. The wind shear can be mechanically induced using fans or by confining the air to a chamber with strategically positioned openings. Figure 4-13 illustrates a laboratory tornado maker.

As the pan of water is heated, the air in the chamber rises and escapes through the opening at the top. Cooler air from the outside enters through the four vertical slots, which are placed in such a manner that a counterclockwise wind shear is produced. As the water begins to boil, the steam facilitates observation of the air movement. Cylinder- or rope-shaped "micro tornadoes" will form and dissipate between the pan and the top opening.

Laboratory tornadoes have been generated on a larger scale by using big window fans to produce the updrafts and wind shear and using dry ice to make "clouds." A floor-to-ceiling "micro tornado," produced in this way, exhibits behavior remarkably similar to an actual twister: a snakelike funnel cloud appears, undulates, moves across the floor, and finally disintegrates.

Although laboratory tornadoes are not screaming, violent, destructive whirlwinds, their effects can be observed by placing such things as loose, fine dirt in their paths. Experiments with micro tornadoes done by Eagleman and others have demonstrated that the strongest winds occur in the direction of tornado movement. This explains many of the effects observed in real tornadoes.

THE OMAHA TWISTER

As the cold front moved eastward across Nebraska on May 6, 1975, it steadily intensified. By the time the clear, cool mass of air behind the front neared Omaha, the line of clouds was sharply defined (Fig. 4-14), and Mother Nature was about to explode into one of her most dramatic temper tantrums. The skies darkened over eastern Nebraska and Kansas, and the clouds unleashed a deluge of rain and hail.

The first twisters touched down in northeastern Nebraska, near the South Dakota border. Dam-

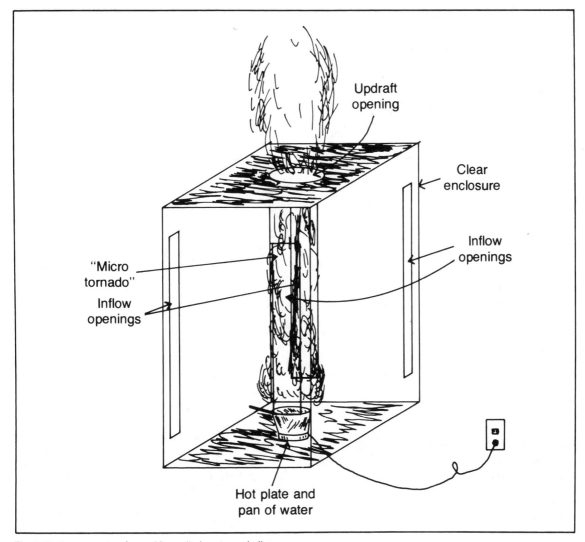

Updraft opening

Clear enclosure

Inflow openings

"Micro tornado"

Inflow openings

Hot plate and pan of water

Fig 4-13. An apparatus for making a "micro tornado."

age was reported in several small towns. The rain and hail continued to batter Omaha, driven by winds of near hurricane force. At about 4 o'clock in the afternoon, the storm began to let up, and conditions became quiet—too quiet. The western sky got lighter, but it wasn't a normal color. Instead of the azure-blue of improving weather, the horizon acquired a bizarre yellow-brown-green hue. The clouds seethed as the turbulence increased. Then, a funnel cloud formed.

A tornado warning was disseminated. Observers watched with awe as the viciously spinning, cone-shaped cloud stretched toward the landscape. The civil defense sirens were activated. Amateur and citizen's band radio operators observed and reported the storm's progress as a second funnel descended from the angry sky (Fig. 4-15).

The second funnel cloud reached the ground with a thunderous roar, and proceeded to follow a southwest-to-northeast track directly into the suburbs of Omaha. People took shelter wherever they could. The storm passed near a hospital and then

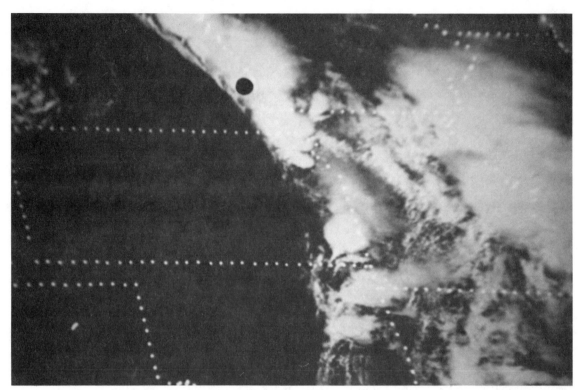

Fig. 4-14. The line of thunderstorms that produced the Omaha twister of May 6, 1975, viewed from space. Metropolitan Omaha is shown by the black dot at top center (courtesy NOAA/National Environmental Satellite Service).

Fig. 4-15. The Omaha tornado looked like this as it touched down (courtesy Gary J. Campisi).

138

blew a restaurant to pieces, killing an employee who took refuge in one of the bathrooms. Although she had chosen one of the safest places in the building, the whole structure was decimated. Only a storm cellar is entirely safe from the murderous winds of a twister.

The storm moved on, wrecking businesses and demolishing homes. Automobiles and trucks flew through the air along with pieces of wood, brick, and turf. The funnel cloud grew in size, a boiling black mass of confusion and terror. Windows exploded like gunshots, and debris filled the atmosphere to a height of thousands of feet. The storm skipped over a freeway and turned northward along West 72nd street. Two more people died in the tornado as it roared northward through the western suburbs of Omaha. One woman was sitting in her living room as the house collapsed. A man was killed on a street corner.

Finally, the funnel narrowed and retreated back into the cyclonic vortex high above. The 9-mile path of the twister began on a golf course, ended on another golf course, and destroyed hundreds of buildings in between. The whole ordeal lasted hardly more than 15 minutes. The duration of the winds was less than 60 seconds at any one place.

Silence and peace again prevailed in Omaha. The sky gradually cleared, and the sun shone down on the scene of ruin. As night fell, a chill crept into the air. A cold front had arrived—one of dozens in any given year.

The death toll was only three people, in spite of the fact that the storm had racked a densely populated area. The tornado warnings had saved dozens, or perhaps hundreds. As the dazed residents of Omaha surveyed the damage of their property, they gave thanks that their lives and health were still intact, but property damage in the wake of

Fig. 4-16. A pickup truck, totaled by flying debris (courtesy Gary J. Campisi).

Fig. 4-17. The remains of a school recreation area following the Omaha tornado. Note the metal pipes bent by the wind (courtesy Gary J. Campisi).

the Omaha twister was almost beyond comprehension. Cars and trucks were wrecked by the score (Fig. 4-16). Metal structures had been bent by the shear force of the moving air (Fig. 4-17). National Guardsmen were called out to keep order and to prevent the looting that always seems to follow a natural disaster (Fig. 4-18). In the hardest-hit areas, the rubble was piled so deep that people couldn't even walk through it (Fig. 4-19). Wherever the whirlwind had struck, the destruction was almost surrealistic.

As the sun rose on the morning of the next day, May 7, the smashed remains of previously handsome homes and buildings stood out starkly against the clear prairie sky. The sounds of rebuilding filled the spring air.

Events such as the Omaha tornado have oc-

curred throughout history and will certainly take place many more times before we learn how—or if—we can protect our homes and businesses against the wrath of the atmopshere's greatest storm. Meanwhile, all we can do is try not to be killed. The Omaha storm, while one of the most destructive in history in terms of property cost so few lives because warnings were issued effectively and taken seriously.

TORNADO-PROOFING

Is it possible to construct buildings strong enough to withstand the winds of a tornado? Would it be cost effective? In recent years, meteorologists have determined that the winds of tornadoes do not blow with sonic or supersonic speeds as was once thought. The worst storms generate winds of about

Fig. 4-18. National Guardsmen keep order in a tornado-stricken neighborhood (courtesy Gary J. Campisi).

Fig. 4-19. Rubble awaits a formidable clean-up task. The damage shown here is characteristic of F4 winds (courtesy Gary J. Campisi).

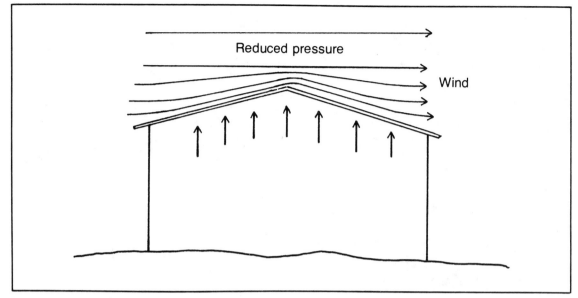

Fig. 4-20. High winds create a drop in pressure above a roof, resulting in an upward force.

300 to 350 miles per hour. Perhaps tornado-proof houses can be built, at least for storms of F3 force or less.

It is not likely that large buildings, enclosing gymnasiums, arenas, or shopping malls, can ever be constructed with the reinforcement necessary to resist tornadic winds. The massive roofs would be torn off by the tremendous overall pressure resulting from the *airfoil effect* at 200 or more pounds per square foot. Small homes might be designed to withstand F3 or perhaps even F4 winds, but special construction methods and precautions would be necessary.

Experience has shown that the first part of a

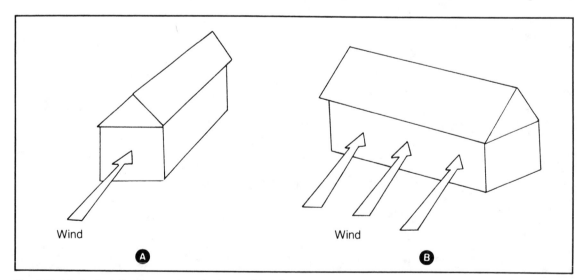

Fig. 4-21. Ideal orientation for a rectangular house (A) and an example of poor positioning (B), showing the relative force produced by southwesterly winds.

142

house to be damaged is the roof. An F1 or F2 storm will often remove part or all of the roof because of the lifting effect (Fig. 4-20). As air flows across a surface, the pressure is reduced. Flat roofs, or roofs with shallow peaks, are the most vulnerable. Steep roofs impede the flow of air and are therefore more resistant to damage. All roofs should be secured with hurricane clamps during the construction process. Attic vents help to equalize the pressure above and below the roof during strong winds.

The orientation of a house affects its susceptibility to damage by winds and debris. A rectangular house will receive the least damage if a short wall faces an oncoming tornado. In that case, the exposed surface area is small, and the overall force is minimized. A single-story house generally has less wall area, and better immunity to wind damage, than a multistory house.

The optimum orientation for a home is southwest-by-northeast in the United States (Fig. 4-21A). The worst angle is northwest-by-southeast (Fig. 4-21B). This is based on the fact that tornadoes most often approach from the southwest, and that the strongest blast occurs from that direction. (Some storms, of course, do not follow that rule.)

It is probably not worthwhile or even possible to build a home that will endure the freakish forces of an F5 tornado. Such severe twisters rarely strike any single place, even in the heart of "tornado alley." The chances of your house getting hit by a "maxi twister" are vanishingly small, but if you insist on full property protection against a direct hit by the most intense possible tornado, you can have it; put your whole house—roof, garage, and all—underground.

Chapter 5

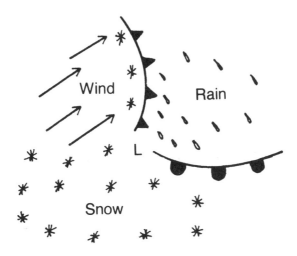

The Wrath of Old Man Winter

Hurricanes and tornadoes are spectacular storms because of their extreme violence. The wind screams and roars; people run for shelter, and terror prevails. Neither hurricanes nor tornadoes, however, are as powerful or widespread, overall, as the huge cyclonic systems that march across the continents of the temperate latitudes in the late fall, winter, and early spring.

A typical winter storm expends more energy than the worst hurricane and can cause widespread damage and death. Somehow, winter storms usually don't make sensational news. The terrifying Omaha tornado of 1975 killed three. A quite ordinary 1984 blizzard was blamed for more than 20 deaths in the midwestern and northeastern United States. The story is repeated every year. Winter storms are dangerous, and the peril is worsened by the fact that not enough people take winter weather seriously.

For reasons of geography, the middle southern latitudes are battered by vicious snowstorms much less frequently than the middle northern latitudes. Between the Tropic of Capricorn and the Antarctic Circle, most of the earth's surface is covered by ocean. Although mighty cyclones occur in this region, especially between the 40th and 50th parallels, the snow lands on salt walter and melts, and few permanent land dwellers are struck. The main exception is the extreme southern part of South America, where blizzards, ice storms, and fierce gales occasionally take place.

In the northern hemisphere, the vast continents of Europe, Asia, and North America comprise much of the world's total land mass. A sizable proportion of each continent is situated in the prime winter storm track. The great cyclones, spun off by the Aleutian and Icelandic low pressure systems, move along with the jet stream and hammer at the populated regions intermittently between September and May. The worst thrashings occur from late November until early April; January and February present the greatest danger of all.

At any given place, the length of the winter storm season depends primarily on two factors: the latitude and the distance from the ocean. The farther north, the longer and colder the winters get, in general. An inland place has a longer and more severe winter storm season than a coastal area, even if both locations are at the same latitude. (An especially interesting example is a comparison between the climates of southern Italy and the plains of Nebraska, which are on the same line of latitude.) Topography and altitude also have an effect; mountains deflect the air and alter temperature and wind patterns. Perhaps the most dramatic variable of all, however, is plain coincidence. The jet stream must take the blame for that. A ridge can produce a warm, dry winter with little snow but the risk of a subsequent summer drought. A persistent trough can result in above-average snowfall with consequent wintertime inconvenience, terrible heating bills, and spring flooding.

One winter may bestow a ridge in the west and a trough in the east. The next winter might give just the opposite situation. Predicting which of these persistent patterns, if either, will develop is almost as difficult as predicting whether a coin will show heads or tails on the next flip. The science of long-term weather forecasting is improving, but still inexact.

Let's suppose, for the sake of optimism, that someday we are able to say in August what will happen in January. Suppose we get to the point where we can claim absolute accuracy for a 6-month general forecast. That still won't solve the fundamental problem: we'll have to live with whatever comes. Perhaps we are capable of anticipating Old Man Winter's next move—but we will probably never be able to stop him from making it.

THE RAINS AND GALES OF AUTUMN

Sometime during the months of October and November, most regions get a brief warm spell. Most, or all, of the leaves have fallen from deciduous trees, and the days are rapidly growing shorter and crisper. There is an intermission that we fondly call Indian Summer. Shortly thereafter, the wind veers sharply, the sky becomes overcast, and the temperature plummets. Raindrops beat against the windows.

Not every winter begins like this, but most of them seem to do so. A strong cyclone, the first in the winter series, pushes through. In Canada, it can happen as early as mid-September. At progressively lower latitudes, the first storm arrives progressively later, perhaps after Thanksgiving in such places as Oklahoma or Virginia. In the extreme southern United States, these rainy gales represent the deepest part of the winter season. Similar patterns prevail in Europe and Asia.

The month of November can produce some early-winter storms that rival hurricanes in intensity. As early as 1641, a vicious November gale from the southeast battered and flooded parts of New England. In 1950, a monstrous cyclonic system, called the Great Easterly Gale, moved through the Ohio Valley and New England. In some locations, sustained winds reached more than 70 miles per hour and gusted to over 100 miles per hour. Tree damage was reduced to some extent because the leaves had fallen, but structural damage was severe. The midwestern United States is characteristically hit by westerly winds of near hurricane force on at least one occasion every October or November. The Pacific Coast is not spared; this is where storms in North America make landfall, and their violent winds and high tides have been well publicized. For the West Coast in November, however, the strongest windstorms are still to come.

European history contains numerous accounts of terrible gales that have caused widespread damage to forests and buildings. November was known in old English lore as the "windy month." A storm in the eighteenth century sent residents of southern England under tables and into closets as the houses shook, windows burst, and debris filled the air. Some homes in the countryside were blown completely away. The storm was accompanied by hurricanelike tides along the western coast, and the system even had a lull followed by a wind shift. It is possible that the storm had originated in the tropics as a late-season hurricane.

The reason for this change in storm activity, so dramatic in October and November in most places, is a change in the positions of the jet stream and polar front. Since late spring, the principal path of the stream has been well to the north of the most heavily populated parts of North America and Europe. In September, the jet stream starts its southward migration. In October, its latitude changes more rapidly, and in November, it moves equatorward over the middle latitudes with decisive speed and force. The stream also develops a greater tendency for irregularity—sharp cyclonic and anticyclonic bends—which breeds low-pressure storms that are, in general, larger and deeper than those of the summer months. The storms do not begin to diminish in strength until March.

THE RAIN BEGINS TO FREEZE

During November, many regions of the world experience their first sleet and freezing rain. The "ice belt" progresses toward the south through December. Sleet and freezing rain are among the most dangerous of winter's array of nasty weather phenomena, primarily because they make it dangerous to drive motor vehicles. After the care-free driving of summer and fall, it takes a while to get used to the change in road conditions that winter inevitably brings. The most treacherous slipperiness often takes us by surprise.

Sleet resembles tiny hail. Sleet pellets are about 1/16 inch across, although they can get as big as about 1/8 inch. As rain changes to sleet, it begins to make a louder smattering noise as the wind blows the pellets against window panes. The little white balls of ice accumulate on car hoods and windshields. The streets acquire a grayish-white color.

In a cloud, rain is normally frozen, especially at high altitude. As the ice pellets fall, they melt because of the warmer temperature at lower heights, but if the temperature at ground level is cool enough—about 40 degrees Fahrenheit or below—the rain does not melt before it reaches the ground (Fig. 5-1). This is *sleet*.

Freezing rain occurs for a different reason. The ice pellets melt as they fall, just as they do in an ordinary rain. The precipitation arrives at the ground in liquid form, but freezes as soon as it lands. Freezing rain is most likely to fall when the temperature near or at the ground is colder than the temperature at a moderate altitude (Fig. 5-2).

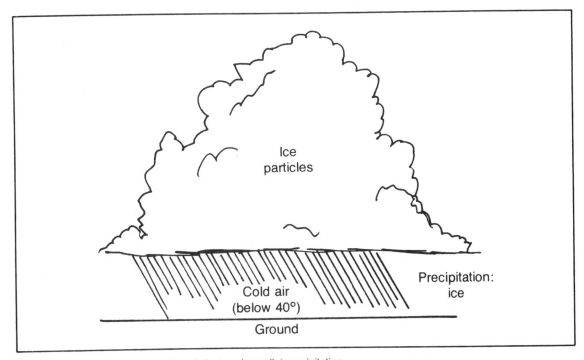

Fig 5-1. Conditions for the formation of sleet, or ice-pellet precipitation.

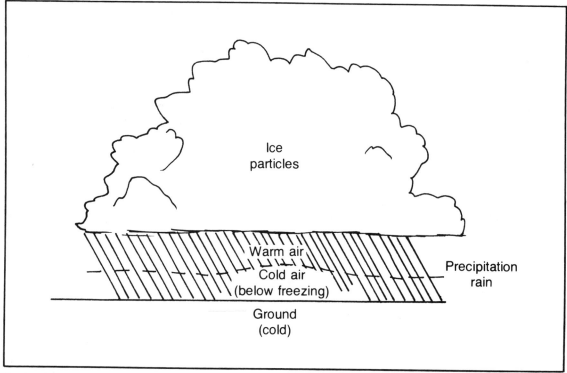

Fig. 5-2. Conditions that favor the occurrence of freezing rain, or glaze.

Freezing rain can produce a coating of ice more than an inch thick on every tree, house, utility wire, automobile, and road. If the icing is heavy, it is called an *ice storm*.

Sleet makes driving conditions adverse, but an ice storm makes them even worse. The ice storm is doubly dangerous because tree branches and utility wires may break and fall on a motor vehicle, smashing it or charging it with hundreds of volts of electricity.

Ice storms occur more frequently in some places than in others. In the United States, the southern and eastern regions are hit most, although the Midwest gets its share. Ice storms are less common west of the Rockies and in the far north.

The most severe ice storms can produce a layer of glaze that lasts for days. In 1978, an ice storm in southern New England kept things glistening for a week. The effects of an ice storm are worsened if snow subsequently falls, because the snow sticks to the ice, increasing the thickness and

weight of the layer. An ice storm accompanied by high winds can wreak tremendous damage to trees and utility lines. Power and telephone service is characteristically interrupted by ice storms.

Sleet or ice storms sometimes precede a snowfall and sometimes follow it. From the point of view of a driver, it is better if sleet or ice falls on top of the snow rather than underneath the snow. If the ice is on top, the plow gets rid of the ice as well as the snow. Children prefer the ice on top, too: they like to walk and slide on the snow without sinking in! For those who must shovel the stuff, however, it doesn't make much difference.

THE SNOW COMES

Almost everybody enjoys the first snow of the winter. The whole world changes. Everything gets brighter and quieter. A dark, loud city becomes more cheerful and quiet—in some cases even boisterous. For some people, it is the first time they have ever seen snow. The sleds, skis, and

148

other winter recreational apparatus are put to use, but the snow is a nuisance in some ways, especially if it is heavy (Fig. 5-3).

The time of the first snowfall varies, depending on the location. In the mountains, snow is possible at any time of the year at high elevations. In the northern sections of the United States, it usually comes in late November or early December, but sometimes not until January. The first white blanket might be less than an inch deep, or more than a foot (Fig. 5-4). The flakes may fall gently, making an even coat over the landscape, or high winds can drive the snow into drifts, reducing visibility and making it difficult to find a highway.

Much of our planet is covered by snow all the time. Mountain peaks, the Arctic Ocean, and the Antarctic continent are almost 100 percent blan-

keted by snow all year round. In the northern hemisphere, snow falls at least once a year over about 50 percent of the land. We can draw a line around the globe, representing the demarcation between regions where it normally snows and regions where it doesn't snow very often (neglecting mountain peaks). This is done by defining areas where the average temperature is below freezing during the coldest 30-day period of the year. Figure 5-5 shows the freezing line for the northern hemisphere. The effect of the oceans and continents is obvious—the severest winters are found in the interiors of North America, Europe, and Asia.

There are many different types of snow. In English, we have only one basic word for it, but in some languages there are several. Some snow is powdery and dry, and some is heavy and wet. Some

Fig. 5-3. A man clears away a heavy early-winter snow in Rochester, Minnesota (courtesy Jim Welch, Rochester Post-Bulletin).

Fig. 5-4. A single snowfall may accumulate to more than a foot.

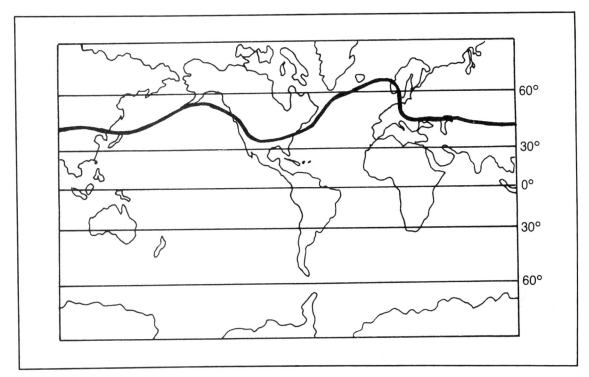

Fig. 5-5. The northern-hemisphere freezing line.

crystals are as fine as flour, while others can stick together to form true flakes measuring an inch or more across. The finer crystals tend to develop when it is very cold and the large, wet flakes at near-freezing temperatures. For this reason, an early-winter or late-winter snow is likely to be wet. Powdery snow falls most often in the "hard winter" months.

The moisture content of new-fallen snow is expressed in terms of the amount of water after melting. For dry, fluffy, powdery snow, the water-equivalent ratio is about 15:1, meaning 15 inches of snow will melt down to 1 inch of water. Wet snow has a ratio as small as 5:1. The wet snow is not only stickier, but it weighs more. If conditions are just right, an early-season or late-season snow storm can cause damage. The effects are similar to those of an ice storm. A particularly destructive storm of this type took place in the upper Midwest in 1966.

The trees began to bud early in 1966. By late March in southern Minnesota, it seemed that spring had arrived, but March is notorious for heavy snow,

and the month lived up to its reputation. Rain changed to wet snow late one evening. Meteorologists warned that a heavy snowfall was probable—8 inches or more. The flakes piled deeper by the minute, accumulating at the rate of more than 1 inch per hour. That is considered an extremely rapid rate of accumulation in nonmountainous regions.

The branches of the trees began to droop under the increasing load. By morning, 11 inches had fallen. The tree damage was extensive. Large elms and oaks were devastated as if by a hurricane. Smaller trees were doubled over (Fig. 5-6). The situation was worsened by gale winds. Utility poles snapped as the wind blew against wires coated with a 2-inch layer of the tenacious white stuff. Snow shovels broke from their handles. The roads were impassable.

Saturated snow can do more than damage trees and break power lines. The winter of 1977-1978 produced snows so heavy in New England that several roofs collapsed. The most sensational of all was

151

the ruin of the Hartford Civic Center. That casualty was caused by the weight of already wet snow further saturated by rain.

ANATOMY OF A WINTER STORM

A winter storm is a low-pressure system covering a large area and containing a warm front and a cold front. The circulation is counterclockwise in the northern hemisphere, and clockwise in the southern hemisphere. A cold front extends equatorward from the center of the system, and a warm front runs in a generally east-west direction. Rain usually falls between the warm and cold fronts, except during the coldest part of the season, when it might be either rain or snow. Behind the cold front, high winds are most likely to occur, and there is light snow or no precipitation. It is here that blizzard conditions occasionally arise. On the polar side of the system, snow falls. In a large storm, this is where the heaviest accumulations take place. Figure 5-7 shows the typical pattern for nothern-hemisphere and southern-hemisphere winter storms.

Three things determine the type of weather that accompanies a winter storm at a given place: the temperature, the storm orientation with respect to the locale, and the direction of storm movement.

The overall temperature dictates the relative sizes of the snow area and rain area. Early-season and late-season storms will have rain everywhere except well to the poleward side of the center. Mid-season storms have smaller rain areas, and in some of them the precipitation is all snow. Of course, latitude affects the temperature of a storm system, as does the proximity of an ocean.

The center of a storm may pass to the north or south of a place, or right through. These three

Fig. 5-6. Wet, sticky snow gives everything a weighty coat, causing damage to trees and utility wires.

152

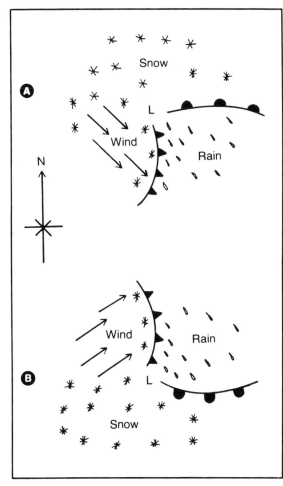

Fig. 5-7. Typical winter storms in the northern (A) and southern (B) hemispheres.

situations are shown in Fig. 5-8 for a northern-hemisphere storm that moves from west to east. Town "X" lies to the south of the storm track. The first precipitation will be rain, accompanied by winds generally out of the south. As the front nears and then passes, the rain will change to snow and taper off. There is a good chance of high winds behind the cold front. Town "Y" lies directly in the path of the storm; the weather there will be similar to the sequence of events at X, except that the snow will probably be heavier. Town "Z" will get heavy snow, along with winds that back from southeast to east to northeast.

The third factor that determines how a storm will behave is the direction in which it moves. The storm of Fig. 5-8 would produce different weather at any town if the movement was from south to north, for example, instead of from west to east. Usually, a storm advances in a direction between southeast and northeast, depending on the position of the jet stream.

You can draw a "model" storm system (Fig. 5-7A) on a piece of clear plastic or tracing paper and experiment with various paths and directions of movement to see what kind of weather the system will produce. Then, the next time a winter storm approaches your area, you can try to predict the weather by watching the progress of the system on a weather map. If you happen to live in one of the few places in the southern hemisphere that gets continental winter storms, you would use the "model" of Fig. 5-7B.

RAIN CHANGES TO SNOW

During a winter storm, the precipitation sometimes changes from rain to snow as the cold front passes and the temperature drops. The wind characteristically veers from south or southeast to west or northwest as the changeover takes place.

The rain-into-snow type of winter storm is common in the Midwest and West because the jet stream normally flows eastward or southeastward over these regions. Figure 5-9 shows two typical midwinter jet stream paths over the United States. At A, a ridge lies offshore in the Pacific, and a massive trough dominates the center of the continent. This brings moderate but wet weather to the west, and severe cold in the Midwest and South. The Atlantic coastal area escapes the grip of the cold. At B, a strong ridge prevails in the west with a deep trough in the east. This results in warm, dry weather in California and Arizona, while all of the eastern states have unusually cold conditions. Storms move along with the jet stream, and the storm centers are usually somewhat to the north of the stream.

Consider the situation in a Midwestern town, located under the jet stream or just to the south of it as a winter storm passes. The first sign of the approaching low-pressure system is a gradual increase in high cloudiness. The clouds begin as cirrus or cirrostratus and thicken until the sky is dark and gray. The temperature remains constant or rises slightly as the warm front passes. The wind blows from the south or southeast. Rain falls behind the front.

As the cold front approaches, the wind veers, and the temperature drops. When the front arrives, the temperature goes below freezing, and the rain changes to snow. Wet roads acquire a layer of glaze ice as the water freezes, and driving conditions

become treacherous. When the cold front moves through the area, the wind shifts to the west or northwest and increases in speed. Visibility deteriorates as the snow begins blowing and drifting. If the storm system is intense, blizzard conditions are likely. If the jet stream pattern is similar to that shown in Fig. 5-9A, snow might fall as far south as Texas and northern Mexico. If the flow is more like that of Fig. 5-9B, the Great Plains states will be hardest hit, and snow will blanket much of the southeast.

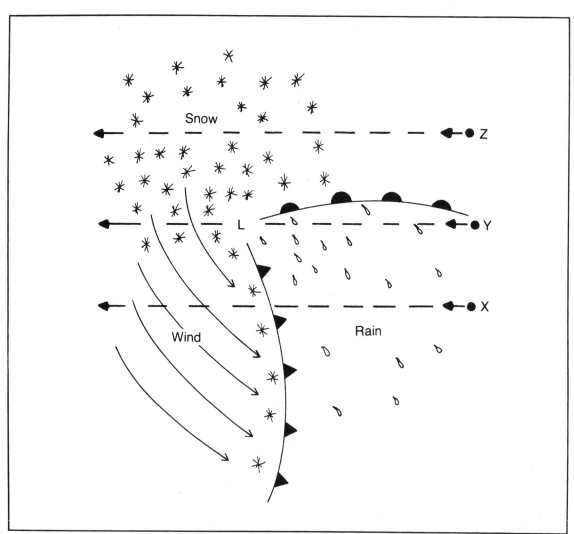

Fig. 5-8. As a winter storm moves by three different towns X, Y, and Z, the sequence of events is determined by the part of the storm that strikes a given place.

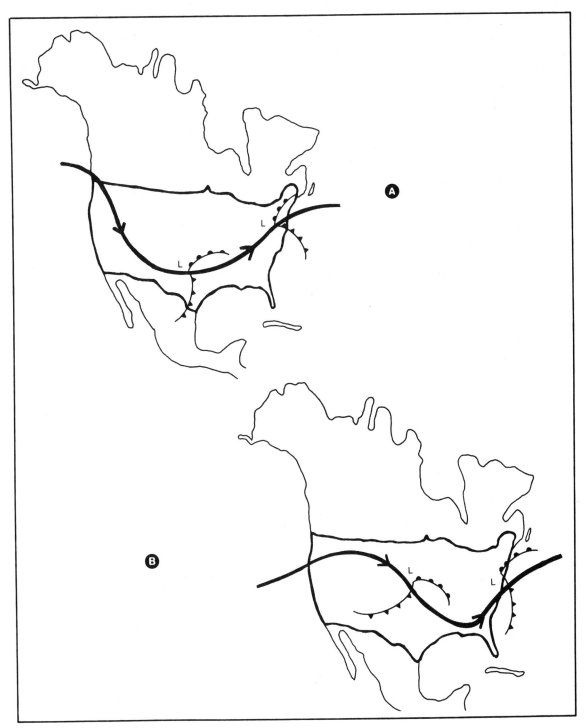

Fig. 5-9. Two typical wintertime jet stream patterns over North America. At A, a central trough; at B, a ridge in the west with a trough in the east.

SNOW CHANGES TO RAIN

Along the eastern seaboard during the winter, the jet stream flow is usually toward the northeast. This brings a different sequence of winter storm events to this part of the country most of the time.

Suppose you are located in Connecticut as a low-pressure system follows the jet stream path shown in Fig. 5-9A. The first signs of the storm are high clouds, such as cirrostratus, along with an increasing easterly or northeasterly wind. The clouds gradually become thicker and lower, and snow flurries begin. As the storm center approaches, the winds increase, and the snow falls heavily. A strong storm can produce hurricane-force winds and high tides along the coast.

When the center of the low-pressure system passes to the west and northwest of Connecticut in the hypothetical situation of Fig. 5-9A, the wind veers to a southerly quarter, and a warm front arrives. The temperature rises, and the precipitation changes to mixed snow and rain, and finally it is all rain. Only in an extremely cold system does the precipitation remain as snow following the warm front.

New England is famous for its ice storms, and the snow-into-rain scenario of Fig. 5-9A presents ideal conditions for such an event. As the warm front passes, all of the trees, utility lines, cars, and rooftops are still cold. If the temperature rises from well below freezing to just above, the rain will freeze on everything. Residents of the East Coast, especially southern New England, are wise to keep ice chisels in their cars' glove compartments.

SNOW DUMPERS

If the center of a low-pressure system passes off to the southeast and east of Connecticut, Rhode Island, and Massachusetts, a different thing happens. A situation of this kind often develops when the jet stream is situated in a manner similar to that shown in Fig. 5-9B. The Atlantic waters provide a rich supply of moisture for the circulation, because much of the storm system lies offshore. Heavy snow develops. Inland, the wind backs from northeast to northwest or west.

In January 1978, an intense storm moved up the coast and out to sea past Cape Cod. Most of New England was buried in a foot or more of snow. Hartford got 14 inches. A few days later, another system, even more severe, followed a similar path. Up to 30 inches of snow fell in parts of New England. Boston was battered by 90-mile-per-hour gusts. People skied in the streets.

Winter storms are given names in New England, just as hurricanes are named in the tropics. In a typical year, there are about 15 storms. The names are given because there are often two or three storms in progress at one time over the United States. The two "snow dumpers" of 1978 were called Jerry and Larry—two stormy brothers. The distinction of "worst northeastern winter storm in memory," however, belongs to March 12, 1888. From Washington, D.C., to the tip of Maine, the region was immobilized by snow accumulations of up to 50 inches. Some drifts were as deep as 40 feet.

Water always exacerbates the snow-dumping capability of a winter storm. Monsters such as the blizzard of 1888 and Larry of 1978 demonstrate this well. The Atlantic Ocean, however, is not the only attractive feeding ground for snowstorms.

As the glaciers retreated during the waning centuries of the most recent ice age, the present-day landscape was carved into the central and northern parts of North America. The glaciers left five puddles in the heart of our continent—Superior, Michigan, Huron, Erie, and Ontario—the Great Lakes. They are famous for the snowstorms they spawn. A large area of the country is affected. Heavy snows regularly fall in northern Wisconsin, northern Illinois, Indiana, Ohio, Pennsylvania, and New York state, as well as a large part of Michigan. The most dramatic accumulations occur right along the southern and eastern shores of all five lakes.

Figure 5-10 is a satellite view of a lake-effect snowstorm. Following the cold front of a low-pressure system, the northwest wind howls across the open water, picking up moisture. The water precipitates as snow over the land areas on the leeward sides of the lakes. Swaths of snow-dumping clouds are clearly visible downwind of all five lakes in this photograph. Most of Superior and

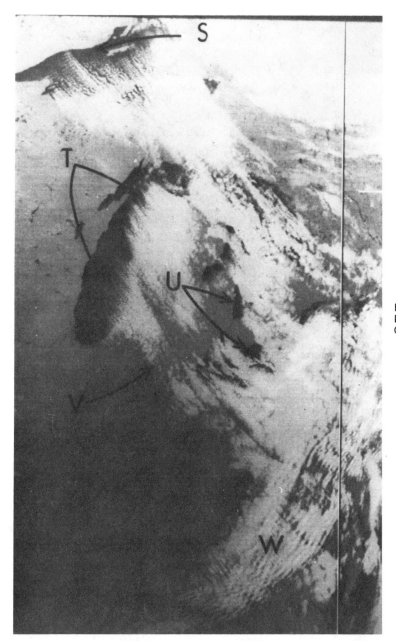

Fig. 5-10. A snowstorm over the Great Lakes (courtesy U.S. Department of Commerce/NOAA).

Michigan can be seen; Huron, Erie, and Ontario are practically obliterated by the snow clouds they have made.

Great Lakes snowstorms can produce accumulations of as much as 3 feet. The problem is compounded by bitter cold temperatures and by high winds, which can sometimes reach hurricane force. This creates true—and deadly—blizzard conditions. A series of storms spawned by Lake Erie in 1977 gave the city of Buffalo, New York, a somewhat undeserved reputation for severe blizzards. The dry, powdery snow drifted completely over cars and trucks, whipped along by 85-mile winds. Temperatures fell below zero.

In recent decades, the lake effect has been increasing because of the activities of man. Much of the Great Lakes area is peppered with cities and industrial complexes. The Great Lakes have been getting warmer because of industrial heat pollution. This warmth has made the lakes better fodder for snow-hungry northwesterly winds that sweep down from Canada during the winter. Ironically, many of the cities most responsible are the hardest hit.

The Atlantic and the Great Lakes have produced some giant snowstorms because of the interaction among wind, water, and land, but Old Man Winter has still another ingredient for snow making: mountains. When moisture-laden air sweeps up the side of a mountain range, the resulting snow accumulations can be hard to believe.

The Berkshires, in New England, and parts of the Appalachians, are well known for their deep snows. The ski resorts of Colorado, Utah, and other Rocky Mountain states are also famous for their snow, but to see snowmaking at its optimum, we must go to the Pacific Coast. A fine example is Mount Rainier, near Seattle.

All along the west coasts of continents and islands in temperate climates, the prevailing winds blow in from the ocean, resulting in copious amounts of precipitation. The three largest areas of this type in the world are Europe, a large portion of Chile in South America, and much of the west coast of North America. The temperate west coasts of North and South America are mountainous, and the mountains literally draw the moisture out of the air by a process known as *orographic lifting*. This is part of the reason why the Pacific Northwest gets abundant rainfall.

As the saturated ocean air sweeps up a mountainside, the air expands and therefore cools. At a certain height, the temperature gets below the dew point. Then clouds form, and rain or snow falls (Fig. 5-11). The scene of a mountain range, its peaks in the clouds, is familiar to people in many parts of the world. At the latitude of Mount Rainier, the temperature near the summit is almost always cool enought to result in snow. Snow falls all year long; the largest amounts occur in the colder months, when Pacific-spawned storms are the most intense.

In a single year, the snowfall on the slopes of Mount Rainier can exceed 80 feet, and a single storm can drop 6 feet or more. Similar conditions exist up and down the coast from central California to Alaska. The same is true along a sizable stretch of the South American Andes. The coastal regions of Europe receive less snowfall because the region is less mountainous, although plenty of heavy snowstorms take place in the Alps and other inland mountain ranges.

SNOW BREAKS LOOSE

It is a sunny, crisp morning as we sit in our warm mountain cottage. The ground glistens with new-fallen snow. We have a hot breakfast and get ready for the work of shoveling our way outside; the snow blocks the doorway, and we'll have to climb out of a window to clear it. The roof, too, needs to be shoveled off before the snow begins to freeze around the eaves.

There is a sound like thunder in the distance. It's too cold for lightning, though. Perhaps it is a high-flying jet airliner. We walk over to a window and peer up at the sky. No signs of a jet. Then we see what is making the noise: a whole section of the mountain is in motion. A white cloud of snow is racing toward the valley below. It is an *avalanche*. We are relieved that it doesn't seem to be heading our way. If it were, we realize, there would be nothing we could do but pray!

We have all heard stories about monstrous avalanches—almost every ski season, someone gets hurt or killed by this phenomenon. Avalanches take place in the mountains where snow accumulates to a significant depth and is subjected to certain forces. Avalanches seldom occur on smaller hills, and never on flat ground.

The snow pack on a mountain looks stable, but it has been built up as the result of several individual storms. Different storms produce slightly different types of snow, and the snow also changes with time under the pressure of its own weight. The result is that the snow pack on a mountain slope accumulates in layers during the course of a winter, in much the same way as the earth is built up over thousands or millions of years from plant and animal remains.

Layered material is not uniformly stable; the boundaries between components are "weak spots." This wouldn't cause a serious problem all by itself on flat land, but on a sloping surface the situation is different. Gravity pulls not only straight down on the snow, but sideways (Fig. 5-12). If the force is great enough, and a certain snow boundary is sufficiently weak, a massive section of one or more snow layers will break off and start sliding. The cleavage can be started by a falling tree, a passing skier or snowmobile, the vibration from a high-flying airplane, or a small animal hopping across the snow-covered slope.

After a fracture forms, it can propagate with amazing speed—in some cases hundreds of feet per second. The fracture may grow to be more than a block long. The top snow layer alone, or several layers, might be involved in the avalanche. The disturbance of the initial snow movement can cause other large pieces of snow to begin avalanching,

like a stampede. Some avalanches ultimately become larger than a football field and travel up to 300 miles per hour.

As the snow catapults down a slope, the air is driven before it, producing a damaging wind ahead of the avalanche (Fig. 5-13). The wind itself can level trees and hurl loose objects through the air. In extreme cases the wind acquires the speed and wrenching force of a tornado. The wind blast covers a much larger area than the avalanche itself and presents a significant danger to life and property.

In ski resort areas, people try to prevent avalanches by releasing unstable snow packs before they get large enough to be dangerous by literally shelling the snow on slopes known to be avalanche prone. A few small, deliberately instigated avalanches are better than a single "maxi avalanche" that strikes a populated place.

THE BIRTH OF A WINTER STORM

During the winter months, storms spin off from the Aleutian and Icelandic low-pressure systems in unending succession. The two permanent lows reach their greatest intensity in January and

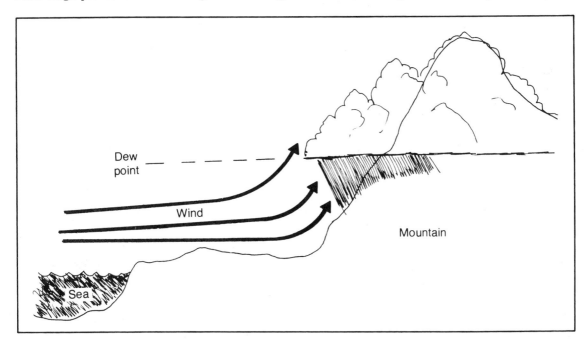

Fig. 5-11. As moist air blows in from the ocean and up the side of a mountain, clouds form and rain or snow falls.

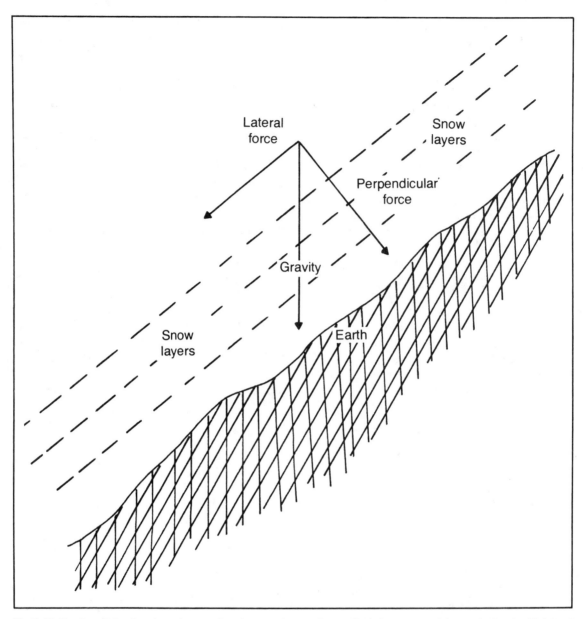

Fig. 5-12. Gravity puts tension along cleavage lines between layers of snow. On a slope, some of the gravitational pull is lateral as well as perpendicular to the earth.

February. The slowly inrushing air begins to spiral because of Coriolis acceleration, and a vortex is produced (Fig. 5-14). The prevailing winds carry the disturbance eastward, and it eventually makes landfall. In North America, the centers of the winter storm systems come ashore between southern California and southern British Columbia.

Although winter storms produce relatively little snow along the immediate Pacific Coast, high winds and heavy rains are common. Wet weather can penetrate far inland, drenching the deserts and steppes.

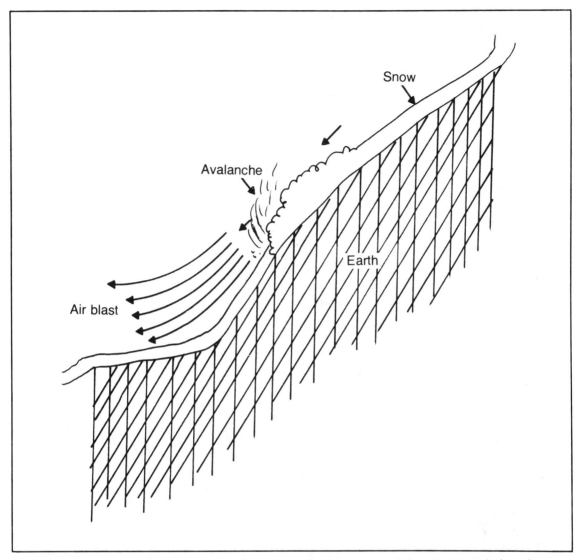

Fig. 5-13. An avalanche sets up a wind blast as the snow displaces the air. This wind can be extremely damaging.

When the jet stream is displaced southward from its average position over the west coast, the deserts of California and Arizona temporarily turn into monsoon zones. Unaccustomed to the sudden climatic change, rivers overflow their banks. The strong on-shore winds pile up the Pacific waters, causing destruction. It seems that, almost every year, we read about luxurious seaside California homes sliding down a mud bank into frenzied water. Meanwhile, people along the coasts far to the north

enjoy a blanket of snow, followed by crisp, clear weather for several days.

As the storm system moves eastward, cold air from the continental Arctic begins to feed the circulation. The rain may change to snow, covering the plains of Texas and Kansas with wind-driven snow before continuing on to the southeast and east. The upper Midwest may get heavy snow, followed by bitter cold. Ultimately, the storm follows the jet stream up the east coast, making things sloppy for residents of New England, and then moving out into the waters of the Atlantic.

A similar sequence of events takes place in Europe. If the jet stream is displaced to the south, the normally mild climates of Spain and southern France turn foul. The system then moves across southern Europe and into Asia Minor. Several storms of this kind, following each other like the links of a chain, caused a major blizzard and windstorm, and much inconvenience, in Yugoslavia during the 1984 Winter Olympics.

If the jet stream is located at, or to the north of, its average position over the west coast of North America, the California and Arizona deserts are spared the effects of Pacific storms. Their residents enjoy the mild, sunny winter weather for which the region is famous. As a system makes landfall, rain and gales pound the coasts of Washington and Oregon; then the storm moves into the Rockies, across the central plains, the Ohio Valley, and New England. It is these storms that occasionally produce some of the worst blizzards in the civilized world.

In Europe, storms move inland in the vicinity of the British Isles, northern France, and Germany, and continue on into the vast agricultural heartland of the Soviet Union. These systems can turn into blizzards. Russian winter storms are as fierce as their Midwestern counterparts Napoleon, and Hitler after him, found that out at great cost.

Blizzards and cold temperatures strike early in the plains of eastern Europe, largely because of their distance from the moderating oceans. The climate of the region is similar to that of the Dakotas and Minnesota. In 1941, the year of Hitler's ill-fated military campaign in Russia, the winter seems to have arrived early, with unusual severity.

Heavy rains came first; fields and roads turned to mud. Then the temperature dropped below freezing, and the mud hardened like concrete. Finally the snowstorms began, moving across the continent in an almost unbroken chain. The first snows came on October 6 and continued for a week. The temperature plummeted below 0 Fahrenheit; by mid-December the thermometer read 40 below. The heavy snow and bitter cold were accompanied by gale-force winds—a true blizzard. Thousands of Germans died of exposure and frostbite.

WINDCHILL

Today, we recognize the fact that the cooling

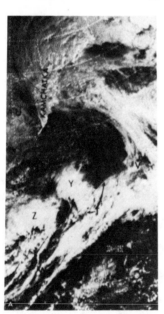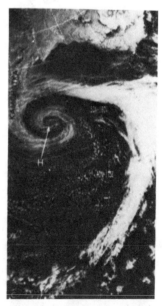

Fig. 5-14. Development of a winter storm over the north Pacific. The Kamchatka peninsula of Russia is visible at the left of each of these satellite photographs (courtesy U.S. Department of Commerce/NOAA).

162

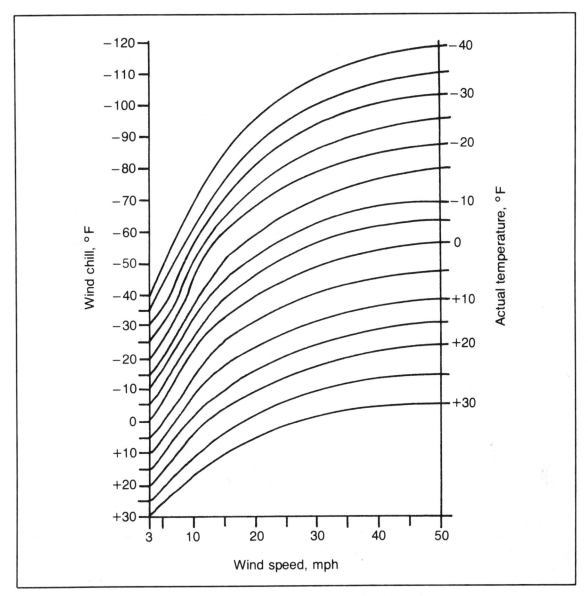

Fig. 5-15. Wind chill temperatures as a function of actual temperatures and wind speeds.

power of the air is increased by wind. Exposed flesh, as well as other warm or hot objects, are affected more severely as the wind speed increases at a given temperature. The effective temperature, taking the wind into account, is called the *windchill factor*.

At a given actual temperature, the windchill figure is defined as the air temperature that would cause the same amount of cooling to exposed human flesh as a person walking moderately in calm air. It is assumed that there is no sunlight to heat the skin, and that the body temperature is normal. Figure 5-15 is a graph of the windchill factor as a function of temperature and wind speed.

Actually, the windchill factor is a somewhat subjective expression of equivalent temperature, because people do not normally sit around unclothed in raging blizzards. Moreover, the windchill function is not the same for machines like automobile engines and electronic equipment, which have temperatures different from that of human flesh. The windchill temperature is, however, a valuable guide to the relative danger of combined cold and wind. It is especially important to know the likelihood of frostbite to hands and face.

In general, a significant danger of frostbite exists if the windchill factor is −30 degrees Fahrenheit or below. The cold can do some harm, however, at any effective temperature below freezing. An unprotected person can die of exposure at +45 degrees in a strong wind. In extreme conditions, the risk is obvious, and residents of the blizzard-swept northlands have coined a little rule known as the "30-30-30 law:" at 30 below with a 30-mile wind, bare skin freezes in 30 seconds.

On the Russian front during the hard winter of 1941-1942, the effective temperature was probably about −100 Fahrenheit. Similar brutal conditions have caused civilian deaths in the United States. In parts of Minnesota and northern Wisconsin, for example, blizzards have brought temperatures of −30 to −35 along with gale winds, resulting in winchill figures of −100 to −110.

Although we tend to think more of windchill in a howling blizzard than in a light breeze, it doesn't take very much wind to cause a significant drop in the effective temperature. For example at +30 degrees Fahrenheit, a wind speed of only 5 miles per hour will result in a windchill figure of +27 degrees, while a 15-mile wind will bring the windchill temperature down to +11 degrees. If the wind speed is 50 miles per hour, the effective temperature is reduced to −7 degrees. At wind speeds of more than about 50 miles per hour, the air does not acquire further cooling power.

It can be seen from Fig. 5-15 that the effects of wind become greater as the actual temperature drops. Suppose it is 30 below zero: a 15-mile wind causes a drop of 40 degrees in the effective temperature, making the windchill −70. At 30 above, the same wind produces an effective drop of only 19 degrees.

WHAT IS A BLIZZARD?

Meteorologists define blizzards according to the temperature and the wind speed. Blizzards are characterized by blowing and drifting snow, limited visibility, and the risk of frostbite and overexposure to cold.

When the temperature drops below +20 Fahrenheit, accompanied by a wind of 35 miles per hour or more, and blowing snow, blizzard conditions are said to exist. The windchill temperature drops below −20.

If the thermometer reading descends to +10 Fahrenheit or lower, and the wind speed rises to 45 miles per hour or more along with blowing snow, a severe blizzard is in progress. The windchill factor in a severe blizzard is −38 or colder.

Although the meteorologist does not rigorously define still more severe categories of blizzards, we might do well to consider that conditions can get a lot worse than those just described. Winds in some blizzards have been known to gust to over 100 miles per hour, and temperatures can fall below −40 degrees Fahrenheit in some parts of the world normally considered temperate. We might categorize blizzards on a scale of 1 to 5, in a manner similar to the Saffir-Simpson scale for hurricanes or the Fujita scale for tornadoes. Table 5-1 is one possible, although not official, scheme for categorizing winter storms.

Blizzards of force 1 and 2 sometimes occur in the northeastern United States, and are frequently observed in the midwestern and mountain states. Blizzards of force 3 are rarely observed in the Northeast, but are not uncommon in the Midwest and mountains. Storms of force 4 or 5 almost never occur in the Northeast, but once in a while they hit the Midwest and mountains. When a winter storm attains such strength, travel is utterly impossible, and anyone caught unprotected is in very serious trouble.

Blizzard conditions do not necessarily come in conjunction with heavy snow. A snowfall of 2 feet produces more inconvenience than an accumulation of 2 inches, and a heavier snow naturally increases the difficulty of travel by car, train, or bus. It is not

Table 5-1. Blizzard Intensity Scale. All Temperatures and Windchill Factors Are in Degrees Fahrenheit.

Designator	Windchill Factor	Description of Conditions
0 Storm	Above −20	Temperature above +20. Wind speed less than 35 mph.
1 Blizzard	−20 to −37	Temperature +11 to +20. Wind speed 35 mph or more.
2 Severe	−38 to −55	Temperature +1 to +10. Wind speed 45 mph or more.
3 Dangerous	−56 to −69	Temperature −9 to 0. Wind speed 50 mph or more.
4 Very Dangerous	−70 to −87	Temperature −19 to −10. Wind speed 50 mph or more.
5 Extremely Dangerous	Below −87	Temperature −20 or below. Wind speed 50 mph or more.

the snow, however, that presents the greatest risk to life, it is the extreme cold, exacerbated by high winds. A blizzard with light snow can actually be more dangerous than one with heavier snow, because people are more likely to attempt travel when the snow accumulation is not great. They forget that the snow can drift. A 2-inch snow, whipped along by gale-force winds for a few hours, can pile up into drifts that are practically invisible in the storm, but more than deep enough to stop a car.

"BLIZZOGENESIS"

The Germans, aware that the Russian winters were severe, were nevertheless unprepared for such Arctic weather in the autumn of 1941, just as Napoleon's armies weren't ready in 1812. Some historians have argued that the severe winter of 1941-1942 was partially responsible for the ultimate defeat of Hitler's troops on the eastern front, and for Napoleon's defeat 130 years before. History is filled with examples of how weather can influence the aspirations of mankind. Today, we worry more about our automobiles than army divisions, tanks, and guns when a blizzard threatens, but the winter storms still affect us.

Why do some winter storms become so much more severe than others? For one thing, wintertime low-pressure systems vary somewhat in sheer size and magnitude, just as do tropical cyclones.

Some systems are larger and have lower central pressure than others, but individual systems can intensify or moderate as a result of jet stream effects.

A cyclonic bend in the jet stream—a turn from right to left in the northern hemisphere—frequently causes winter storm systems to intensify to the point where blizzard conditions develop. The counterclockwise flow of air enhances the circulation of a low-pressure system, increasing the speed of the winds. Also, a cyclonic bend is likely to be accompanied by atmospheric divergence, which causes the barometric pressure to drop more than it otherwise would. Cyclonic bends in the jet stream are common over the United States and eastern Europe during the colder months.

A blizzard can also develop from a low-pressure system that is unusually strong from the very beginning. The jet stream circulation extends down to the ground, producing the strong winds and low temperatures necessary for blizzard conditions. This type of storm normally moves faster than the other, producing higher winds but less snow in any given place.

Most blizzards reach their maximum intensity once they have arrived at the point in the jet stream nearest the equator. The storms can remain severe for the remainder of their eastward or northeastward trek across the continent. As a blizzard nears the eastern coast, the snow accumulation increases, but the temperature moderates as warm ocean waters pump moisture into the circulation. A blizzard thus changes somewhat during its lifetime. The "midwestern type" of blizzard generally has higher winds and colder temperatures than the "eastern type."

Blizzard conditions sometimes occur following a winter storm that we would not consider a true blizzard. An exceptionally strong high-pressure system can produce bitterly cold temperatures and winds that gust to about 40 miles per hour. The highest winds blow on the northern side of the center, where the movement of the system complements the wind circulation. The result, if a snow has just fallen, is similar to a blizzard even though there is no precipitation. The sky may even be bright and sunny, but visibility is severely restricted within a few feet of ground level. These conditions can be dangerous because, although the weather doesn't look too bad, the drifting snow and low windchill factor nevertheless exist.

WATCHES AND WARNINGS

Meteorologists issue blizzard watches and warnings in much the same way as they do for hurricanes, severe thunderstorms, and tornadoes. If a hurricane, severe thunderstorm, or tornado watch is posted, the chances are small that any given place will be hit. The situation is different in the case of a blizzard however. Because blizzards are such large storms, a watch is frequently followed by a warning—and then an active storm.

A blizzard watch might be issued for either of two different reasons: when a storm is expected to mature into a blizzard, or when an existing blizzard might strike within a day or two. If a storm has matured into a blizzard and is expected to strike within 24 hours, a warning is posted. A severe blizzard warning is disseminated if winds of more than 45 miles per hour are expected in conjunction with temperatures lower than +10 degrees Fahrenheit.

You can tell, to some extent, how severe a blizzard will be by checking the barometric pressure as the center of the storm passes nearby. If the weather maps in your local newspaper contain in-

formation about the barometric pressure, you can check the figures at the storm center. If a winter storm has a central pressure of 1000 millibars (29.5 inches) or less, you can expect a blizzard; if the pressure is lower than 992 millibars (29.3 inches), you should be prepared for the possibility of a severe blizzard. Occasionally, blizzards develop central pressure below 980 millibars (28.9 inches). If you see this kind of barometer reading, you can expect extreme blizzard conditions, with heavy snow and winds that may reach near hurricane force.

EFFECTS OF THE WIND

In a blizzard, the wind creates havoc for reasons other than the dangerous windchill factor it generates. High winds change the character of the snow, ruin visibility, and in the worst cases cause structural damage.

Blowing and drifting snow always accompanies a blizzard. A strong wind along with subzero temperatures would be bad enough without snow. Windblown snow reduces visibility and becomes packed together, making driving conditions poor (Fig. 5-16). The wind sometimes sculpts the packed snow into strange cornices that hang precariously from rooftops (Fig. 5-17).

In some blizzards, snow has been known to drift so high that whole cars, trucks, and even houses are buried. Of course, the greater the amount of snow that falls, the deeper the drifts will be, but in a prolonged blizzard with especially high winds, a little snow can produce heavy drifting. When all of the ingredients of a blizzard—wind, cold, and snow—combine for several days, the activities of civilization come to a complete halt. Buffalo, New York, experienced a situation like this in the winter of 1976-1977.

Snow drifting can be controlled to some degree by means of barriers. Drift control is especially useful to prevent roads from becoming impassable. Temporary fences, especially designed for drift control, are used in the Midwest to keep roads clear. The snow is slowed down as it passes through the vertical wooden slats of the fence. This creates a deep drift on the lee side of the fence (Fig.

Fig. 5-16. Blowing snow reduces visibility and can make a paved road difficult to see (courtesy Merle Dalen, Rochester Post Bulletin).

Fig. 5-17. Crystals of windblown snow break down and become packed more tightly than fresh snow. This causes them to stick together, sometimes forming odd shapes.

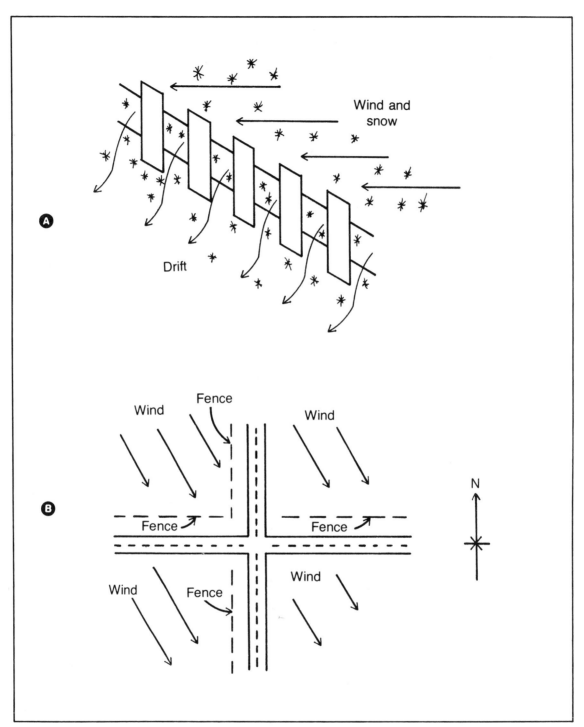

Fig. 5-18. A snow fence, consisting of slats about 1-inch wide and 1-inch apart, causes snow to drift in a controlled manner (A). In temperate regions, snow fences are placed along the north and west sides of roads (B).

5-18A). Because the worst blowing and drifting in midwestern blizzards are almost always caused by west or northwest winds, snow fences are erected on the north sides of roads running east and west, and on the west sides of roads running north and south (Fig. 5-18B). The fences are positioned far enough from the roads so that the artificial drifts are formed before the snow gets to the road surfaces. When spring arrives, the fences can be rolled up and put in storage. Permanent barriers, consisting of rows of evergreen trees on either side of the road, are also frequently seen in regions where blizzards are common.

In some blizzards, the wind can get so strong that it damages buildings and blows down utility wires and telephone poles. Gusts can reach hurricane force even though the wind does not make much noise because the snow muffles the sound. Windows can be broken by the force of the wind, presenting a significant danger to people indoors. In the fiercest blizzards, roofs are sometimes removed from poorly constructed buildings. Power outages are common, and the problem of repair is worsened by the high winds and the severe windchill factor (Fig. 5-19).

AFTER THE STORM

Following a heavy blizzard, the clean-up task begins. Mailboxes and fire hydrants are dug out first (Fig. 5-20); then the plows get busy.

Before the proliferation of motor vehicles in civilized countries, our modern, frenzied snow-removal programs would have been considered ridiculous. Decades ago, sled-type runners replaced wheels on vehicles until the snow melted in the spring, but today, millions of dollars are spent every year to clear snow off of streets and highways. There is an almost incredible variety of plows, blowers, and shoveling devices available for the serious task of keeping our modern transportation system moving.

Sometimes, despite all of our snow-removal machinery, a blizzard defeats us. We clear a spot, and 5 minutes later it is drifted in again. Nature forces us to take a day or two off and slow down. It's hard for some adults, but children don't seem to

have a problem with it—especially if school is cancelled.

PROTECTING YOURSELF IN A BLIZZARD

People die needlessly in snowstorms and blizzards. Some insist on travel when roads are impassable, some attempt to shovel a whole driveway in spite of the fact that they never get any exercise, a few people get lost between a farm house and barn. When people die in winter storms, however, there are usually complicating factors.

Most people who lose their lives in blizzards die from frostbite or hypothermia. *Frostbite* occurs when skin actually freezes, or when the circulation is restricted because of excessive cold. *Hypothermia* is an abnormally low body temperature. Either condition, if severe, mandates prompt medical treatment.

If a blizzard is raging, it is best not to go out in it, but in some cases it is necessary. Proper clothing then becomes crucial for protection against frostbite and hypothermia.

The chief warning sign of frostbite is numbness and/or whiteness, especially in extremeties such as fingers, toes, and ears. For protection against frostbite in the fingers, mittens are better than gloves. Feet can be kept warm with two or three pairs of socks, soft shoes, and rubber boots. For ear protection, a thick fur cap is excellent. A parka with a hood is even better. It is important that hands, feet, and head be kept dry.

Hypothermia causes confusion and drowsiness. The risk of hypothermia can be minimized by dressing in layers, as well as by taking all of the precautions for guarding against frostbite. It also helps to make sure you have had enough to eat. The body's demand for calories is increased in cold weather. All high-calorie foods (except alcohol), consumed in moderate quantities, help to maintain body temperature. Cheese and nuts are excellent; so is a good cup of hot chocolate. For most people, choosing a suitably appealing high-calorie food is not a difficult problem.

Several years ago, the body of a man was found in a street in a small town following a severe blizzard. He had evidently been unable to get his bear-

Fig. 5-19. The high winds of a blizzard keep utility repair crews occupied (courtesy Jerry Olson, Rochester Post-Bulletin).

Fig. 5-20. After a severe snowstorm, mailboxes and fire hydrants must be freed immediately.

ings because of near-zero visibility. The storm was blamed for the death, but an autopsy revealed that the man had been drinking heavily. Alcohol increases the danger of hypothermia, largely because it impairs judgment. It is difficult enough to get around in a blizzard without getting drunk. Alcohol also causes the capillaries to dilate, which increases the rate at which body heat is lost through the skin.

BLIZZARDS AND CARS

Most of the deaths in blizzards occur in conjunction with motor vehicles. Poor conditions increase the probability of single-car and multiple-car accidents. Also, there is a risk of getting stranded. Ideally, all travel should be suspended during a blizzard and resumed only when the storm is over and the snow has been cleared from the roads. Unfortunately, however, emergencies sometimes arise, necessitating travel in spite of the worst blizzard conditions. Snowmobiles are made especially for such situations, but few people own them, and they are therefore forced to use more conventional motor vehicles.

For traveling in a blizzard or snowstorm, larger cars are better than smaller ones. Pickup trucks are better still. Vehicles with a lot of ground clearance (high chassis) are better than cars with very little ground clearance.

If it becomes necessary to drive in a blizzard, certain supplies will be of help in case you get stuck:

☐ An amateur or citizen's band radio transceiver can be used to call for assistance.

☐ A shovel can be used to clear away snow if the situation is not overwhelming.

☐ One or more warm blankets can protect passengers against the cold.

171

☐ Several bags of sand, placed in the trunk, add weight to a car and improve traction. Also, the sand can be used underneath the tires if the car gets stuck.

☐ Tire chains are of obvious value.

☐ A flashlight is useful to improve vision at night.

☐ A supply of storable, high-calorie food will help to maintain body heat (besides preventing hunger).

☐ A jug of water will alleviate thirst (snow should not be relied on for its water content).

☐ A large thermos bottle of hot soup or coffee will help keep people warm.

Even if the roads are free from ice, windblown snow can be slippery. Common-sense safety rules for driving in blizzards are:

☐ No alcohol or drugs should be consumed.

☐ The gas tank should be kept at least ¾ full.

☐ Headlights (low beam) should be switched on.

☐ Drive at a slow speed and accelerate gradually.

☐ Brakes should be applied gently to prevent skidding.

☐ If a skid occurs, brakes should be released.

☐ Following distance should be greater than usual.

☐ Low gear should be used when going down hills.

Every year, hundreds or thousands of people get stranded in blizzards with their cars, and the experience can be frightening. We are used to warm, comfortable cars and homes. Many people spend whole days indoors during the winter, except for the minute or two that it takes to run from the parking lot to the office in the morning, and from the office to the parking lot in the evening. It is possible to go from one place to another in subzero cold and not spend more than a few seconds outside. It's enough to foster overconfidence, but that secure feeling vanishes quickly for the passengers of an automobile that gets stuck in a snowstorm during the night in some isolated place.

The following safety rules will be of value to people who are marooned in a severe snowstorm or blizzard:

☐ Passengers should stay with the vehicle. An on-foot attempt to get help can result in a catastrophe, unless a house or other source of assistance is within a short distance.

☐ The passengers should stay inside the vehicle as much as possible to avoid windchill.

☐ Attempts can be made to free the vehicle, but overexertion should be avoided. Sweating can worsen the danger of hypothermia. Wet clothes conduct heat away from the body more rapidly than dry clothes.

☐ The engine should be run for only about 10 minutes per hour. This will conserve gas while keeping the inside temperature reasonably safe (although not comfortable).

☐ The exhaust pipe outlet should be kept clear to prevent engine stalling.

☐ A downwind window should be kept open to provide ventilation and minimize the chances of the passengers getting carbon monoxide poisoning.

☐ Snow should not be eaten because it reduces body temperature.

☐ The emergency flashers (but not the headlights) should be on. Inside lights should be shut off.

☐ Alcohol and drugs should be absolutely avoided.

☐ After the rescue, everyone should be carefully and immediately examined and treated, if necessary, for frostbite and hypothermia.

More complete information covering driving and safety in blizzards can be obtained from a variety of sources. The Wyoming Department of Civil Defense, P. O. Box 1709, Cheyenne, Wyoming, has an informative brochure. The American Red Cross publishes information about first-aid treatment of frostbite and hypothermia.

MOUNTAIN WINDS OF WINTER AND SPRING

In the western United States, high pressure often dominates during the winter and spring months, bringing the characteristic clear, cool weather to the southwestern deserts during this time of year. The northern Rockies and Great

Plains get bitterly cold. These conditions result from a strong ridge in the jet stream. The high-pressure systems can get intense, with barometer readings of more than 31 inches near the center. The winds spiral outward from the center, blowing from the west on the northern side and from the east on the southern side (Fig. 5-21). Similar situations develop over parts of Europe and Asia.

Strong, cold westerly winds, after passing over the mountains at a high altitude, become warmer as they descend into valleys and onto the foothills or prairies. The winds can get gusty, and once in a while, even violent. A warm westerly wind, blowing down from the mountains, is called a *chinook*. Chinooks are most common from January through March.

Chinook winds have been known to cause the extremely rapid melting of snow. Temperatures can rise from near 0 Fahrenheit to well above freezing in just a few minutes. The warmth and

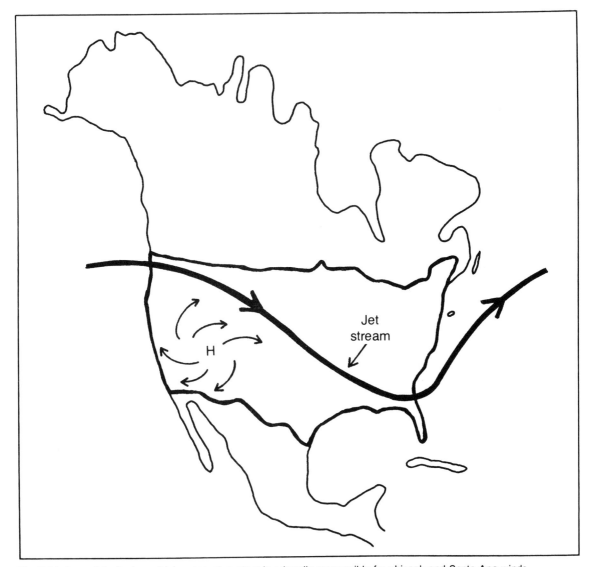

Fig. 5-21. A persistent, strong high-pressure system is primarily responsible for chinook and Santa Ana winds.

dryness of the chinook, combined with its high speed, affects the snow like a gigantic electric hair dryer. (Perhaps you have used a hair dryer to hasten the defrosting of a freezer compartment.) Several inches of snow can disappear in a short time.

The chinook wind provides relief from the bitter cold of winter, but it can also cause considerable damage. During the late winter of 1982-1983, chinook gusts reached 137 miles per hour in some parts of Colorado. That kind of wind can certainly be called a storm! The peculiar gustiness of a chinook—perhaps 20 miles per hour one moment and 80 miles per hour a few seconds later—makes it different from a hurricane, thunderstorm, or blizzard. Sometimes chinooks seem to have a twisting nature, resembling a series of small, invisible tornadoes. Vortex action is occasionally reported by observers as they watch loose dirt or snow blowing around. A chinook storm usually occurs without precipitation.

On the opposite side of the high-pressure system, a similar effect takes place because of the mountains in southern California. The primary difference is that the wind is warmer and drier because of the more southerly latitude. As the wind descends into the valleys near the coast, the speed and temperature increase. Gusts of more than 80 miles per hour are not unusual in the Santa Ana area, and for this reason, the wind has been called the *Santa Ana wind*.

A severe Santa Ana storm struck large areas of southern California during January 1984, resulting in much damage to trees and buildings. The problem was exacerbated by fires that burned out of control, whipped along by the hot, dry wind from the east. In desert areas, the Santa Ana wind picked up sand and carried it high into the air. Buildings and motor vehicles got a thorough sand blasting, and people venturing outdoors risked injury.

Winds similar to the chinook and Santa Ana occur frequently in, or near, most mountainous parts of the temperate zone. In central and southern Europe, the Urals in Russia, and the vast region of western China and Tibet, high-pressure systems sometimes dominate and produce dry, warm, gusty winds. The same thing also happens in the Andes of southern South America.

Mountains provide violent winds in other ways on a local scale. Cool air, descending along a mountain slope, picks up speed like water running downhill. I recall an experience of this phenomenon in southern California on a night in January. The evening was clear after a magnificant desert day. Then a hissing, rushing sound seemed to come from the windows. A glance outside revealed what it was: wind. It quickly turned into a series of howling, almost screaming gusts. Then, after a few minutes, it was calm again. The wind had been violent—patio furniture, some of it made of iron, was strewn about as if it were newspaper. Gusts were probably about 80 miles per hour. Such "mini mountain storms," striking without warning but with much force, can be dangerous.

WILD MARCH

March, like November, is famous for its wind. Winter begins to lose its grip, and people look forward to sunny skies and gentle breezes. The skies are relatively sunny in March in many parts of the world, but the breezes aren't always gentle.

The jet stream begins its retreat in earnest by the end of February, and brutal cold waves are not as likely or as frequent as before. It seems that everywhere, from Maine to California, and from Seattle to Miami, it is windy a lot of the time. On a late-March day, the winds can reach whole-gale force despite warm temperatures and sunny skies. Trees whip around, and moderate structural damage sometimes occurs (Figs. 5-22 and 5-23).

In the Midwest, northern mountains, and northeast, March is famous for snow as well as wind. Blizzards, with wet, heavy snow and fierce gales, are the hallmark of March in many places. Sometimes March brings tremendous snowstorms. The blizzard of 1888 struck the northeastern United States with well-documented severity. Numerous clubs were organized by storm "veterans" to commemorate the storm of March 12, 1888. They couldn't forget the devastation that the blizzard wrought on the industrialized world. Inhabitants of other northern regions recall their own March storms.

Residents of river valleys are acquainted with another feature of March: the floods produced by melting snow. If the winter has been snowy and a few warm days come in March, the result can be a catastrophe. Spring floods carry an extra wallop because the water is dangerously cold, and massive ice floes are carried along by the fast-moving current. These chunks of ice, moving at a few miles per hour, can practically demolish a house or small building.

March has still another nasty habit in places where the ground freezes in the winter. When water freezes, it expands. This is not much of a problem in November and December, because in most places the soil is resilient enough to alleviate the pressure as the liquid turns into solid. When the frost melts and the water volume decreases, however, pockets form in the earth (Fig. 5-24), causing extensive damage to paved streets and highways. In March, much of the Midwest, as well as northern New England, becomes peppered with signs marked "DIP" or "BUMP." More than one passenger has been injured while driving over a buckled road.

In March, the days grow noticeably longer in the northern hemisphere, and the sun describes an increasingly larger and higher arc across the sky. Shadows are shorter at noon than they have been for several months. On March 20 or 21, it becomes official: the North Pole is now in sunlight. The sun precisely follows the celestial equator. In Minneapolis, the length of a shadow at noon is equal to the height of the object that casts it. It is spring!

Then April arrives. We flip the pages of our calendars, and realize that April is, astronomically, the first full month of spring. Even the name of this month sounds gentle and springlike, but only fools believe that winter is entirely over on April 1.

MUD SEASON

Severe snows have occurred in April. A good example is the storm that buried the upper Midwest

Fig. 5-22. Florida palms strain against a March gale.

175

Fig. 5-23. Sometimes the winds of March cause minor damage. A traffic light was swung around so hard that it snapped in two.

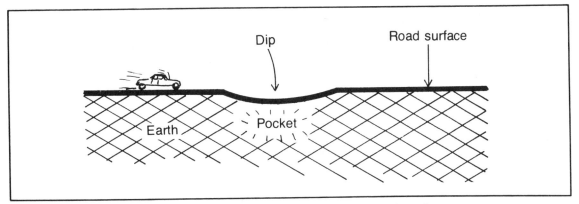

Fig. 5-24. Dips or bumps in paved roads result from the melting of ground frost in the spring.

in 10 inches of snow in the second week of April, 1973. Snow is a novelty in November. It is pretty at Christmas. It gives us our winter sports, making January and February endurable. In March, most people are tired of snow; it has gotten "old." An April snowstorm is downright depressing! April can also bring high winds and river flooding, and in some parts of the country, April is the worst month for tornadoes and severe thunderstorms.

Although winter can continue well into April, the coldest weather has passed by then, and the precipitation normally falls as rain. If April has a trademark, it is showery weather. After the snow has melted, leaving the ground wet and still frozen in places, the rains provide the final ingredient for a perfect mud season.

The upper Midwest, the Great Lakes region, the Ohio Valley, and northern New England have the muddiest Aprils in the United States. The wooded, hilly country of Vermont and New Hampshire is well known (at least by the people who live there) for the early spring mud season. Much of Europe is in the same predicament in April. If the mud season is severe, farmers must delay planting because tractors get stuck in the mud. In the worst cases, roads get washed out, and in hilly regions, mud slides can become a serious threat.

April is fickle. After a dry winter, rains are welcome, and after a wet winter, the rains are dreaded. April does not always bring raw, wet, chilly weather, however; sometimes the month is dry and hot. If the preceding winter has been dry,

and the rains of April do not come, we fear another kind of trouble: drought.

By the end of April, winter has pretty much gone away. A light dusting of snow can fall in late April or early May in the United States and Europe, but it melts quickly. Spring really comes, and before we know it, we're hot. Late April and early May can bring record heat waves with low humidity. A hot spell in April 1980, brought temperatures of 100 degrees Fahrenheit to (of all places!) northwestern Minnesota and eastern North Dakota.

We all know that violent winds, hail, lightning, killing cold, torrential rains, heavy snows, and other stormy weather phenomena can affect us. When the weather has a temper tantrum, we notice right away. Visibly violent weather presents comparatively little danger to the human species, however. The greater challenge lies with the factors we don't so easily see.

The weather on our planet has not always been the way it is today. There have been periods of incomprehensible cold, and times when the world was almost totally covered by jungles. In an 80-year lifetime, the climate does not change much, and this has, perhaps, led mankind to care too little about long-term climatic fluctuations.

If we think for a moment, we can figure out that two things are certain about medium- and long-term weather on earth. First, the climate on our planet goes through changes over periods of a few, several thousands, or millions of years. Second, our

177

species has been, and will continue to be, affected by these changes.

What will the changes be? How will we cope with them? We ought to consider these equations, and in Chapter 6, we will look at medium-term weather variability—the kinds of variations that affect us over periods of several years. These include heat, cold, floods, and droughts. In the final chapter, we will see what might happen in the distant future.

Chapter 6

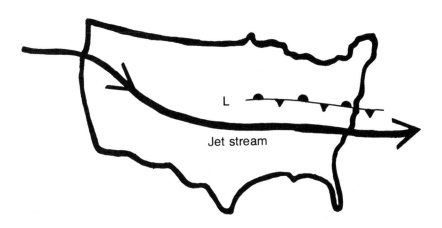

Jet stream

Hot, Cold, Wet, Dry

We are a remarkably adaptable species. We can survive in the Arctic or at the equator, in deserts or at a rainy seashore. Some humans even live, temporarily, in Antarctica, in space, or undersea. No other species has spread over the world like ours. No other species can tolerate the weather extremes that we can—but the weather occasionally gets too adverse, over a period of months or years, even for us.

History is full of examples of climatic fluctuations. The drought period of the 1930s is well remembered even today. At this moment, deserts are creeping across parts of the world, driving people out and causing mass starvation and terrible suffering. Floods have ravaged mankind since the beginning of recorded history. Heat and cold waves still kill people, even in the modern industrialized nations.

The balance of nature is tenuous. If our atmosphere had developed with a little more carbon dioxide, Earth might resemble Venus today: a pressure cooker. If there had been less air, our

planet could have become like Mars: a frigid desert. The balance can be easily upset by various events, some of which are within our control and some of which are not. We seem to be learning the difference the hard way.

HEAT WAVES

The morning promises a hot day, like the previous several days have been. By 8 o'clock, the thermometer already reads 85 degrees Fahrenheit in the shade. By late morning it is up to almost 100, and there is not a cloud in the sky. It's too hot to do anything except swim, but there are no clean lakes nearby; the pools don't open until noon, and they will be overcrowded anyhow. No golf, no tennis, no outdoor sports are practical. Although the weather is sunny, we dare not think about trying to get a suntan. At 2 o'clock in the afternoon, the electricity goes off as the temperature nears its maximum of 112 degrees Fahrenheit. Too many air conditioners are running, and the electric company is blacking out selected areas in a rotating sequence. Perhaps we can fill up that little "kiddie pool" we bought on impulse last fall. We find it and, after an agonizing few minutes, inflate it and turn on the garden hose. The water pressure is unusually low. Everyone else has the same idea. We are having a heat wave.

Heat waves have always been a problem for inland parts of much of the temperate zone. In the United States, heat waves occasionally develop everywhere, although the Pacific northwest, right along the coast, is relatively immune. Forested and mountainous areas are less severely affected than open plains and prairies, steppes, and deserts.

In the past, severe heat waves claimed thousands of lives in the United States, and millions of lives in less developed, hotter parts of the world. India and other nearby countries are particularly

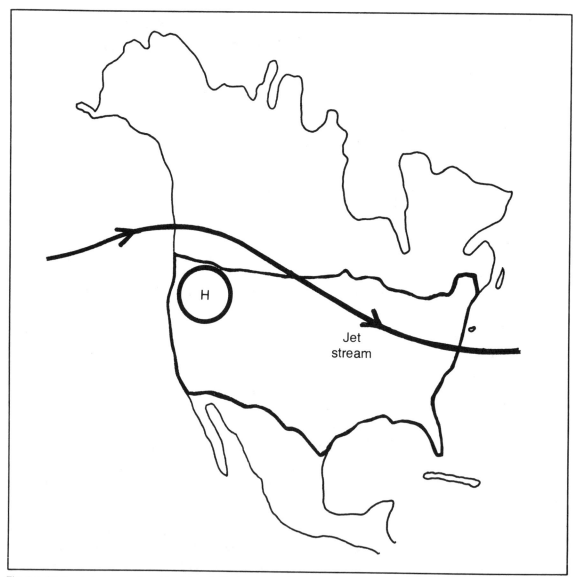

Fig. 6-1. Heat waves are produced by ridges in the jet stream during the summer months. Here the heat wave occurs in the West.

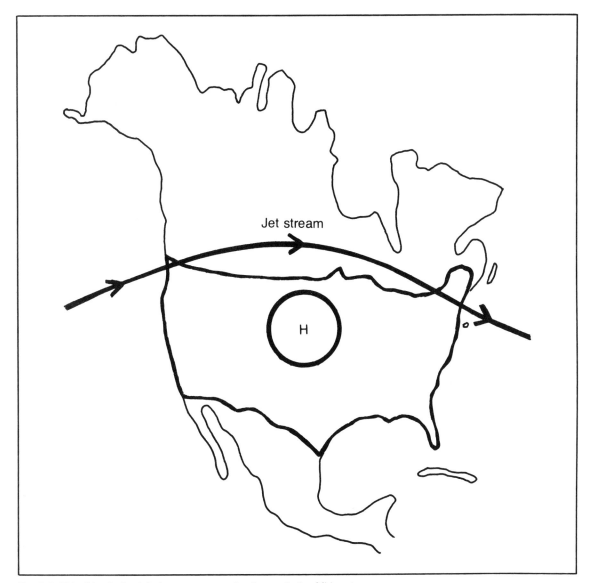

Fig. 6-2. This ridge in the jet stream causes a heat wave in the Midwest.

hard hit by heat waves just before the monsoons commence. Certain interior regions of Africa, Asia, South America, and Australia are regularly visited by these events. Heat waves, unlike violent storms, kill quietly—and slowly.

The principal cause of a heat wave is a persistent ridge in the jet stream (Fig. 6-1). The worst heatwaves occur in summer (obviously), but unusually warm weather can develop at any time of year.

A heat wave near a coastline is normally less intense than the effects of a ridge in or a near the middle of a continent. A pattern such as that shown in Fig. 6-1 causes extreme temperatures in the western states. If the jet stream gets oriented as shown in Fig. 6-2, the Midwest has a heat wave. The pattern in Fig. 6-3 results in hot weather in the eastern states.

Why does high pressure cause heat waves?

Part of the reason is that high-pressure systems are associated with mostly fair or clear weather. This allows the sun to heat up the earth, which in turn heats the air near it. Another reason is that frontal systems are blocked by ridges and high-pressure systems, so that the air becomes stable over a large region. Without any change in atmospheric circulation, the air gets increasingly hotter until the energy radiated into space is the same as the energy received from the sun.

Heat waves are sometimes accompanied by high levels of relative humidity. In the United States, the Eastern Seaboard has the muggiest heat waves when the Bermuda high-pressure system fans the continent with moist Atlantic and Gulf air (Fig. 6-4). The circulation on the western side of the Bermuda high is generally from the south or southwest. The immediate coast is spared because

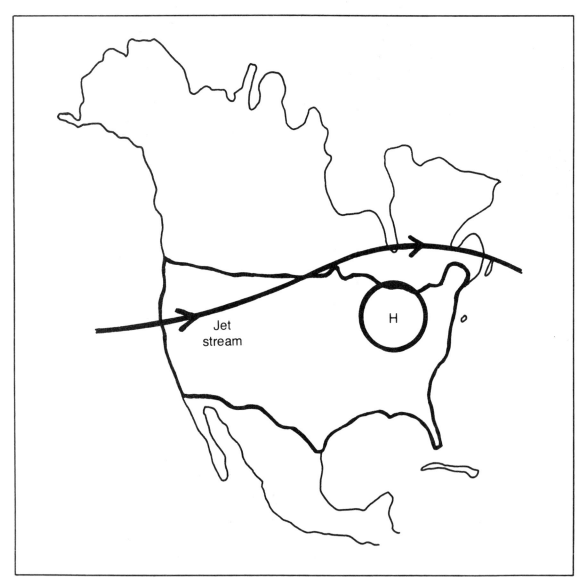

Fig. 6-3. A heat wave in the East occurs from this fluctuation of the jet stream.

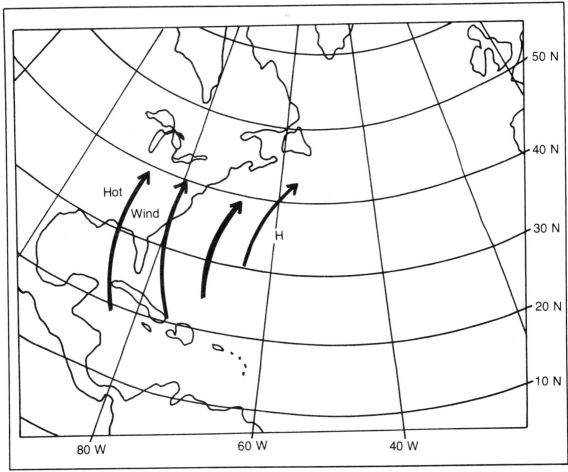

Fig. 6-4. The Bermuda high brings heat waves to the eastern seaboard.

of the moderating effect of the water, but the air becomes very hot over interior regions. Because of the shape of the United States' east coastline, the more northerly sections, such as New Jersey, New York, and New England, are often hit the hardest.

Heat waves are made worse by the activities of man. This is largely because we have cut down the trees that, generations ago, kept the temperature from soaring to deadly levels. A tree is a very effective air conditioner. Bare soil, concrete, and blacktop are excellent heating devices when they are exposed to sunlight, and large cities, therefore, get hotter than rural countryside.

In major urban areas, such as the Washington-Boston megalopolis, hot weather is frequently accompanied by air pollution. The high temperatures and sunshine cause ozone to form from oxygen. This reaction is triggered by the components in automobile exhaust. The ozone gives the air a characteristic chlorine smell, and if the concentration is high enough, it irritates the eyes, throat, and lungs. Other pollutants accumulate because of the stability of the high-pressure system, which keeps frontal cyclones from bringing in fresh air.

A severe heat wave is not only uncomfortable, but dangerous. Meteorologists define a heat wave according to the maximum expected temperature for the day. Anything over body temperature (98.6 degrees Fahrenheit or 37 degrees Celsius) makes it official. In some parts of the United States, high temperatures have exceeded 110 degrees Fahrenheit for several days in a row, causing major health problems for people, and killing livestock and wildlife.

The Heat-Humidity Comfort Index

Hot weather is more uncomfortable when the humidity is high, compared to when it is low. This is because we are cooled by the evaporation of sweat, and water evaporates less readily as the humidity rises. A *comfort* (or discomfort) *index* has been devised that takes both temperature and humidity into account, giving an apparent or effective temperature value.

The *heat-humidity comfort function* is shown in Fig. 6-5 for actual temperatures ranging from 70 to 120 degrees Fahrenheit. The relative humidity is shown on the horizontal scale. When the humidity is very low, the apparent temperature is lower than the actual temperature. For example, if it is 80 degrees and the relative humidity is 10 percent, it feels like 75 degrees. When the humidity is very high, it feels hotter than it actually is. If it is 80 degrees and the relative humidity is 90 percent, it feels like 88 degrees.

The heat-humidity index, like the windchill factor, is not purely imaginary. When our bodies aren't cooled effectively by sweat evaporation, we really do get hotter. If the heat-humidity index is greater than the skin temperature (normally about 90 degrees Fahrenheit), we get miserably hot. Even when the apparent temperature is 80 degrees, most of us are uncomfortable.

Although our body cooling systems work best when the humidity is low, it is not necessarily true that we will be comfortable in dry weather. Suppose it is 110 degrees Fahrenheit and the humidity is zero; then it feels like 99 degrees. That's hot, as any permanent resident of the desert southwest will tell you. Dry heat can, in fact, be more dangerous than muggy heat, because people are less aware of how high the temperature really is. This might lead to a sense of overconfidence, with potentially serious consequences. Dehydration and heatstroke have claimed lives in hot, dry weather as well as in hot, muggy weather.

How to Cope with Heat

Extremely hot weather has detrimental physiological and psychological effects on people. The most dangerous potential problem is heatstroke. Less deadly, but still unpleasant, effects include dehydration, cramps, exhaustion, drowsiness, irritability, and depression.

In hot weather, it is important to stay hydrated. This is especially true for children, who tend to run around with almost complete disregard for the weather. An easy way to see if you are severely dehydrated is to weigh yourself at frequent intervals. A pint of water weighs about a pound. Thus, for example, if you suddenly lose 4 pounds, you have lost 2 quarts (about 2 liters) of water. That might not be very serious if you are a linebacker for a professional football team, but for a 5-year-old child it represents a significant water loss.

The best way to drink water is a little at a time. Other liquids can be substituted for water, but they may not relieve thirst as effectively as water, and some beverages have side effects. Beverages containing caffeine or theobromine, like iced coffee or tea, should not be consumed in large quantities for obvious reasons. Beer is all right in moderation, but large amounts of alcohol hinder the body's ability to regulate its temperature. "Hard" drinks must be avoided because they can actually worsen dehydration. Pure orange, grapefruit, or tomato juice, as well as other fruit and vegetable juices, are excellent.

Some physicians believe that salt tablets will help prevent exhaustion and cramps in hot weather. More recently, however, there has arisen some disagreement about this. Your family doctor should be consulted concerning the advisability of taking salt tablets or any other nutritional supplement to help you deal with the heat.

Heavy foods, or large quantities of food, should be avoided in extremely hot weather. This is true for the same reasons that high-calorie foods are desirable in cold weather. A large meal can put extra stress on an already overtaxed body. Moder-

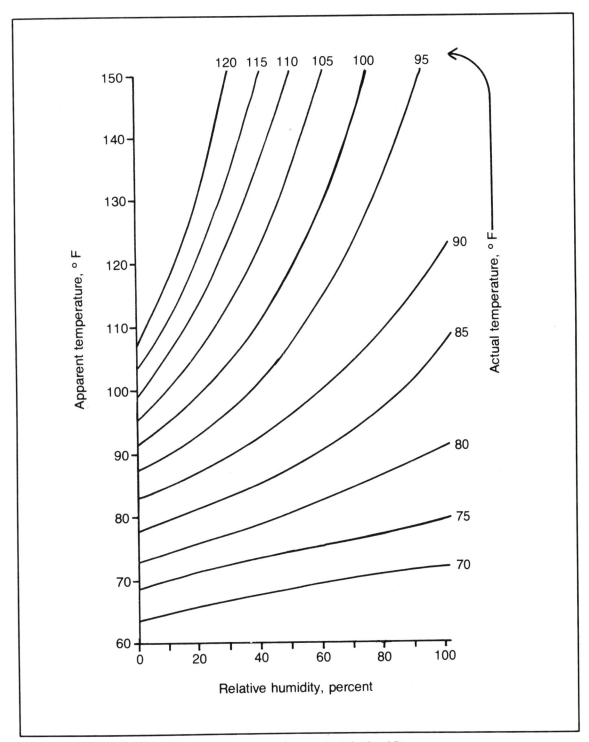

Fig. 6-5. Discomfort index as a function of actual temperature and relative humidity.

185

ate meals at frequent intervals are better than large meals spaced far apart in time. Light foods such as salads and fruits are better than heavier fare like gigantic steaks. During heat waves, people's taste for food automatically changes in this way.

The problems of drowsiness, irritability, and depression are difficult to cope with directly. A little iced coffee or tea may help alleviate these symptoms (as long as your doctor doesn't forbid you to have caffeine). The best thing to do is to try to keep cool—literally and figuratively.

As previously mentioned, *heatstroke* represents the most dangerous threat during a heat wave. In heatstroke, the body actually loses its ability to control its core temperature. The result is a high fever of 105 degrees Fahrenheit (40.5 degrees Celsius) or more. Sweating stops, and the victim appears pale or gray. Unconsciousness usually occurs. Unless a heatstroke victim receives first aid and medical attention immediately, he or she may die. For more information, the most current American Red Cross first-aid publications should be consulted, because first-aid procedures change as medical knowledge advances.

Cooling Degree Days

We all know how terrible our electric bills can get during a heat wave. In some cases the monthly electric bill exceeds the mortgage payment. Of course, it is better to run the air conditioner than to die of heatstroke, but the thermostat should be adjusted for the highest tolerable temperature. This not only conserves energy, reducing the probability of brownouts or blackouts; it also narrows the margin between indoor and outdoor temperatures, minimizing thermal shock for people going in or out of the building.

The severity of a particular summer, in terms of heat, is measured according to an average figure called *cooling degree days*. This figure is based on the average temperature relative to 65 degrees Fahrenheit. A single cooling degree day represents one day for which the mean temperature is 66 degrees. If the average temperature on a given day is 75 degrees, it represents 10 cooling degree days.

The figure is added cumulatively over a period of time. Figure 6-6A is an example of a degree-day graph for a hypothetical week. Figure 6-6B shows the graph for a whole season (May through September). The slope of the curve indicates the relative energy consumption that is required to keep the indoor environment comfortable.

Heat Islands

The temperature is affected not only by natural weather factors, but by the nature of the terrain, geography, and the type of material that makes up the surface. High in the mountains, severe heat waves never occur. Deadly hot weather is unlikely near the seashore, on the leeward shore of a very large lake such as Superior, or in areas with vast, dense forests. Severe heat is worsened by open plains, prairies, or steppes, especially if there is not much vegetation. Large cities are the worst of all.

In most cases, the interior of a city is somewhat warmer than the surrounding countryside. This happens for two reasons. First, the abundance of concrete, asphalt, and other man-made materials cannot cool itself as effectively as vegetation or soil. The man-made materials do not absorb much water, and therefore they cannot be effectively cooled by evaporation. Second, there are sources of heat within a city, such as automobiles, electric lights, and power plants, that are much less concentrated in rural places. In the downtown area of a large city, the temperature is several degrees Fahrenheit higher than in the countryside a few miles away. The highest temperatures are observed near the center of a city. A hypothetical example of this effect is shown in Fig. 6-7. The heat zone in a city is known as a *heat island*.

Heat islands are of obvious benefit in cold weather. The expense of heating during the winter is generally lower in a metropolitan area than in the country, but in the summer during a heat wave, the heat island makes the situation worse. It might be 105 degrees Fahrenheit on a farm 40 miles outside the city, 109 degrees in the suburbs, and a scorching 112 downtown. Because of this effect, people

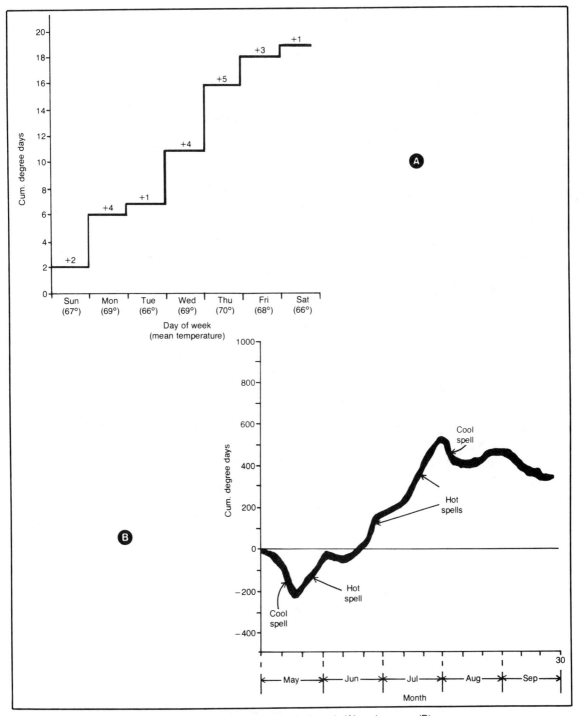

Fig. 6-6. Accumulation of cooling degree days for a hypothetical week (A) and season (B).

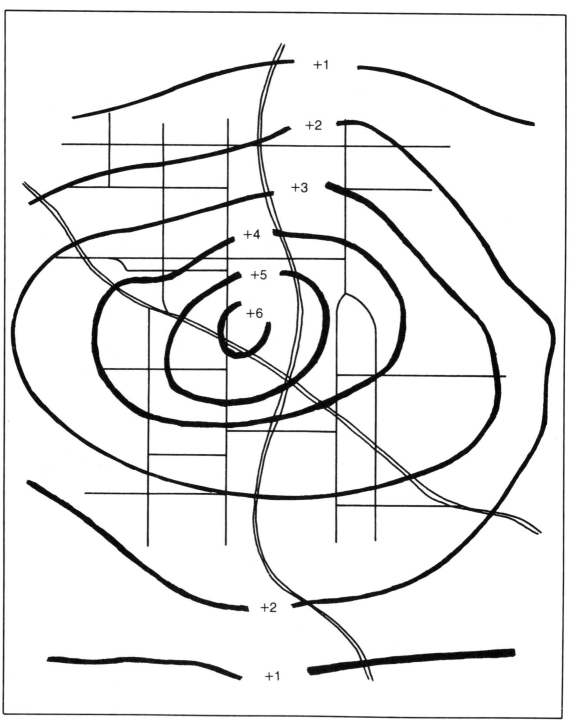

Fig. 6-7. In a large city, a heat island is produced. In this hypothetical case, the center of the city is 6 degrees Fahrenheit warmer than surrounding rural areas.

188

flock to rural areas during heat waves.

Hot-Weather Records

Every state in the United States has experienced, in some location, a heat wave. Even Alaska has had a temperature reading of 100 degrees Fahrenheit. This occurred on June 27, 1915, at Fort Yukon, with an elevation of about 400 feet. Strangely, the record high temperature in Hawaii is also 100 degrees. This apparent paradox can be explained. The islands of Hawaii are relatively small, and their climate is moderated by the cool waters of the Pacific and by the persistent trade winds at that latitude. Inland places at low elevation, such as Fort Yukon, can become hot despite the distance from the equator, because the sun shines almost 24 hours a day in the summer, and the cooling ocean is relatively far away.

The highest temperature ever recorded in the United States belongs to Greenland Ranch, California. The thermometer soared to 134 degrees in the shade on July 10, 1913, at this place in the desert. The location is below sea level, and vegetation is practically nonexistent.

Table 6-1 shows record high (and low) temperatures for each state in the United States through the year 1981. Some interesting things can be noticed from this table: the western states have generally had higher maximum readings than the eastern states; North Dakota has experienced a 121-degree reading while Florida has only reached 109; even Maine has been up to 105 degrees.

Heat Waves in the Sea

Global weather patterns are influenced by factors we do not completely understand. Hot and cold spells, fluctuations in precipitation, and frequency of storms are affected by some common things. One of the most interesting, noticed for hundreds of years by natives of the eastern Pacific, is a strange rise in the water temperature. It occurs at unpredictable intervals, lasting from 1 to 3 years. This oceanic heat wave, given the Spanish name El Niño (The Child), is believed by some scientists to be responsible for many recent climate-related problems around the world. An El Niño event began in 1982 and ended in early 1984.

An El Niño event is actually a combination of atmospheric and ocean phenomena. Areas of high and low pressure change position, and the ocean temperature in some locations rises by several degrees Fahrenheit. Atmospheric winds and ocean currents change course, bringing wet weather in some areas and drought to others. During 1982 and 1983, floods, triggered by tropical storms and excessive rainfall, battered Peru and Ecuador in South America, parts of the west coast of North America, and the southeastern United States. Dry weather caused dust storms and crop losses in Mexico, southern Africa, and much of Australia and Indonesia. In southern India, the monsoons failed, bringing starvation.

Normally, high pressure prevails in the eastern Pacific, and low pressure dominates the western Pacific (Fig. 6-8A), which is why western South America is rather dry, while Indonesia is covered by wet rain forests. Ocean temperatures are warm in the west and cooler in the east. In the spring of 1982, this pattern began to reverse itself. A massive, warm, low-pressure system developed in the east, and a cooler, high-pressure area formed in the west (Fig. 6-8B). Is the redistribution of the ocean temperature the cause or the result of El Niño? It is not known with certainty, but the consequences have been vividly evident.

The Pacific heat wave produced some beneficial effects, as well as widespread hardship. Although the frequency of tropical cyclones increased during 1982 and 1983 in the Pacific because of the low pressure off the coast of South America, there were fewer hurricanes than usual in the Atlantic Ocean, the Caribbean Sea, and the Gulf of Mexico. High-level air currents, generated by the effects of El Niño, moved across Central America and over the storm spawning grounds in the Atlantic, Caribbean, and Gulf. Some meteorologists believe these upper-atmosphere winds sheared off the tops of the storms before they could mature into hurricanes.

Apparently, El Niño events affect weather all around the world, even in the temperate zone and perhaps in the Arctic and Antarctic. The severe

State	High	Low
Alabama	+112	−27
Alaska	+100	−80
Arizona	+127	−40
Arkansas	+120	−29
California	+134	−45
Colorado	+118	−60
Connecticut	+105	−32
Delaware	+110	−17
District of Columbia	+106	−15
Florida	+109	−2
Georgia	+113	−17
Hawaii	+100	+12
Idaho	+118	−60
Illinois	+117	−35
Indiana	+116	−35
Iowa	+118	−47
Kansas	+121	−40
Kentucky	+114	−34
Louisiana	+114	−16
Maine	+105	−48
Maryland	+109	−40
Massachusetts	+107	−35
Michigan	+112	−51
Minnesota	+114	−59
Mississippi	+115	−19
Missouri	+118	−40
Montana	+117	−70
Nebraska	+118	−47
Nevada	+122	−50
New Hampshire	+106	−47
New Jersey	+110	−34
New Mexico	+116	−50
New York	+108	−52
North Carolina	+109	−29
North Dakota	+121	−60
Ohio	+113	−39
Oklahoma	+120	−27
Oregon	+119	−54
Pennsylvania	+111	−42
Rhode Island	+104	−23
South Carolina	+111	−20
South Dakota	+120	−58
Tennessee	+113	−32
Texas	+120	−23
Utah	+116	−50
Vermont	+105	−50
Virginia	+110	−29
Washington	+118	−48
West Virginia	+112	−37
Wisconsin	+114	−54
Wyoming	+114	−63

winter of 1983-1984 might have been triggered, in part, by the decaying phases of the cycle. Effects in the polar regions are harder to observe because of the lack of meteorological observation stations there, and because knowledge of "normal" polar weather is not very well established. One scientist, observing the effects of El Niño and endeavoring to devise a method of predicting the events, has said that the weather is always abnormal in some way or other, making it difficult to distinguish between cause-effect and coincidence.

One thing is certain about El Niño: the events will happen again in the future, and the medium-term weather will be affected in many parts of the world.

COLD WAVES

At the opposite end of the temperature spectrum, prolonged cold spells have caused inconvenience, suffering, and death in the same measure as excessively hot weather. The winter of 1976-1977 was unusually cold in the Midwest because of a persistent trough in the jet stream. The polar air mass advanced far toward the equator and stayed there for several weeks in January and February of 1977, producing continued below-zero temperatures in the Dakotas, Minnesota, and Wisconsin. High winds exacerbated the situation. Windchill temperatures fell to, and stayed at, values of about −90 degrees Fahrenheit. (A similar cold wave seems to have taken place in eastern Europe in the winter of 1941-1942, causing hardship to the armies of the Third Reich.)

A deep trough in the jet stream often occurs when the North Pacific high-pressure system intensifies. The clockwise circulation around the northeastern part of the system pumps arctic air into the continent of North America. Depending on the center of the high-pressure region, the cold wave may affect primarily the Midwest (Fig. 6-9A) or the East (Fig. 6-9B). Cold waves in some parts of the country are often accompanied by warm weather farther west, because the Pacific high represents a ridge in the jet stream. For example, a brutal cold wave in the upper Midwest might occur along with warm, sunny weather in California and Arizona. For those residents of the desert South-

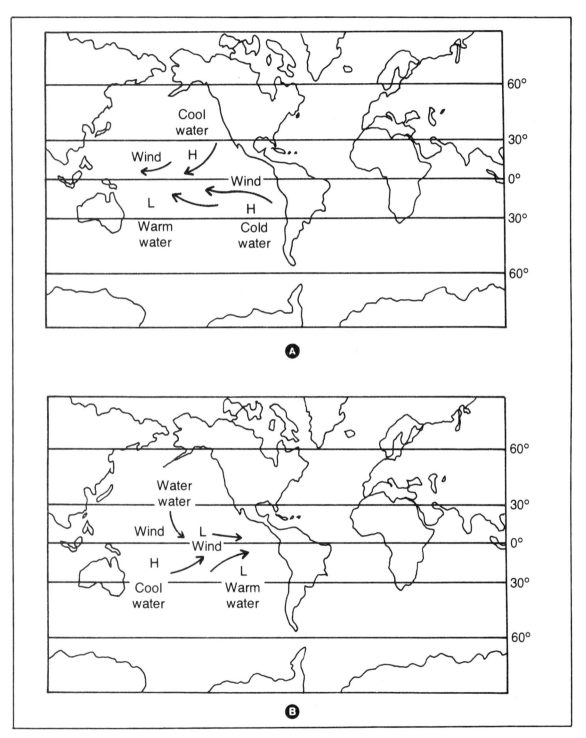

Fig. 6-8. At A, normal wind and water in the Pacific. At B, wind and water characteristics during an El Niño event.

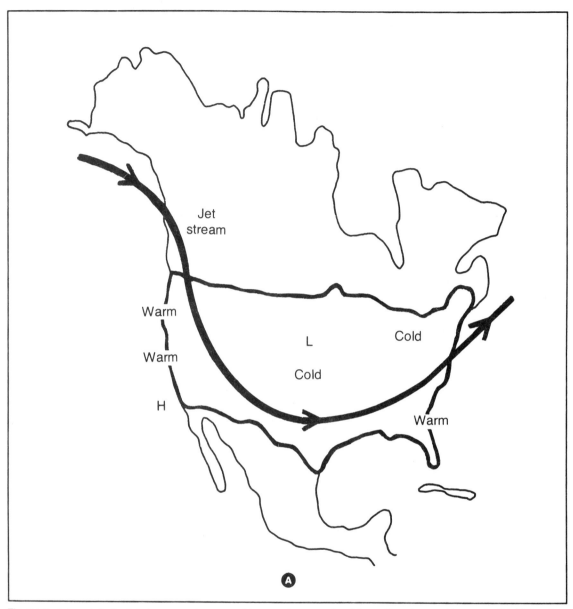

Fig. 6-9A. A trough in the jet stream produces a cold wave. An example of the pattern for a cold wave in the Midwest.

west whose livelihood depends on tourism, such events are welcomed.

A similar jet stream trough can develop over eastern Europe in conjunction with an intensification of the Bermuda high. Spain and Portugal might then have balmy, fair weather, while rains drench Norway, Sweden, Holland, and Poland, and bitterly cold storms sweep across the Russian plains. In the southern hemisphere, the effects of jet stream troughs are less brutal in terms of cold temperatures, but the tip of South America is frequently blasted by raw, wet gales as storms sweep around troughs in that region.

Cold waves, like heat waves, are moderated

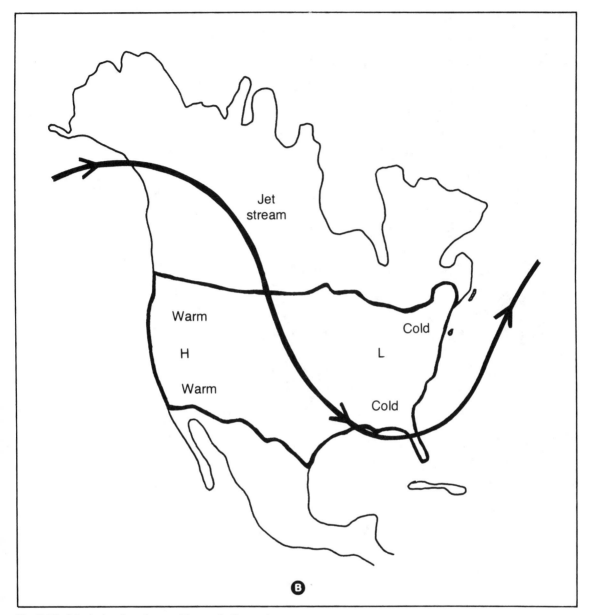

Fig. 6-9B. A typical pattern for a cold wave in the east.

by the presence of the ocean. Below-zero readings are rare at any coastal location in the United States. In England, below-zero temperatures are almost unknown, despite the relatively high latitude, because of the moderating effect of the warm Atlantic current that originates in the Gulf of Mexico. Even as far north as Anchorage, Alaska, the weather is much warmer because of the proximity of the ocean than it would otherwise be. The difference is illustrated by comparing the wintertime temperatures at Anchorage, Alaska, and an inland place at approximately the same latitude, such as Yellowknife, in the Northwest Territories of Canada. The mean January temperatures are +12 degrees Fahrenheit

Fig. 6-10. A lone jogger, undaunted by a subzero Minnesota cold wave (courtesy Jerry Olson, Rochester Post-Bulletin).

at Anchorage and −20 degrees Fahrenheit at Yellowknife. That is a difference of 32 degrees Fahrenheit over a span of less than 2 degrees of latitude.

Because jet stream troughs frequently develop, and persist, over inland parts of large continents in the winter, conditions often become favorable for severe, prolonged cold waves in the upper-midwestern United States, central Canada, and eastern Europe. A less populated, but still famous, haven for cold waves is Siberia. Much of Siberia, however, lies within the arctic circle, and is therefore not a true part of the temperate zone.

Cold weather is the norm in that part of the world.

Cold waves make things difficult in many ways. All but the most hardy joggers (Fig. 6-10) must suspend their activities or exercise on indoor tracks. Of more concern than exercise, however, is the high cost of keeping warm. Energy bills rise to astronomical levels during severe cold snaps.

Heating Degree Days

The severity of a cold season is determined in much the same way as the severity of a hot season. Relative demand for energy during a winter is cal-

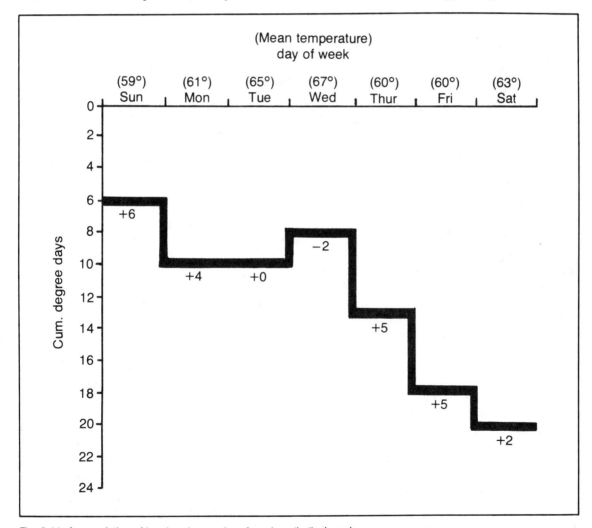

Fig. 6-11. Accumulation of heating degree days for a hypothetical week.

culated according to the accumulation of *heating degree days*. The basis for determining heating degree days is a mean temperature of 65 degrees Fahrenheit. A single heating degree day represents a day for which the average temperature is 64 degrees. If the mean temperature is 55 degrees for a day, we have 10 heating degree days.

Figure 6-11 shows an example of the accumulation of heating degree days for a hypothetical week. Note that on Wednesday, the mean temperature was actually above 65 degrees, reducing the cumulative total. Figure 6-12 illustrates an entire season (October through April). The most severe cold waves correspond to regions in the graph at B having a steep downward slope. The slope of the curve is an indication of the amount of energy required to keep the indoor environment comfortable.

In most places at temperate latitudes, the number of heating degree days is greater each year than the number of cooling degree days. In New England, for example, the number of cooling degree days is normally a few hundred for each warm season, but the number of heating degree days is several thousand. The same holds for most of the United States, with the exception of Hawaii, Florida, and parts of the desert Southwest.

Cold Weather Records

Surprisingly, every state except Hawaii has had at least one cold wave severe enough to put the thermometer below zero Fahrenheit. Even Florida has experienced a reading of −2; it occurred in Tallahassee, in February 1899. Tallahassee is located fairly far inland, away from the moderating influences of the Gulf of Mexico. The coldest temperature in the 48 states was observed in Montana: a bitter −70 at Rogers Pass, on January 20, 1954.

The coldest temperatures occur when several factors combine. Elevation is important, since the temperature drops with increasing height above sea level. Hawaii, for example, has had a temperature as low as +12 Fahrenheit atop Mauna Kea. An inland place will get chillier during a cold wave than a spot near a large body of water, which is why the record cold temperatures are lower in the center of the country than along the coasts. Latitude obvi-

ously has an effect; Minnesota has been colder than Arkansas. Of course, the severity of the cold wave itself makes a big difference. Table 6-1 shows the record cold temperatures for all 50 states through 1981.

The effects of cold weather are increased by wind. During a cold wave, it is effectively chillier if a strong wind blows. The apparent temperature, based on the actual temperature and the wind speed, is called the windchill factor, and was discussed in Chapter 5. Record low windchill factors are almost always much lower than the record low temperatures. Every single state has experienced windchill temperatures below 0 Fahrenheit.

How Will We Keep Warm?

In recent years, the cost of energy has been increasing rapidly, mostly because of the dramatic rise in the price of petroleum. Alternative energy sources are becoming more attractive, especially for heating purposes. We have to stay reasonably warm to survive! This problem will get more attention in future years, as some forms of energy become unavailable or unaffordable. Among the most promising alternative energy sources is the sun.

In some places, solar energy is a practical and effective source of heat for small buildings. The best locations are those at which the sun shines much of the time. In general, the weather is sunnier in the western United States than in the east, and the sunlight is more intense in the southern part of the country than in the northern part. Solar energy, however, can be used to a limited extent even in regions where cloudy weather is common.

Solar energy can be harnessed directly by placing large windows on the south side of a building, in conjunction with heat-absorbing and heat-retaining floors, walls, and furniture. When the sun shines through the windows, visible light and shortwave infrared penetrate the glass. Objects in the room get heated and radiate longwave infrared, which cannot pass back out through the windows (Fig. 6-13). This longwave infrared radiation continues long after the sun has gone down or the weather has turned overcast. Direct solar heating systems can be very effective in sunny climates,

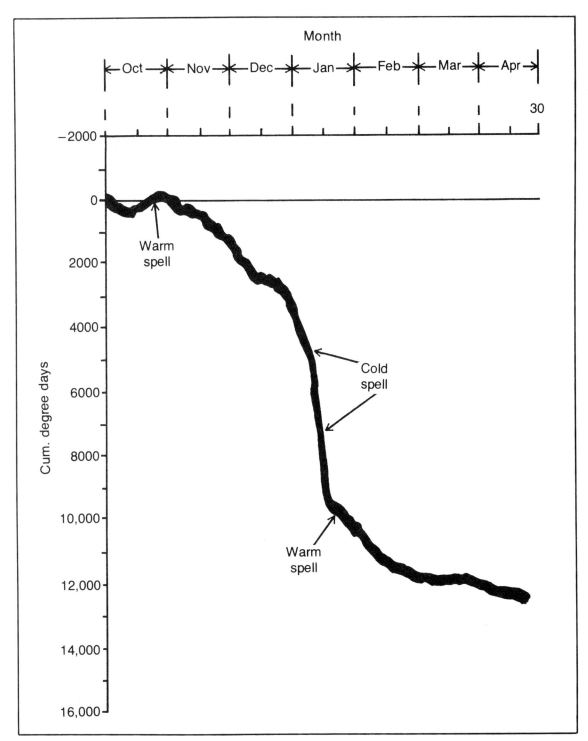

Fig. 6-12. Heating degree days accumulation for a hypothetical season.

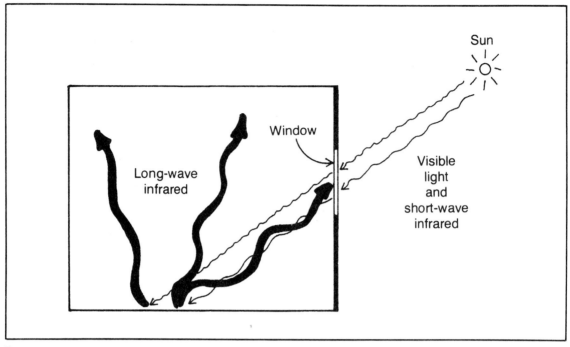

Fig. 6-13. Sunlight, shining through the window in an enclosed room, helps to heat the room.

even if the outside temperature is extremely cold.

In a less sunny location, indirect solar heating can be used. An indirect system uses solar panels to generate electricity for heating, and also for general power needs. An indirect solar energy system can be totally independent of the utility company, or it can be interconnected with the commercial power line.

The wind can be harnessed to provide heat by generating electricity. Farmers have been using the wind as a source of energy for hundreds of years. A single wind-driven generator can produce several kilowatts of power. Such generators are available from commercial sources.

Other means of keeping warm, all of which will certainly be considered in the coming decades, include woodstoves, fireplaces (if they are efficiently designed), geothermal heat, and nuclear power. Natural gas, although a petroleum product, may someday be replaced by hydrogen derived from electrolysis or from chemical reactions. Some scientists have suggested that massive reflectors could be put in space to direct solar energy to

earth-based power plants. The list of new ideas is almost endless.

Unfortunately, all-out efforts to find new energy sources are restricted to a few enthusiastic people. A very real crisis awaits us in the future unless we find a viable substitute for petroleum. We have gotten used to living in warm houses and working in warm office buildings, but our winters are, and will continue to be, as cold as they have always been. A warning sign of what could happen presented itself in the winter of 1972-1973, when a cold wave struck much of the United States at the same time many of the oil-producing countries refused to sell crude to the United States.

Conservation is important if a house or building is to be kept warm at an affordable price. Heat loss can occur because of radiation, conduction, or convection. Radiation loss can be detected by photographing a structure in infrared light. Conduction loss can, in some cases, also be detected in this way. Convection contributes to heat loss when a building is not airtight. If you place your hand at the base of your front door on a blustery day and feel cool air currents, you have convection heat loss. A professional should be consulted regarding the insulation of a particular house or building.

TOO MUCH WATER

We rely on water for our very existence. Water makes it possible to grow food crops, and it provides a source of electrical energy. Much trade is carried on by boats navigating rivers and oceans. When we run short of water, we notice it, but too much water can be just as bad as too little. Floods are responsible for millions of dollars of damage and numerous deaths every year. Most people who live on river flood plains know what can happen, even if they haven't been there long enough to see a real catastrophe.

In July, 1978, following a wet spring in the upper Midwest, a line of heavy thundershowers developed in southern Minnesota along a stationary front oriented in an east-west direction. As the skies darkened, the weather reports told of possible heavy rain, but conditions did not appear too bad. Cumulonimbus clouds moved toward the north and bore down on the city of Rochester and the surrounding area. The late-afternoon sun shone on the clouds, giving them a strange reddish-brown color, then the rain began, driven by a 50-mile-per-hour southeast gale.

Most heavy thunderstorms last for about 20 to 40 minutes, and few, it any, of the residents of Rochester thought that this one would be an exception. The rain became heavier, seeming to come down in sheets instead of drops. Small trees bowed under the sheer force of falling water as the wind subsided. The rain continued without the slightest sign of a letup: 1 hour, 2 hours, 3 hours.

At about 11:00 that night, the Zumbro River had grown from a quiet little stream to a mighty river. Within its newly claimed banks lay about one-third of the city of Rochester. Residents were awakened by evacuation orders, and some were also greeted, upon arising, by water in their basements and garages. By midnight, about 7 inches of rain had fallen—more than some hurricanes produce. It was the worst flood in the history of the city. I was lucky enough to be living well above the flood plain of the river, but it was nevertheless a sobering thing to see familiar landmarks under water. Route 63, which runs north and south and forms the main avenue (Broadway), looked like a boat launching ramp in the vicinity of North 16th Street; it just ended at the shore of a muddy lake.

The event just described is called a *flash flood*, because it happens so fast. Flash floods are especially dangerous because of the rapidity with which they strike. In the Rochester flood, the water level rose so quickly that its vertical progress was plainly visible. When water rises that fast, a strong horizontal current is produced. Floating debris then becomes a deadly hazard.

There are other types of floods. After a snowy winter, a period of warm weather can produce flooding because the ground cannot handle the water runoff. This type of flood usually takes place over a longer span of time than a flash flood, but can cause more damage because of its duration and also because of ice floes that are carried with the current.

Flood activity is not restricted to rivers. The ocean can flood because of tidal effects produced by changes in barometric pressure. The most spectacular type of ocean flood is the surge that accompanies a hurricane. Such a storm surge strikes with overwhelming suddenness and fury, and is responsible for most of the damage and death in a major tropical storm. This type of flood is most likely in bays or estuaries, such as the Galveston-Houston area (Fig. 6-14). The nature of storm surges is discussed in Chapter 2.

Local floods sometimes occur in desert areas. Even the Sahara gets an occasional deluge, and small lakes can form in some places if the rain accumulation is significant (Fig. 6-15). Such floods can cause problems for people living in or near the area, but, after a short time, an ephemeral desert flood lake evaporates, leaving things as they were.

Tributaries and Flood Plains

Floods result from the combination of two ingredients: a river or stream, and too much water. Certain types of rivers and streams are more susceptible to flooding than others, however. Floods

Fig. 6-14. The Galveston-Houston area is prone to floods resulting from storm surges. This photograph shows the bay as seen from Apollo 9 (courtesy NASA).

are most common in regions where the rainfall varies significantly. The most flood-prone rivers and streams are those with many tributaries or which run through a flat plain.

Figure 6-16A illustrates the Ganges river and its numerous tributaries. The Ganges regularly floods during the monsoon season because a large part of India gets its drainage via tributaries of this river. A heavy rain anywhere upstream will cause a rise in the water level downstream. The people who dwell in the narrow flood plain of the Ganges are used to the annual inundation and treat it as a perfectly ordinary event. In recent years, some measures have been taken to reduce the damaging effects of flooding along this river.

Figure 6-16B shows the Yangtze and its flood plain in China. Because the flood plain is so low, the water level does not have to rise very much in order to cause massive flooding. The Yangtze does, however, rise tremendously on occasion: crests have been almost 100 feet above normal. A quarter of a billion people—a population as large as that of the whole United States—live along the lower part of the Yangtze. Killer floods struck in 1931 and again in 1954. The people of the Yangtze have, in recent years, undertaken to protect their lives from the uncontrollable floods that occasionally take place in the river valley.

Several of the world's rivers are famous for the beneficial effects of their flooding; an example is the Nile. For those who dwell next to the Nile today, the flooding is less fierce than in ages past. In a country largely covered by deserts, the annual Nile flood was, for thousands of years, a vital link in the food chain. Now a great dam controls the waters of the Nile, taming the destructive effects of its

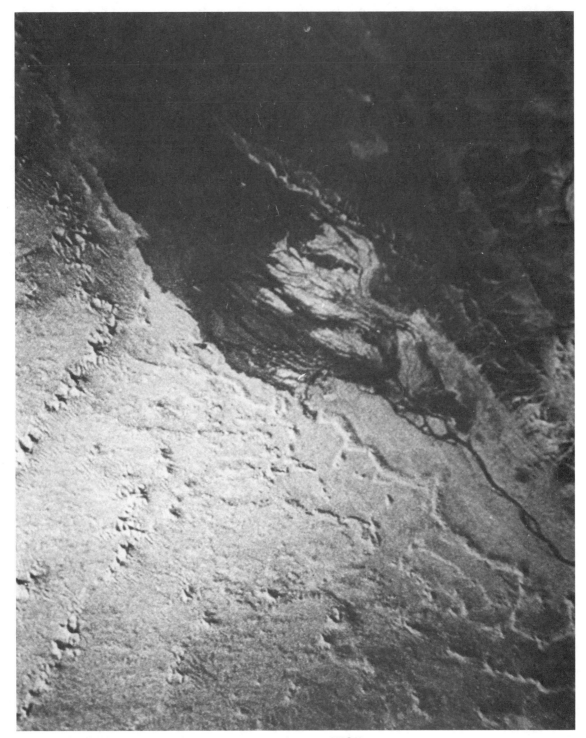

Fig. 6-15. An ephemeral desert lake as seen from space (courtesy NASA).

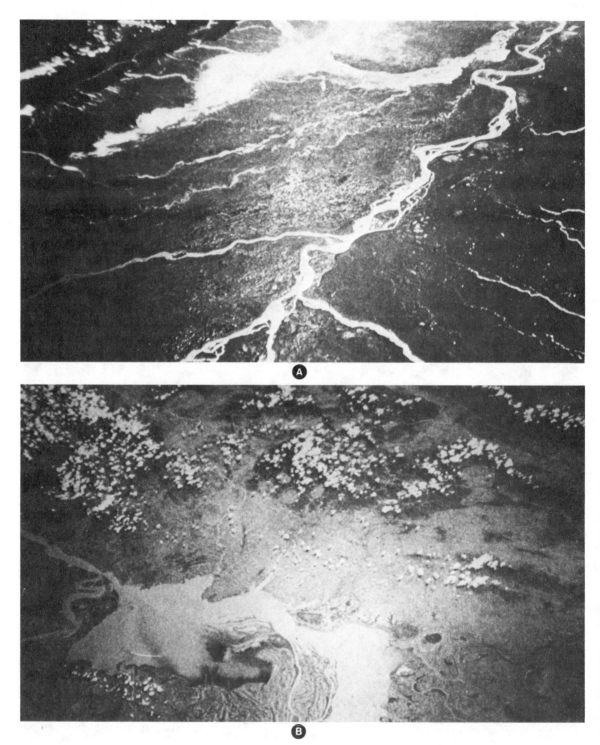

Fig. 6-16. Two different rivers. At A, the Ganges in India; at B, the Yangtze in China (courtesy NASA).

Fig. 6-17. Lake Nasser, the reservoir created by the Aswan High Dam, as seen from space (courtesy NASA).

irregular floods, but also perhaps upsetting the natural fertilizing process.

Dams

The most devastating of all floods occur downstream from large dams. Ironically, one of the primary purposes for building a dam is to control flooding. The Aswan High Dam in Egypt was built to regulate the level of the Nile, reducing flood damage in the valleys and providing water for irrigation. Behind the dam, a massive reservoir has been formed (Fig. 6-17). The Aswan High Dam, completed in 1970, is one of the largest in the world. If the dam were to break, the colossal reservior known as Lake Nasser—all 100 million acre feet of it—would spill down the Nile to the Mediterranean Sea. Most of the people in Egypt live along the Nile flood plain, and they would be killed by such an event, but not before witnessing a sight that would surely seem to represent an act of wrath by a supreme being.

Dams have burst. A grisly example of what can happen to a dammed river is the Johnstown, Pennsylvania, flood of May, 1889. A large earthen structure called the South Fork Dam held back a reservoir about 2 miles long, on the shores of which a resort complex was built. The dam was inadequately maintained, and a rainstorm caused it to disintegrate. A wall of water cascaded down the river, carrying away everything in its path. Johnstown, a few miles downstream from the dam, was obliterated, and several other communities suffered the same fate. The destruction can be compared to the effects of a nuclear detonation.

Earthen dams are the most commonly built, primarily because they are less expensive than concrete dams. They are also more easily destroyed by a phenomenon known as *overtopping*: a swollen reservoir literally pours over the top of the dam, eroding it away almost instantly (Fig. 6-18). Proper dam construction prevents overtopping and minimizes the probability of a catastrophe such as the Johnstown flood, but no dam is indestructible.

Flood-producing Weather

Two types of weather phenomena can produce flooding: excessive rainfall and a rapid snowmelt. In both cases, the situation can build up gradually over several weeks or months, exploding into a flood suddenly because of a single rainstorm or warm spell. Sometimes both of these weather factors act together to produce a "maxi flood."

Heavy rains are associated with some low-pressure systems. As a warm or cold front progresses around the center of a temperate-latitude cyclone, the front slows down and may practically stop. The bad weather associated with a slow-moving front lasts longer, at a given place, than the precipitation that accompanies a fast-moving front. The result is a larger accumulation. Another factor is also involved: fronts tend to slow down or stall as they become aligned in the direction of movement of the cyclone. Thus, instead of sweeping past points in its path, the front hovers in about the same position for days. Figure 6-19 shows a situation of this kind that would generate a series of rainy days in the Ohio Valley.

In some low-pressure systems, heavy rains occur on the poleward side of the center. This situation is particularly true of extratropical hurricanes. A noteworthy example of a hurricane that generated flooding is Diane of 1955. This storm passed south and east of New England while moving toward the northeast (Fig. 6-20). Heavy rains, fed by the winds blowing in from the Atlantic Ocean, caused great destruction. In fact, Diane was one of the most destructive New England hurricanes in history, not because of her winds, which were comparatively weak, but because of the torrential rains that fell on already saturated ground.

Whenever there is a winter with unusually heavy snow, the skiers love it, but other people (besides those who have large driveways to shovel) hate it. The residents of the flood plains fear the arrival of spring. If a warm spell comes, streams and rivers begin to swell. If the onset of the warm weather is very rapid, the ground cannot absorb the runoff, because there is too much water and the ground frost has not had time to thaw. Warm spells are frequently followed by cold fronts, and the associated weather can bring heavy rain. In such a case, when all the potential flood-generating factors conspire together, the result can be a catastrophe.

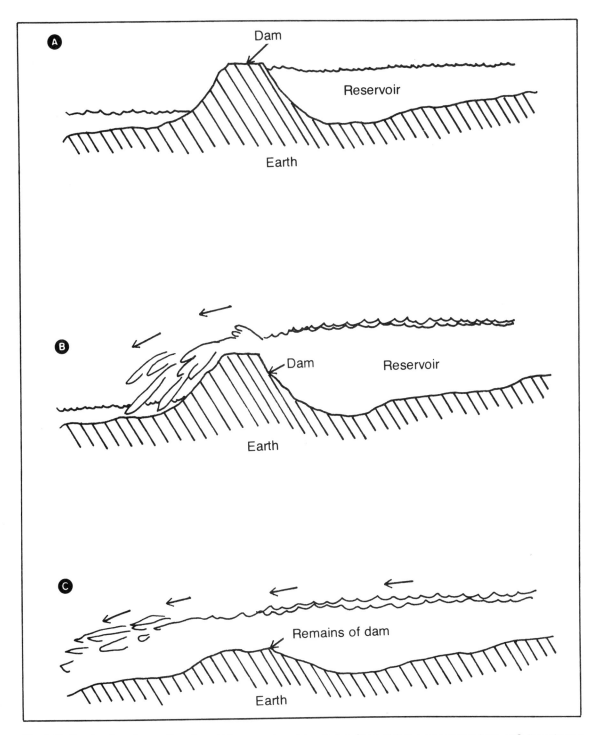

Fig. 6-18. Overtopping of an earthen dam. At A, reservoir and dam before flood; at B, the water bursts forth; at C, flow of water erodes the dam, causing the reservoir to disappear and sending a wall of water downstream.

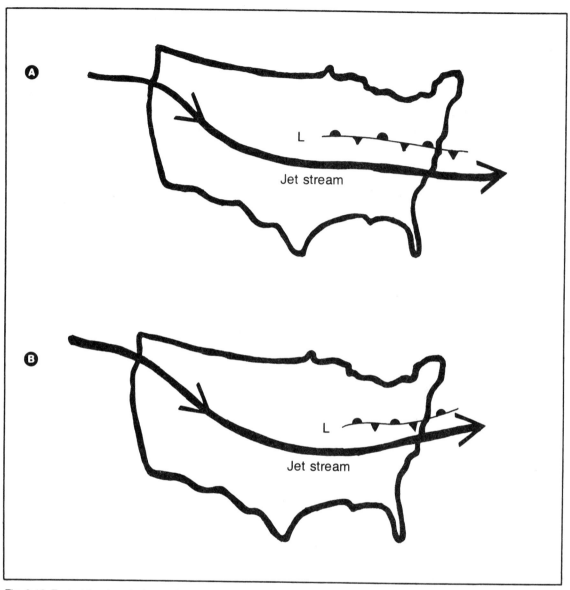

Fig. 6-19. Typical flood-producing stationary front. The low-pressure system moves slowly. The maps at A and B represent conditions 24 hours apart.

Safety in a Flood

Some floods strike with little or no warning, but others can be predicted several hours in advance. Spring flooding, caused by the melting of snow, is the easiest to forecast. Flash floods resulting from rainstorms are more difficult to predict, but meteorologists can usually tell when a flash flood is likely. Dam-burst floods are the hardest of all to predict in terms of the time of strike. Because of this, and because of their extreme violence, dam-burst floods, while rarities, are the most dangerous.

Some common-sense safety rules during a flood are:

☐ If a flood warning is issued, residents of the flood plain should evacuate if advised to do so. In some cases, authorities, such as the police, will assist in carrying out an evacuation.

☐ Property protection measures can be taken within reason, but people should realize that their lives are more important than their possessions. Flood waters can rise with extreme rapidity. Valuables can be moved to a second floor or a place near the ceiling of the first floor if time permits.

☐ When evacuating, the main electrical switch or switches should be turned off.

☐ If utility wires are down, they should be avoided because of the possibility of electrocution via conduction through muddy water.

☐ No one should try to swim in the flood waters, except when it is unavoidable in the course of a rescue. Besides being dirty and perhaps dangerously cold, debris is often present.

☐ Beware of using a boat in a flood, especially if the water appears to be fast moving. It is better to evacuate before it is necessary to use a boat.

☐ After the water has receded, check with local authorites concerning the safety of drinking water.

DROUGHT

The winter has been unusual: there has been practically no snow, and the weather was strangely warm. A ridge in the jet stream is responsible.

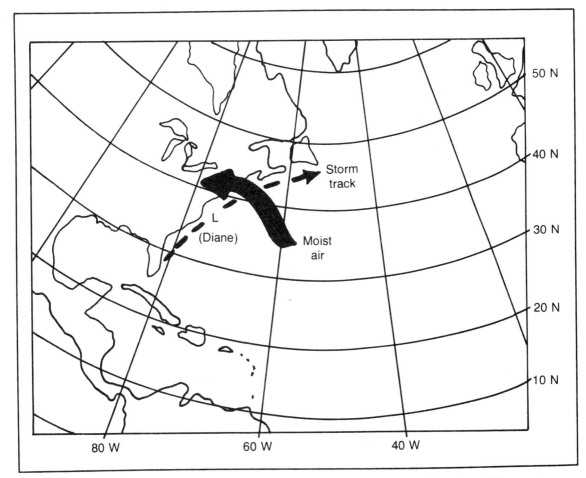

Fig. 6-20. Hurricane Diane caused massive flooding in New England as she passed south and east of the coast.

Temperatures rise into the mid-70s during March, and the spring rains do not come. In April, high winds carry loose topsoil into the air, creating massive dust storms. By the middle of May, the whole countryside is parched and hot. Crops fail. We are having a drought.

Throughout history, droughts have been feared more than floods. There is always plenty of high ground to run to, or to grow crops in, when it rains too much, but during a drought there is no reprieve. The entire human community is placed at the mercy of the weather. If food plants won't grow, we can't eat. For a time, food reserves can be used, but a whole country cannot survive for very long on stockpiles of grain.

In the United States, we have not experienced a truly severe drought since the 1930s. In some parts of the world today, however, dry weather is slowly starving millions of people. Most of us tend to think of Africa especially, and to some extent Asia, when we imagine severe, prolonged drought, but it could—and someday it might—happen in the industrialized world.

The Drought Belt

Some parts of the world have a much drier climate than others. In some cases this is because of geography; for example, we often find deserts on the lee sides of mountain ranges. Persistent high pressure, however, centered near 30 degrees north and south latitude, has also created a state of unending drought in certain places.

You can look at a map of the world and see for yourself how many major deserts are near 30 degrees north and south latitude. The Sahara in northern Africa is probably the best example. Deserts also exist in southern Africa. Progressing eastward around the north 30th parallel, we find the deserts of Saudi Arabia, Iran, Pakistan, Tibet, the southwestern United States, and northern Mexico. In the southern hemisphere, Australia is largely covered by deserts, and the climate of west-central South America is quite dry.

Not all regions near 30 degrees latitude have desert climates. Florida and most of the Gulf Coast, eastern China, and eastern Australia get a fair amount of rainfall, although not as much as many people think. These regions are not deserts because the ocean-atmosphere machine brings in tropical water and air.

Places that do not get much rain show more variability of precipitation from month to month and year to year than places that get a lot of rain. Some deserts get an entire year's rainfall in a single deluge. In other places, there is a wet season and a dry season. Most of the precipitation in southern California comes during the winter months, and in India and Pakistan, summer monsoons bring most of the rain for the year.

In recent decades, the world's deserts have been visited and populated by man. This is especially true of the southwestern United States. The desert eco-system is fragile, and it is not yet clear whether or not our invasion will do significant harm to the environment. It has been said by some ecologists that nature makes forests while man makes deserts. There is evidence that the world's deserts are expanding, but we do not know yet whether that is because of us, or because of natural changes in the earth's climate.

We do know that the environment on our planet has changed, is changing, and will continue to change. The Sahara desert was apparently much smaller at one time than it is today. As recently as 5,000 years ago, some scientists believe, much of the Middle East was green and fertile. Perhaps the empire of ancient Egypt fell, in part, because of the relentless expansion of the desert.

Semiarid regions occasionally experience droughts that render them practically deserts. These droughts are the most damaging to mankind because we rely on semiarid places for much of our food supply. During the 1930s, a prolonged drought occurred in the central United States, resulting in near famine. Other droughts, less severe, have taken place since then, at strangely regular intervals.

Drought Cycles

Temporary droughts, such as the one that took place during the 1930s, occur when the high-pressure belt is closer to the pole than normal. The conditions that produce a temporary drought are the same as those that cause a heat wave: a persistent ridge in the jet stream over a continent. The desert belts literally move northward in the northern hemisphere. Summer rainfall decreases while the temperature increases.

Figure 6-21 shows the summer rainfall and temperature variability for the period 1900-1975, averaged for the "wheat belt" states of Oklahoma, Kansas, Nebraska, South Dakota, and North Dakota. The Dust Bowl of the 1930s shows plainly on the graph. There have been other, lesser droughts during the twentieth century. The periods 1912-1914 and 1952-1957 were characterized by above-normal temperatures and below-normal rainfall. Interestingly, these drought periods are spaced at intervals of about 20 years. It is quite possible that this is a coincidence, but the period of the middle and late 1970s (only part of which appears in Fig. 6-21) brought another round of dry, warm weather to much of the United States.

Why would drought seem to recur about every 20 years? There is another natural phenomenon that displays a similar cycle: sunspots. The number of sunspots varies from year to year, reaching a maximum approximately once every 11 years. Each succeeding maximum is of opposite magnetic polarity from its predecessor. Thus, the so-called sunspot cycle is actually a 22-year periodic event.

Could it be that the sunspot cycle somehow affects our weather? Some climatologists think so, and recent studies have shown that the radiation from the sun fluctuates along with the cycle. It would not take much of a change in solar radiation to warm the earth by a few degrees Fahrenheit. This might push the subtropical high-pressure belts toward the poles—exactly what causes drought, but many climatologists are rather skeptical about the sunspot theory of drought. Here is what some of the experts have said in *Climate Change to the Year 2000,* published in 1978 by the National Defense University press.

"... I am not convinced that a solar-drought effect has been demonstrated ..."

"... I think that the evidence is mounting that

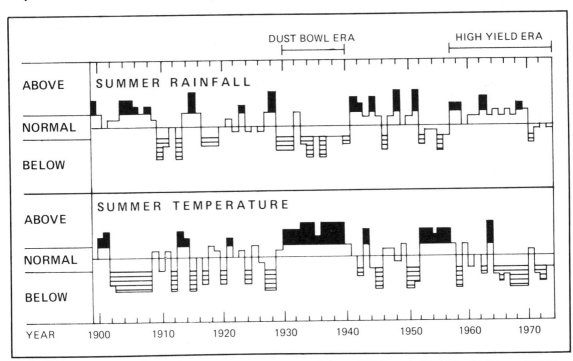

Fig. 6-21. Yearly rainfall and temperature in the "wheat belt" states from 1900 through 1975 (after D. Gilman, NOAA).

there is a 22-year cycle in droughts and that it is related to sunspot activity. However, predictions of the relative intensity and regional distribution patterns lie beyond our scientific knowledge . . ."

". . . While I do not believe that sunspots are related to drought, there is a statistical behavior of drought that suggests a pattern of repetition . . ."

". . . Droughts seem to be related to solar influences . . . Power spectrum analysis shows a very notable 22-year rhythm and a weak one near 11 years . . ."

". . . The 20-year periodicity seems to be a well-documented climatic feature . . . The expected warming towards the end of the century would seem to increase the probability of drought . . . *"

The Effects of Man

Figure 6-21 clearly shows an interesting fact: the 1930s drought was much worse than any of the others. The reason is not certain, but perhaps improper farming techniques had something to do with it. We found out that Ohio-Valley methods do not work in the Great Plains. The "wheat belt" states have a drier climate than the land to the east. Man changed the land, and this might have significantly affected the temperature and rainfall. After the Dust Bowl disaster, we changed our farming methods, and this may be why we haven't had another Dust Bowl. We certainly want to believe, anyway, that this is correct, because it implies that we have some control over things. If not, we may have another Dust Bowl—possibly as early as the 1990s.

Droughts seem to be associated with above-normal temperatures. At least, this has been the case for the American Midwest during the twentieth century. But what comes first? Do higher temperatures cause droughts, or do droughts cause higher temperatures? Or are both heat and dryness caused by something else? The exact cause-and-effect relationship is not known, but if drought is caused by temporary global warning—perhaps because of increased solar radiation—we might have a problem. Evidence has been mounting that man's activities are making our planet hotter. Pollutants, especially carbon dioxide, are the main culprits.

Our atmosphere retains a certain amount of heat. Some of the heat originates inside the earth, but most of it comes from the sun. When visible light and shortwave infrared strike the surface, especially land, the earth is warmed and emits longwave infrared. Some of the longwave infrared is radiated back into space, but some is trapped by the atmosphere, in a manner similar to the way a greenhouse works. For this reason, the phenomenon is called the *greenhouse effect*. Some gases, notably carbon dioxide, produce more greenhouse effect than others.

The atmosphere contains mostly nitrogen and oxygen. These two gases together comprise 99 percent of the weight of the sea of air surrounding our planet. Carbon dioxide makes up only a fraction of 1 percent of the atmosphere, but it is responsible for much of the heat retention. It wouldn't be necessary to add very much carbon dioxide to increase the amount of that gas by 1/10. That small increase would make a big difference in the way our atmosphere holds the longwave infrared radiation.

The Environmental Protection Agency is concerned that the burning of fossil fuels in particular is raising the concentration of carbon dioxide in our air. In the next 100 years, they think, the average temperature of the earth might rise 3.6 degrees Fahrenheit above what it would normally be. Eventually, the temperature might rise as much as 9 degrees. A change of less than 4 degrees might not sound like much, but it would have an impact on our climate. A 9-degree increase would not only have profound environmental effects, but it would be very noticeable—especially during the summer.

Consider the daily summer weather in Miami, Florida. We choose this city because the temperature is regular and predictable in the summer: the high is around 90 degrees and the low is about 80 degrees. That's warm, but a low of 89 and a high of 99 is plain hot!

---

*From *Climate Change to the Year 2000* (National Defense University, 1978), pp., 53-54.

A global warming trend would cause the rainfall to change over many parts of the planet. The dry regions, now near 30 degrees north and south latitude, would probably move closer to the poles. The zones of the trade winds, prevailing westerlies, and polar easterlies would change. Perhaps a new circulation belt would develop near the equator, producing unbelievably hot deserts at latitude zero. Previously fertile farmland would turn into desert. The level of the oceans would rise. Many of the world's major coastal cities would be inundated. Some regions would benefit from a rise in the average temperature of the earth, however. The increase in carbon dioxide concentration might aid plant growth by improving photosynthesis.

The main problem may not be the warming trend itself, but the fact that we won't be prepared for its effects because we don't know exactly what they will be in various places. Scientists are trying to determine just what will happen if the world gets a certain number of degrees warmer. We can then act accordingly when, or if, the climate changes.

Not all scientists believe that the earth will get warmer because of greenhouse effect. In fact, a few experts have said that the earth might, instead, get cooler—and we could be the culprits. Factors that might contribute to global cooling include a possible natural tendency toward cooling, particulate pollution, volcanic activity, and interstellar dust. In addition, our consumption of fossil fuels may decline as we begin to rely more heavily on alternative energy sources. There is another possible cause of massive global cooling: a phenomenon that some scientists are calling the *nuclear winter*. A large-scale thermonuclear war might blow so much dust into the atmosphere that we would get much less energy from the sun.

The consequences of global cooling might be more serious than the effects of warming. A drop of just a few degrees in the earth's average temperature would reduce the rate of snow melt. This would, in turn, result in more reflection of sunlight into space, since snow, being white, absorbs very little energy. That would cool off the planet still more. By the time the vicious cooling circle ended with restoration of natural thermal balance, we might have another ice age. The agricultural belts would shift toward the equator, and many cities would become uninhabitable, buried in hundreds of feet of snow.

It is worthwhile for us to learn just how our activities affect the climate, not only so we can avoid doing harm, but also because we might be able to counteract undesirable natural changes. It may be possible for us to actually prevent the onset of the next ice age, should our planet begin to cool. Undesirable warming could perhaps also be prevented.

GEOLOGICAL AND ASTRONOMICAL EFFECTS

Short-term and medium-term climate changes sometimes occur as a result of events that we would not consider weather related. History provides us with an interesting example: the cold summer of 1816. This bizarre summer was the kind of thing that warm-weather lovers dread. Climatologists are not completely certain what caused the cold summer of 1816, but one theory holds that volcanic dust was responsible. A short time before that summer, there was a massive eruption. A volcano can spew millions of tons of dust into the upper troposphere, and the dust remains for months or even years, blocking out solar energy. Figure 6-22 gives an idea of the amount of matter released by a volcano. The dust is clearly visible from hundreds of miles up as it blows downwind.

Since 1816, there has not been another comparable cold summer. Some summers are cooler than others, of course, as Fig. 6-18 clearly shows, but the variation is not great enough to cause snow in June and frost all year long at temperate latitudes and at low elevations. Yet, there have been numerous volcanic eruptions, such as Krakatoa and Mount Saint Helens. The effects of volcanic activity on weather and climate are not fully known, but there is no doubt that the dust reduces the amount of solar radiation that can penetrate the atmosphere. A recent eruption in Mexico caused a drop of as much as 10 percent at some solar observatories.

A reduction in solar radiation might be caused by extraterrestrial matter. Space is not a complete vacuum; gas and dust permeate it. We know that large gas and dust clouds exist in space, because we can see them with our telescopes. It is possible that there are smaller clouds through which the solar system might pass in a few years on its way around the galaxy. Such clouds would have to be moving at a different speed or direction than our sun. If the concentration of dust between the sun and the earth were to change, we would get more or less energy from the sun, and this could cause global warming or cooling. There is some evidence that the sun does pass in and out of dust clouds over very long periods of time.

A comet with a long tail (Fig. 6-23) might have a very short-lived effect on our weather if the earth happened to pass through the tail, but comet tails are tenuous. The effect, if any, would probably be slight. If a comet or asteroid were ever to strike our planet directly, however, there would be a tre-mendous, immediate, and long-lasting change in the climate.

Celestial objects have hit our planet numerous times. We know this because we can see the evidence in the form of craters. Most meteorite craters are less than 1 mile across, but some geological formations may be the remnants of much larger craters. Hudson Bay is believed by some scientists to be an ancient, huge crater, largely filled in by millions of years of erosion. A trench in the bottom of the Caribbean may have been formed when an asteroid struck the earth thousands or millions of years ago. The impact of a large meteorite or comet could change the climate within a matter of hours, perhaps starting or ending an ice age, changing rainfall patterns, and possibly even wiping out whole species of living organisms.

The climate on our planet is continually changing. There are many factors that affect our

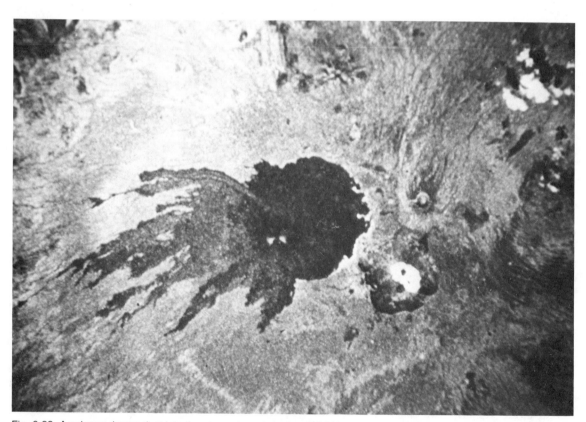

Fig. 6-22. A volcano dumps dust into the atmosphere (courtesy NASA).

Fig. 6-23. The comet Ikeya-Seki (courtesy U.S. Naval Observatory).

environment, and its suitability (or lack thereof) for the existence of humans. The climate fluctuates from year to year and from decade to decade, and we feel the effects of these changes. Medium-term climatic changes are minor, however, in fact inconsequential, compared to the fluctuations we can expect over thousands or millions of years.

Planet Earth is several billion years old, according to modern astronomers, and it has several billion more years of potentially hospitable climate left. We will now examine the history of our planet's climate from the very beginning, and we will look at what might happen in the future—all the way until the end.

Chapter 7

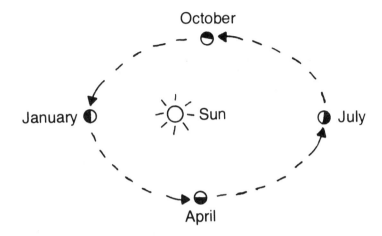

Climatic History and Prognosis

Our universe is restless. The cosmos has always had its own gigantic tempests and our planet is the product of a chain of cosmic storms.

Contemporary scientists believe that the universe began about 10 to 20 billion years ago in a brilliant flash, with a point of energy and matter smaller than an atomic nucleus. There was a fantastic explosion, and the matter was thrown outward, whereupon it condensed into protons, electrons, neutrons, and other particles. Electrons fell into orbit around protons and formed hydrogen, which is still the most abundant element in the universe.

Clouds of hydrogen gas swirled and gradually collapsed under their own weight, heating up from the compression until nuclear fusion began, and stars were born. Billions of years passed, and the stars grew unstable; some of them exploded.

The material from exploded stars, along with virgin hydrogen and still-shining stars, became arranged in enormous eddies, globes, and irregular congregations that we call galaxies. In one pinwheel-shaped galaxy, spinning around like a hurricane 600 quadrillion miles in diameter, a particular gas-and-dust cloud acquired its own spin. At the center, a star formed.

About 93 million miles from the center of this vortex, a small (relatively speaking) spherical chunk of matter, 8,000 miles across, condensed. At first it was so hot that it glowed red and yellow. The outside cooled first. Gradually, the temperature at the surface lowered, approaching a reasonable value. The surface was barren. There was no air, no water, no storms, no climate at all—for a while.

Such, it is thought, was the sequence of events leading to the formation of the earth.

AIR, WATER, STORMS, AND LIFE

Eventually, the earth acquired an atmosphere. Some of the gas was captured by gravity from space, and more came from the interior of the planet. The earth's primordial atmosphere was not like it is today; we would find the mixture of gases unbreathable. Hydrogen and methane, as well as nitrogen, oxygen, and carbon dioxide, were present in large quantities. Out planet was something like Jupiter is today, but smaller.

There were storms in the earth's ancient sea of air, as there are on any planet with an atmosphere. (Jupiter, for example, has unimaginably violent storms; winds of Jupiterian speed would level everything on earth.) Rain fell, lightning flashed, and thunder boomed, but there were, as yet, no plants for the water to nourish and no animals for it to sustain; there were not creatures to hear the thunder. Ultimately, oceans formed on the earth, and all of the ingredients for carbon-and-nitrogen-based life forms were finally there.

It is believed possible that lightning is responsible for the generation of amino acids, of which all life on earth is made. Scientists have created amino acids in laboratories by simulating the conditions just described. Perhaps all life evolved as a result of a single lightning flash, although it is more likely—if in fact this theory is correct—that the event occurred on many occasions and in many different parts of the world.

Violent weather has affected life ever since the first cells began to develop from amino acid chains. We are not concerned, here, about the evolution of life, but instead with the way in which climate and weather have influenced the evolution of life. Let us consider a few examples.

We all know how rain, or lack of it, affects plant life, but the interaction between plants and weather is more complex. A hurricane might blow coconuts off of palm trees as it passes over Haiti. Some of the coconuts would land in the ocean and would be blown along by the storm until they washed up on a distant shore, such as the east coast of Florida. Perhaps this is how coconut trees got to Florida; a single hurricane might have brought them.

Birds, caught in the eyes of hurricanes, are occasionally transported thousands of miles. This has certainly had an effect on the kinds of bird life we see in various parts of the world. Tropical birds have been found as far north as New England in the wakes of hurricanes. In such extreme cases, the birds usually die, but they could survive shorter journeys and produce hybrid, previously nonexistent species.

Suppose that a stroke of lightning sets a tree on fire. Other trees nearby are ignited, and a forest fire ensues. Many acres of wooded land are scorched, but forest fires are part of the ecology. Young trees soon sprout from the blackened land. There is plenty of sun, and the soil is rich in carbon. The cycle repeats.

Wind makes waves on the ocean surface. Some of these have *whitecaps* caused by tiny air bubbles in the water, generated by the agitation. When raindrops fall on the water surface, the disturbance adds air to the water in a similar way by dissolving air in the water. The water must be aerated, or mixed with air, if fish are to survive, because fish need oxygen. If there were no wind or rain, the sea surface would be as smooth as glass, and unless oxygen were available from some other source, fish could not live.

ICE AGES

Figure 7-1 is a time-line diagram of the history of our planet. The earth is, according to recent estimates, about 4½ billion years old.

Let's think, for a moment, about how long a time that is. If we have a cube-shaped box measuring 1 meter high, 1 meter wide, and 1 meter deep (a meter is about 3 feet), the volume of the box would be 1 billion cubic millimeters (a millimeter is about 0.04 inches). Now suppose we have five such boxes, and a huge pile of tiny cubes, each measuring 1 millimeter high, 1 millimeter wide, and 1 millimeter deep.

We decide to fill four of the large boxes, and half of a fifth, with the little cubes. The enormity of this task is apparent when you consider how long it would take you to do this at the rate of one little cube per second; you couldn't do it in your lifetime. In fact, for one person to complete the job, he or she would need over 140 years! Each little cube would represent a full year in the history of the world.

Another way to look at the situation is to consider that the age of the earth is to your life span as your life span is to ½ minute, assuming you live to be 70 years old.

For millions of years after the first appearance of life on the earth, the climate was warm and

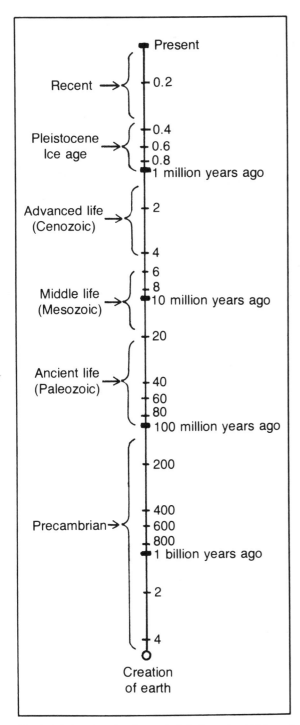

Recent →
- Present
- 0.2

Pleistocene Ice age →
- 0.4
- 0.6
- 0.8
- 1 million years ago

Advanced life (Cenozoic) →
- 2
- 4

Middle life (Mesozoic) →
- 6
- 8
- 10 million years ago
- 20

Ancient life (Paleozoic) →
- 40
- 60
- 80
- 100 million years ago

Precambrian →
- 200
- 400
- 600
- 800
- 1 billion years ago
- 2
- 4

Creation of earth

Fig. 7-1. A time line showing periods in the natural history of the earth. The scale is logarithmic. The Pleistocene ice age is a relatively recent event.

comparatively gentle. There were not many mountains or deserts. Much of the world was covered with lush greenery. The climate presented very little adversity for animals and plants, and animal life reached its pinnacle with the evolution of the dinosaurs. Many of the dinosaurs lived in present-day North America. Others lived in the eastern part of Africa and in the regions we now call China, England, and eastern Europe. These places, with the exception of eastern Africa, now have a climate in which the great lizards would perish.

The ideal worldwide climate did not continue. Unknown events intervened to change it. The reason for this change is one of the greatest mysteries facing earth's scientists, astronomers, and climatologists. By the time of the Pleistocene period, the climate was bleak, like a perpetual winter—much worse even than it is today. This radical change took place quite recently in time: the severe ice-age climate had become fully established about 1 million years ago.

There are many different theories that attempt to explain the cause of the Pleistocene ice age. There have apparently been several different ice ages at intervals of a few thousand years. These ice ages seem to have been superimposed on a much longer cyclic variation in world temperature.

Earth-Orbit Theory

The earth orbits the sun at an average distance of about 93 million miles, but the actual distance changes during the course of the year. Our planet does not go around the sun in a perfect circle. Instead, the orbit is an ellipse, with the sun at one focus (Fig. 7-2). The orbits of all planets are elliptical; some have almost circular orbits, while others have highly eccentric orbits.

In July, the distance between the earth and the sun is 94 million miles; in January it is 92 million miles. This surprises many people who think that summer is warmer than winter because the earth is closer to the sun in summer. In fact, the sun's radiation is only about 6 percent more intense in January than in July. The apparent diameter of the solar disk changes so little that it is not noticeable without special equipment, but the eccentricity of

217

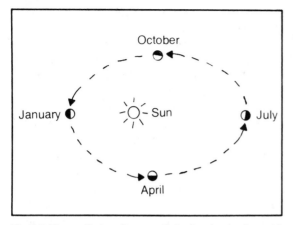

Fig. 7-2. The earth describes an elliptical, not a circular, orbit around the sun. (This illustration is exaggerated.)

tween (but not including) March 20, which is most frequently the first day of spring, and September 23, which is usually the first day of fall, in a nonleap year. There are only 177 days between (but not including) September 23 and March 20, however.

The seasons are caused mainly by the tilt of the earth's axis. The earth's orbit lies in a single plane, known as the *ecliptic plane*. The earth's axis is not perpendicular to the ecliptic. If that were the case, we would always have exactly 12 hours of daylight and 12 hours of darkness; the sun would always follow the celestial equator, rising precisely in the east and setting precisely in the west. There would be no seasons.

The angle between the ecliptic and the earth's axis is about 66½ degrees. Another way of saying this is that the earth is tilted from the perpendicular by 23½ degrees (Fig. 7-3). As the earth revolves around the sun, the northern and southern hemispheres alternately receive more sunlight, then less, because of this tilt. All planets are tilted in this

the earth's orbit does have some effect. The earth moves more slowly when it is farther away from the sun, and more rapidly when the distance is less. Thus, we get a few extra days in the northern hemisphere warm season. There are 186 days be-

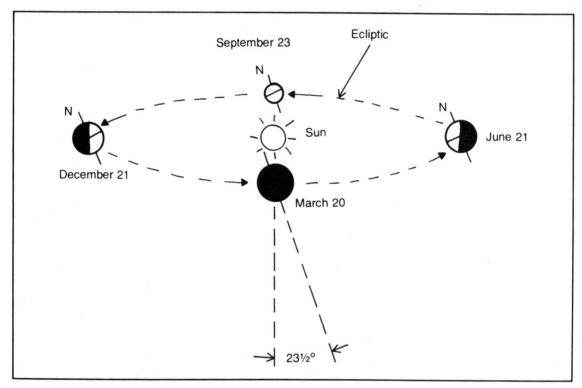

Fig. 7-3. The earth's axis is tilted. This is the primary cause of our seasons.

way, although some (like Jupiter) are tilted less than our planet, and others (like Uranus) have more tilt.

The earth's orbit does not stay exactly the same. In a few thousand years, the earth will be closer to the sun in July than in January. This slow change, insignificant between the birth and death of one human being, is called *precession*. The orientation of the ellipse spins around in space. About 6,500 years ago, the northern hemisphere's warm season was shorter than the cold season, just the reverse of the present situation. The sun was 92 million miles away in the northern hemisphere summer and 94 million miles away in the northern hemisphere winter. The same thing will happen again about 6,500 years from now. Could this affect the climate? Some scientists think so.

The tilt of the earth's axis also changes slightly, just as a top wobbles. At times the tilt is a little greater than it is now; sometimes it is a bit less. The tilt does not change much—only about 1 degree either way of its present extent—but it may affect our climate significantly.

The precession of the earth's orbit, and the wobbling of the axis, have different periods. If both of these phenomena have an influence on climate, then there will be times when their effects add together and times when the effects partially or completely cancel each other. Some climatologists have suggested that when both factors favor cooler weather in the northern hemisphere, a prolonged ice age, lasting hundreds of thousands of years, results. One factor or the other, acting alone, might produce a short-term ice age lasting a few thousand years.

If this theory is correct, we should expect that ice ages would occur at regular intervals throughout history, and this has been verified. Moreover, there appear to be two ice-age cycles superimposed on each other, giving the earth-orbit theory some credibility.

Galactic Plane Theory

Another astronomical phenomenon has been singled out as a possible cause of long-term ice ages. Our sun orbits around the center of the galaxy in much the same way as the earth orbits the sun. Our galaxy lies mostly, but not entirely, in one plane. Seen from a broadside angle, the galaxy looks a little like a hurricane, and the resemblance is more than superficial. Stars are arranged in spiral-shaped "arms," similar to the rain bands in a hurricane. The stars all orbit in the same direction around a highly concentrated central core. Our sun, located in one of the spiral arms near the edge of the galaxy, takes approximately 200 million years to complete one revolution (Fig. 7-4A). Stars nearer the center move faster than the sun, just as the winds blow harder near the center of a hurricane than near the outside.

What has all this got to do with ice ages? As the sun goes around the center of the galaxy, it passes in and out of dust clouds that lie very close to the galactic plane. Seen edgewise, our galaxy looks something like the illustration in Fig. 7-4B. Although the stars are concentrated near the galactic plane (shown as a dotted line), their orbits frequently carry them away from the plane. This is true of the sun, whose orbit is shown by the solid line.

In a spiral galaxy, most of the gas and dust exists in the galactic plane. Therefore, the sun passes through varying concentrations of interstellar matter as it plunges in and out of the plane. Every 100 million years, the amount of interstellar material reaches a peak. Midway between these peaks, it reaches a minimum. Figure 7-5 shows this cycle. Because the earth is about 4½ billion years old, we can figure that there have been about 45 maximums and 45 minimums in the amount of cosmic gas and dust that might have affected our planet.

How much difference does interstellar matter make in the amount of radiation that the earth receives from the sun? We cannot be certain, but some scientists think that the concentration of gas and dust in the galactic plane is sufficient to cause ice ages. We can get some idea of how much interstellar matter there actually is when we realize that if there were none, the center of our galaxy would appear nearly as bright to us as the sun. The intervening matter almost totally obscures our view of the stars near the galactic plane, and espe-

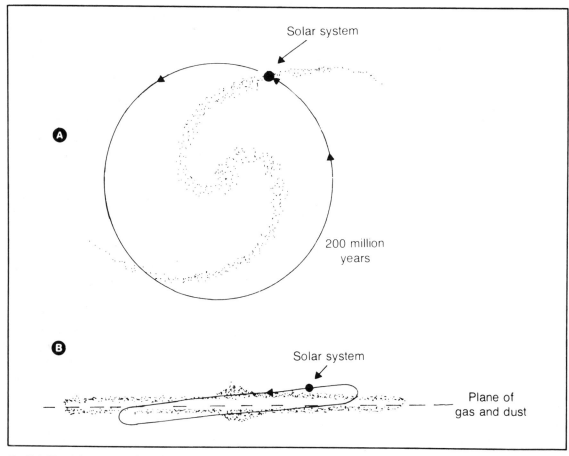

Fig. 7-4. The solar system takes about 200 million years to complete one trip around the Milky Way (A). As the solar system orbits the center of the galaxy, it moves in and out of the plane of gas and dust (B) at intervals of about 100 million years.

cially near the galactic center.

It is possible that the eccentricity of the earth's orbit, the wobbling of its axis, and the amount of interstellar matter all act on our climate. There would be times during which all of these factors would favor cooler weather, resulting in a prolonged and severe ice age.

Solar Radiation Theory

There is yet another possble cosmic reason why the earth has had ice ages: perhaps the sun shines more brightly and generates more heat at some times than at other times. We like to think of our parent star as perfect, but we know today that it isn't. The behavior of the sun is complicated, and

there are things that we still don't understand about it. There is evidence that points to a large-term cycle in the intensity of radiation from the sun.

The sun operates like a huge hydrogen bomb. In the center of the sun, where the temperature is millions of degrees Fahrenheit, hydrogen is converted into helium and energy, but this reaction may not be continuous. It may go on and off at regular intervals. Why would this happen? Astronomers are not certain, but some believe that the sun's temperature is self-regulating, and that the mechanism operates like a thermostat. If the sun starts getting too cool, the furnace (nuclear reaction) is switched on. If things heat up too much, the thermostat stops the reactions. No thermostat is perfect, however. You know that if you set your thermostat at 65 degrees Fahrenheit, the temperature in your house oscillates a degree or two above and below this value. The highest temperature is reached just as the furnace shuts down, and the coolest conditions occur at the moment the furnace goes on. If the sun actually has a thermostat, it probably isn't perfect either.

In 1968, experiments were begun in an effort to verify the existence of a strange kind of particle. Theorists had predicted that massless, tiny subatomic particles, traveling at the speed of light and capable of penetrating the earth in the way light shines through a pane of glass, would be emitted by our sun. These particles, called *neutrinos*, are generated by nuclear fusion reactions.

Neutrinos are hard to detect because they pass through everything so easily. Neutrinos were found in 1968, however, and the only place they could be coming from was space, but something was wrong. According to the calculations of the physicists and astronomers, there should have been a lot more neutrinos than were observed. The sun, they thought, should be the main source of neutrinos in

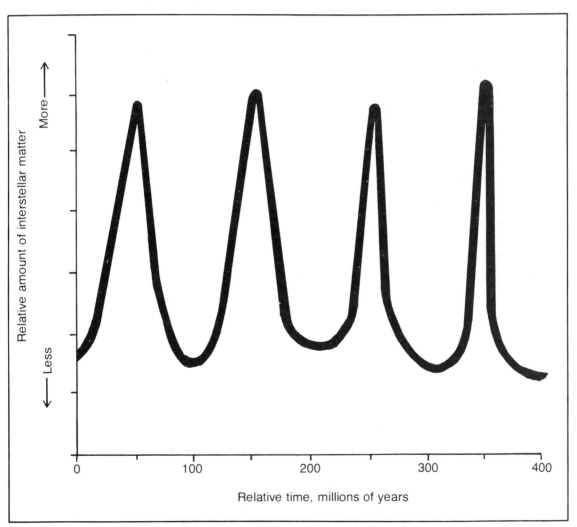

Fig. 7-5. Graph of the amount of matter between the earth and sun as a function of time.

the vicinity of our planet. It appeared that the sun was putting out practically none of the elusive particles. Measurement errors were dismissed as a possible cause of these unexpected results; the equipment had been tested and found to be working properly. It appeared that the center of the sun, from which a barrage of neutrinos was supposed to be coming, was cooler than had been previously thought and that nuclear fusion—the only possible source of solar energy—was not taking place in our parent star.

The only way out of this conflict between theory and experiment was the solar thermostat theory: these days the solar furnace is off. How long has it been off, and when will it start up again? We cannot be sure about that, but if the solar thermostat theory is correct, it might provide an explanation for the occurrence of ice ages. According to the theory, the sun is cooling off right now. The earth's climate was once much warmer than it is today, and perhaps at that time the solar furnace was on. During the ice ages, the solar temperature might have been at a minimum.

Although the solar thermostat theory is a tempting proposition in our effort to unravel the cause of the ice ages, the problem is exceedingly complex. What is the period of the solar radiation cycle? How much does the temperature actually change? These questions must be answered before we know whether or not the solar thermostat theory can explain why we have had ice ages on the earth.

Maverick Star Theory

The stars in our Milky Way do not all move in perfect unison around the center of the galaxy. They move in a random fashion with respect to each other. Besides the sun, the nearest star is about 26 trillion miles away. That is too far for its gravitational field to affect our solar system, but perhaps, long ago, a maverick star came close enough to perturb the orbits of the planets—including the earth.

A tiny change in the earth's orbit would be enough to change the climate greatly. The main problem with the maverick star theory, however, is that the orbital change would be permanent, and the ice ages have always been temporary.

Meteorite Theory

The earth and the eight other known planets are not the only objects that orbit the sun. Millions of chunks of matter, ranging in size from several hundred miles to a fraction of an inch across, swarm around our parent star in orbits of all shapes. Some of these orbits are such that a collision might occur between one of the rocks, known as *meteors,* and the earth.

Meteors enter the earth's atmosphere every day. If it is dark, we can sometimes see the trail of a meteor as it burns up because of friction with the air. Then we say that we have seen a shooting or falling star. Meteors usually vaporize completely before they can reach the ground, but occasionally a large one makes it to the surface, and we call it a *meteorite.* Meteorites have been found everywhere in the world. Some meteorite impacts have been witnessed by people.

Every few thousand years, an especially massive meteorite lands somewhere on our planet. A tremendous explosion occurs, comparable to the detonation of a nuclear bomb. The impact leaves a crater. The famous crater in Arizona, almost a mile in diameter, was formed by a massive meteorite. Other craters have been found and attributed to meteorites.

Very rarely—maybe every few million years—an extremely large meteor, more accurately called an *asteroid,* might strike our planet. The orbit of the earth, the location and tilt of its axis, and the period of rotation might then be altered slightly. Even a very small change in any of these parameters could trigger an ice age or a warm spell.

The meteorite theory is popular among those people who prefer cataclysm to slow change. Statistically, the chances of a major meteorite impact are small over short or moderate periods of time. It is not likely, for example, that we will witness a great cosmic collision within the next few generations, but the earth is billions of years old, and the probability is excellent that there have been several collisions violent enough to have had some effect on the orbit, axis, or rotational speed of our planet.

Meteorites might trigger ice ages by causing geologic disturbances. A violent impact could produce an increase in volcanic activity by upsetting the earth's crust. A long-term rise in volcanism would put more dust into the atmosphere, reducing the amount of solar heat reaching the earth. If this persisted long enough, an ice age could ensue.

Volcanism Theory

Volcanic eruptions have occurred throughout recorded history. We can be affected, even today, by the eruption of a volcano. Mount Saint Helens has provided us with an excellent example of how helpless we can be when a mountain blows up. Whole cities can be destroyed: Pompeii, in the ancient Roman empire, was utterly eliminated by a single eruption of Mount Vesuvius. The nineteenth-century eruption of Krakatoa produced oceanic shock waves that circled the earth. As we have seen, a single volcanic eruption might cause a short-term change in the climate of the whole world.

There is evidence that the general level of volcanism does not remain constant. If this is true, then a long-term change in volcanic activity could precipitate a long-term change in the earth's climate.

Why would volcanism increase or decrease for centuries or millenia? There are several possible reasons. A meteorite impact could, as previously mentioned, cause an increase. Gravitational disturbances might also have an effect.

In recent years there has been concern among some people that the alignment of the planets could trigger earthquakes and perhaps also volcanic eruptions. (Extremists cried that this cosmic event would cause California to slide into the Pacific Ocean, but then, that kind of talk has been going on ever since the pioneers got there.) The planets do not align very often—there are nine of them, all with different orbital periods—and it is possible that ice ages could have been triggered by this kind of astronomical coincidence. A star, passing unusually close to the solar system, might also produce tidal forces sufficient to cause an increase in volcanism.

Mountain Theory

Before and during the age of the dinosaurs, there were not many mountains. The terrain was relatively flat, and mountain-produced weather effects were practically nonexistent. According to some scientists, the continents were joined into one almost contiguous mass. Gradually, the continents moved apart, with the earth's crust literally floating over the more viscous material beneath.

For the Cambrian period of the Paleozoic age, about 100 million years ago, the region roughly corresponding to present-day North America has been given the name *Laurentia*. A huge continent, spanning most of the South Atlantic and Indian oceans of today, has been called *Gondwanaland*. Near present-day Siberia, a small island continent is believed to have existed; geologists call it *Angara*. Europe and Asia were much smaller than they are today, but the scientists have decided that their names haven't changed.

The continents gradually changed shape and position over the next million of years. The unrest was accompanied by the formation of mountains. In the United States, the Appalachians were formed during a period that was followed by an ice age known as the Permian. At that time, the Appalachians were much higher than they are today; they resembled the Rockies and Himalayas. The younger Rockies and Himalayas formed later, along with the Andes, the Pyrenees, and other ranges. The Pleistocene ice age followed.

Some scientists think that the formation of mountains is linked to the onset of an ice age. Mountains alter the flow of the prevailing winds and can produce a change in the locations of cold and warm regions on the earth. Atop high mountains, snow falls all year long, even in the summer. Snow-capped mountains such as the Andes (Fig. 7-6) are necessary for the formation and movement of glaciers, and the ice ages have been characterized by massive glaciation. The movement of glaciers is responsible for many of the land features

Fig. 7-6. One ice age theory holds that mountains, and mountain formation, result in periodic glaciation. This photograph shows the tall, fairly young Andes, seen from space (courtesy NASA).

we see today at middle and high latitudes. The myriad lakes of Minnesota and Wisconsin, for example, were left by glaciers from the most recent ice age.

According to George Gamow, a famous cosmologist and earth scientist, ice ages are the result of general cooling in conjunction with an accumulation of ice in the mountains. When the ice becomes thick enough, it spreads into the lowlands, producing the huge glaciers that cover sizable portions of the continents. According to Gamow, a mountain-building period is going on right now, and this might provide one of the ingredients for another ice age in the future. [1]

Ross Ice Shelf Theory

The continent of Antarctica is almost entirely covered by ice, a vast region of the sea surrounding Antarctica is peppered with icebergs, and McMurdo Sound is overlaid with a massive ice shelf. The reason why this ice shelf has formed is something of a mystery, but one thing is clear: a great deal of water is locked up in this huge ocean glacier, known as the Ross Ice Shelf. It is as large as France and 1,000 feet thick. If this ice shelf were to break free of the continent and float into the warmer waters to the north, the level of the world's oceans would be raised considerably. It could have a profound effect on the weather everywhere on the earth.

There is evidence to suggest that the Ross Ice Shelf has been built up over a period of thousands of years. It is possible that it may someday separate from Antarctica and float into the ocean. A new ice

[1] Wendt, Herbert, *Before the Deluge* (Doubleday & Company, Inc., 1968), pp. 171-175.

shelf might start building up, replacing the old one, and when it got too big to be supported by the continent, it too would break away. This cycle may have repeated numerous times in past ages.

What would happen if the Ross Ice Shelf did move away from Antarctica and cause a rise in the sea level? Much of the low-lying land areas of the world, such as the Atlantic coastal plain of the United States, would be submerged. Jet stream patterns would be altered over North America. Could this trigger an ice age, or would the climate get warmer?

If the Ross Ice Shelf repeatedly builds up and breaks free from Antarctica, how much bigger will it get before the catastrophe happens? It is hard to say, but if the shelf were to lock up significantly more sea water than it now contains, the ocean level would drop. It could have a pronounced effect on the climate in the northern hemisphere if it caused the Bering Strait, the narrow gap between Alaska and Siberia, to close. Ocean currents would then be prevented from passing between the Pacific and Arctic Oceans. The position of the north Pacific semipermanent high would be altered, resulting in a shift of the jet stream over North America. If the jet stream shifted just a few degrees of latitude toward the south, the climate would be much colder than it is today over the United States and Canada. Conversely, if the jet stream were to move northward, the climate would get much warmer in many places.

The mechanics of the Ross Ice Shelf are still largely a mystery. Until we learn more about its behavior, we cannot be certain of its potential effects on past and future world climate.

Oscillation Theory

The fact that there have been many ice ages, spaced at intervals of several thousand years, suggests another possible reason for their occurrence. Perhaps something in the earth's ocean-atmosphere system simply oscillates. This could happen in the absence of any geologic or cosmic changes, because oscillation is a common natural phenomenon resulting from the alternate storage and release of energy.

Imagine a long, flexible spring, hanging from the ceiling, with a heavy weight at the bottom. If the spring is left alone in a state of equilibrium, the weight will not move. If the weight is displaced upward or downward for any reason, however, the spring-weight system will oscillate (Fig. 7-7A). Neglecting the effects of friction, the weight will continue to move up and down indefinitely.

A pendulum provides another example of the oscillation effect. When the pendulum hangs straight down, it does not move, but if it is pulled to one side, it oscillates (Fig. 7-7B). As with the spring, if there is no friction, the oscillation will continue forever.

Some sort of oscillation, similar to that of a spring or pendulum, could occur in the earth's ocean-atmosphere heat engine. There might be essentially no "friction;" warm climate might cause cold climate later, and cold climate might subsequently produce warm climate, indefinitely. Nature would thereby maintain a reasonable balance. The tendency would be toward moderation rather than toward runaway cooling or warming. If we think for a moment, nature must keep such a balance, for otherwise the slightest change in any climate-related factor would precipitate "climatic runaway." The earth would end up like Venus or Mars.

If the oscillation theory is valid, we have to ask ourselves what would cause the initial imbalance. It could be almost anything, such as the precession of the earth's orbit, the wobbling of its axis, or a cosmic event such as a meteorite impact. Perhaps the earth just turned out with a built-in imbalance. We must also ask ourselves how the energy is stored and released—the mechanics of nature's "pendulum." Right now, that is a mystery.

What Is a Glacier?

All of the ice ages have been characterized by glaciation of a large part of the northern hemisphere. Even today, glaciers exist in some of the world's mountainous regions.

Glaciers take a long time to form from snow. For a glacier to develop, the climate must be sufficiently cold so that snow does not melt completely during the summer months. In mountainous areas, this requirement is met primarily because of the altitude, although in Greenland, northern Alaska, Siberia, and Antarctica, there is some snow all year round.

As snow continues to accumulate, more falling than melting each year, the snow is compressed at the bottom of the pack. The individual flakes and crystals lose their identity, and the volume is reduced as the air spaces disappear. Eventually the snow is squeezed so tightly that it becomes ice: not the clear ice that you get in your Martini "on the rocks," but a white, hard mass. Winds blow snow off the craggy peaks of the mountain and into the passes and crevices, increasing the accumulation there. The ice pack becomes deeper and heavier, and a glacier has formed.

We normally think of ice as inflexible and even brittle. You cannot, for example, bend an icicle noticeably without breaking it. On a small scale, ice is like glass, but on a large scale, and over a long period of time, things are quite different. Let's ignore the scaling laws of physics for a moment and suppose that you were a giant a mile tall, and you perceived a year as a minute. Then glaciers would appear vicious to you. Ice would behave a lot like thick molasses. Glaciers literally flow like rivers, except they are many times larger and much slower than rivers of liquid water (or even of the thickest molasses). They still flow, however, and, given enough time, they can eventually cover vast areas of the earth.

If snow accumulates enough to form a glacier and then continues to build up on a mountain as the glacier inches forward, the land at lower altitudes will gradually be swallowed up by the glacier. Eventually the front of the glacier will encounter a climate warm enough to halt its progress; the rate of melting will exactly balance the forward speed of the glacier (Fig. 7-8).

If the rate of snowfall increases along with a cooling trend in the climate, the glacier will move farther and faster. The equilibrium point will move to a lower elevation. If there is still more snow and a still cooler climate, the glacier may move out of the mountain entirely and begin to invade the plains below. This is evidently what has happened numerous times in the earth's past. There is an excellent chance that the most recent glacial invasion was not the last.

The Next Ice Age

It is not my purpose here to support or refute any of these theories concerning ice ages, but only to call attention to the complexity of the problem. The mystery of the ice ages is so complicated, in fact, that we might be tempted to throw up our hands in exasperation and say, "Who cares? Why should we worry about it?" There is a specific answer to that: mankind might have to face another ice age. We need to know if that will happen, and if so, when. We will have to prepare for it.

Many scientists believe that we are in a short-term interglacial age today, and that the long-term cycle favors cool climate. For several billion years, the earth's climate has, they think, been similar to the Pleistocene climate, with glaciers alternately advancing and retreating. At present, there are mountains with glaciers moving forward, and mountains with glaciers that are retreating. It would seem that the period of general glacial retreat is over, but that the major thrust forward has not yet begun.

Fortunately, ice ages don't just start up instantly. It takes hundreds of years for conditions to change that much. Assuming that the interglacial-age adherents are correct, and we are indeed heading for another ice age in a few millenia, what will we observe in the coming centuries? Let's try to imagine the weather and climate in North America as an ice age approaches and establishes itself.

There will probably not be much of a difference until about 3000 A.D. At that time, winters will begin to get more severe, especially in the mountains. The last snows of the season in the northern United States will occur in late May or even early June. The Great Lakes will freeze up every year, as they did in the worst winters of the twentieth century (Fig. 7-9). In the southern United States, snow will regularly fall as far south as south-central Texas and the Gulf Coast states with the exception of Florida. Southern Florida will experience more

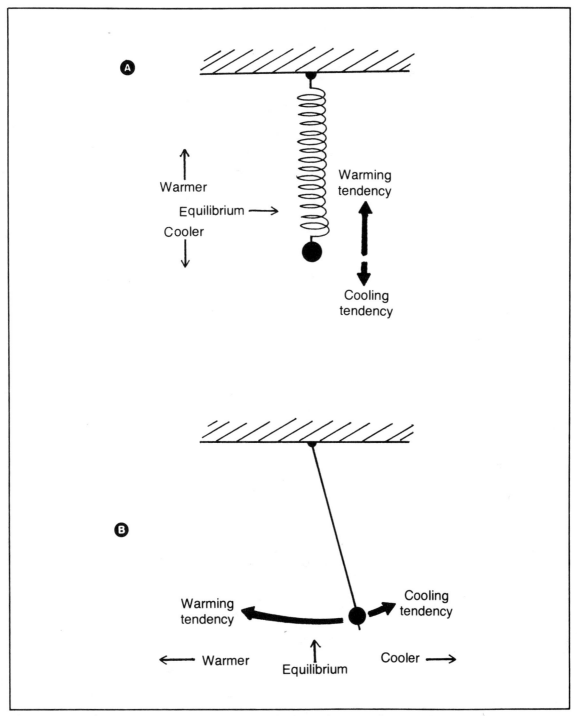

Fig. 7-7. Perhaps the ice ages result from simple climatic oscillation. Here, two models are shown to illustrate how cool climate might eventually produce warm, and vice versa. At A, the spring-and-weight model; at B, the pendulum model.

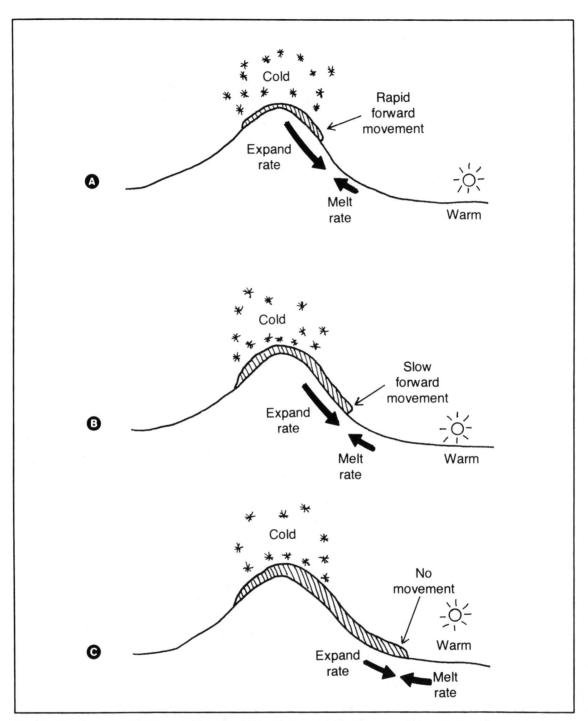

Fig. 7-8. Glaciers expand until the rate of melting is equal to the rate of enlargement. At first (A), the glacier moves forward rapidly. As time progresses, the rate of expansion slows (B) until it finally stops (C) as the rate of melting balances the rate of expansion.

Fig. 7-9. During severe winters, the Great Lakes become partly frozen. The markings in this satellite photograph can be ignored (courtesy U.S. Department of Commerce NOAA).

freezes during the winter, and cold fronts will send a shiver down the peninsula at regular intervals from November through April or May. Similar changes will be observed in Europe and Asia. There will be essentially no change in the equatorial climate.

By 4000 A.D., winters in some parts of the United States will last well into May, and light snow will be possible during any month of the year. Frost will occur on at least one day in every month. The general weather will resemble conditions in 1816. A decided shift in glacial behavior will be noticed: they will all be inching forward as they increase in weight. None will be retreating.

By 5000 A.D., the climate will have become so severe that blizzards will occur in the northern United States at all times of the year. Agricultural belts will have moved south. The glaciers will have

increased their rate of advance, and cities will begin to disappear. In Canada, the glaciers will cover some of the high prairies in the west. Palm trees will have vanished from places such as southern California, Arizona, and Florida.

The climate will continue to grow colder, and the glaciers will keep on advancing. Finally, by about 9000 A.D., a large part of North America will be glaciated, as it has been during previous ice ages (Fig. 7-10). Temperatures will be winterlike, even during the summer, in the icy regions. At last, the equilibrium point will be reached—the rate of melting at the glacial front will exactly balance the rate of advance—and the high point of the ice age will have arrived. Mankind might then look forward to an eventual reversal, and an ultimate return, in a hundred centuries or so, to the ideal conditions that prevailed when world wars were popular.

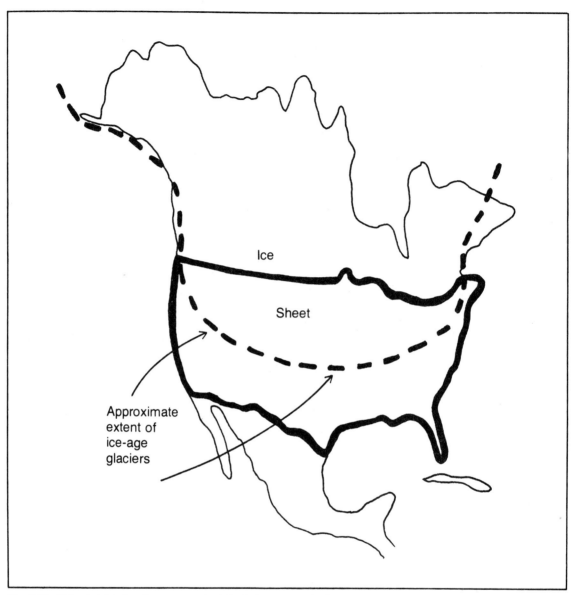

Fig. 7-10. At the height of an ice age, much of North America is glaciated.

The foregoing scenario is, of course, hypothetical. Or is it?

Preventing It

Technology has advanced more since 1800 than during all of the previous history of man. We have learned how to control many aspects of nature—even, to some extent, the weather. Our control has sometimes been deliberate, and often it has been accidental. We are slowly learning, however, how our activities might affect the climate of our planet, and given a few millenia, we may be able to get rid of the accidental effects and make them deliberate. Perhaps we can stop the next ice age from coming—bump the climatic pendulum in our favor!

Various ways of preventing an ice age have already been considered by scientists throughout the world. One idea is to deliberately alter the ocean currents. The Russians have suggested damming the Bering Strait, preventing cold Arctic waters from invading the Pacific Ocean. The United States and Canada have been skeptical, however, of what the effects might be in North America. Although the climate in North America is variable (as it is everywhere else), conditions are generally good for food growing. If the Pacific gets warmer, the jet stream might move south over the continent, shortening the growing season, or it might move north, causing expansion of the southwestern deserts and reducing the amount of rainfall over vast regions.

Some climatologists think that we may already be doing things that will not only prevent global cooling in the future, but actually cause global warming. The burning of fossil fuels produces, among other things, carbon dioxide, which helps to trap heat in the atmosphere. There has not yet been a noticeable change in the earth's climate since the beginning of the fossil fuel era, but it is possible there eventually will be. If another ice age threatens, we certainly won't want to burn great vats of gasoline all over the world to raise the level of carbon dioxide in the air, but there are other ways to raise it. We could probably invent a simple way to make carbon dioxide: the earth has plenty of carbon and plenty of oxygen for this purpose.

Another method of warming the earth would be to change the *albedo*, or reflectivity, of our planet. Albedo is a term familiar to astronomers. It is expressed as a number between 0 (no reflection) to 1 (total reflection), or a percentage from 0 to 100. A very dark object has a low albedo; a bright object has a high albedo. Clouds reflect much of the energy from the sun, as do snow fields and ice caps. Only about one-third of the sun's light and heat reaches the surface, and of this, about nine-tenths is absorbed. We might change either factor to increase the temperature of our planet. The reflectivity of the atmosphere could be changed by reducing the cloud cover; how we could (or if we should) do that is far from certain, but the albedo of the surface could be increased by making it darker.

One method of reducing the albedo of the earth's surface has already been suggested: sprinkling graphite or some other black powder in unpopulated regions such as deserts or the polar ice caps. It would take a tremendous amount of manpower, however, besides a ridiculous amount of the black stuff, to make a significant difference. Besides, a single snowfall would cover up the material and render it ineffective. Not only that, but we must consider the possibility that blackening, say, Antarctica would actually cool the planet by increasing heat loss. A dark object does absorb more available radiant energy than a light object—but conversely, dark surfaces also radiate energy more efficiently in the absence of an external source. During times of darkness, we would not be getting what we wanted, but just the opposite.

Another way to increase the temperature of the earth is by directing more solar energy toward our planet. This could be done by building massive reflectors in space, designed to direct extra sunlight at certain parts of the world. Now that we have the space shuttle, and astronauts have repaired satellites in space and are considering the construction of a space station, that notion is within reason.

Perhaps the most direct method of heating the earth is to do it directly, by means of heat "factories." The only problem is that we already face an energy crisis. We will have to resolve that before thinking about preventing an ice age.

Geothermal energy might provide the solution. Controlled nuclear fusion might also be used, if a fusion reactor has been perfected by then, and if the radiation hazard can be avoided.

Despite all of the gloom-and-doom talk about the threat of another ice age, we should think twice about trying to prevent its onset should the warning signs begin. Although our technology has advanced immeasurably and will continue to advance, it would be presumptuous of humans to ever assume that they knew better than Nature itself what is best for this planet.

Deliberate global warming might have effects more destructive than the ice age itself. The level of the oceans might rise, for example, inundating major population centers such as New York and Tokyo. Temperature distribution, precipitation patterns, and other factors would be affected in ways that would be very difficult, or impossible, to foretell. One final possibility must also be considered: that global warming would not prevent, but in fact would actually cause, another ice age by precipitating some unforeseen natural reaction.

We might be better off letting the ice age come, migrating toward the equator as necessary. Hopefully by the time we are faced with the decision of whether or not we ought to try to prevent an ice age, we will have not only the technology to take action, but the wisdom to do the right thing—even if that means doing nothing.

WEATHER AND CLIMATE MODIFICATION

We have all heard the saying, "Everybody talks about the weather, but nobody does anything about it." It is not strictly true: weather and climate modification have been not only discussed, but attempted, occasionally with apparent success. Sometimes weather/climate modification is done accidentally, and sometimes it is done on purpose. Here are a few examples.

Cloud Seeding

During times of drought, various substances can be added to clouds to increase the chance of precipitation. Dry ice and silver iodide, in powder form, have been sprayed from airplanes or fired from ground-based apparatus. The idea is to produce condensation of water droplets large enough to fall as rain, rather than remaining suspended in the cloud. Results have been promising, but not entirely conclusive; the process often, but not always, seems to work.

Cloud seeding has been used in an effort to reduce the intensity of the winds in the eyewalls of some hurricanes. In some cases the wind speed has diminished by a few percent after seeding. In hurricane Betsy in 1965, seeding was followed by a strange and unexpected course change that brought the storm over the Florida Keys into the Gulf of Mexico when she had been expected to recurve into

the open Atlantic. A few people blamed the course change on the seeding, although the scientific evidence points to natural causes.

The benefits of cloud seeding must be weighed against the potential for harm. If rain is produced in one place, rain might be robbed from another place. Seeding of hurricanes might have unexpected, potentially harmful consequences, such as increased flooding of low-lying areas.

Hail Control

Hail is responsible for great damage to crops and personal property each year. As early as about 1900, farmers, in conjunction with scientists, were attempting to control or alter hail. Because most hail damage is caused by fairly large hailstones, the most common method of hail control has been aimed at reducing the size of the stones.

One early hail control scheme was an attempt to break up the stones, or to get them to fall before they got very big. Blanks were fired from cannons to generate shock waves that might effect this. Later, rockets were shot into hail clouds; perhaps the disturbance would send the hail earthward while the stones were still small. Neither of these methods seemed to do anything except cost money and make a lot of noise.

More recently, cloud seeding has been tried in an effort to interfere with the hail-formation process. Several different countries have used this method, and some believe that it works well enough to be cost effective. The Russians have claimed a high rate of hail-control success—over 80 percent—using artillery to fire shells filled with silver iodide crystals into cumulonimbus clouds (Fig. 7-11). While there is some scientific merit to the cloud seeding theory, and there is reason to think the method has helped somewhat, the results claimed by the Soviets have not yet been reproduced anywhere else. This has led to some skepticisms about their findings, although farmers worldwide would certainly like to believe them.

Fog Control

Clouds form when the temperature falls to, or below, the dew point. Normally this happens at a

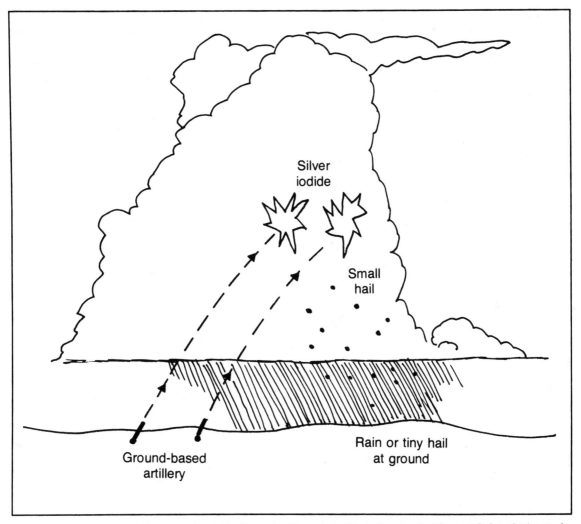

Fig. 7-11. One method of hail suppression is the firing of artillery shells filled with silver-iodide crystals into the heart of a hail-producing cloud.

certain height above the ground, but not on the ground. Occasionally, however, conditions are such that the base or ceiling of a cloud is at the surface. Then we have fog. Fog has contributed to many accidents in aviation and highway travel ever since people began speeding around in airplanes and high-performance motor vehicles. Fog has plagued mariners ever since the first boat floated on the sea.

How might we get rid of fog? Would it be worth the effort and expense? Airlines think that dispers-

ing or burning off fog would save more money than it would cost by reducing the number of cancelled or delayed flights. In harbors, fog dispersal might also be cost effective. The two primary methods of dealing with fog has been to raise the temperature to a level higher than the dew point, and to attempt to literally blow the fog away with gigantic fans, propeller airplanes, or helicopters. Both methods have met with some success. If the fog layer is thin enough, fans disperse it by mixing the foggy air with clear air above (Fig. 7-12A). If the fog layer is very deep, heaters at ground level can raise the ceiling several yards above the surface (Fig. 7-12B).

Deforestation and Reforestation

A tree is an effective air conditioner and also a producer of oxygen. The removal or addition of large numbers of trees can radically alter the climate in a localized area. It is possible that, on a worldwide scale, a sizable change in the tree population could alter the climate of the entire planet.

Deforestation has occurred in many places where man has moved. A good contemporary example is one of the last frontiers in the world: the Amazon river basin. In that region, the soil is poor for farming, but civilization is doing its best to move in anyway. If enough trees are removed from that rain forest, the climate could change drastically. The land's water-holding capacity would be reduced, and the rain forest climate would turn drier. The intertropical convergence zone might shift to the north or south over South America. A similar situation exists in central Africa.

In many parts of the world where lumbering is the major trade, active reforestation programs have been implemented. For every tree cut down, a new one is planted. This is known as *tree farming;* the idea is to replenish the lumber supply so we won't eventually run out of wood. Reforestation has

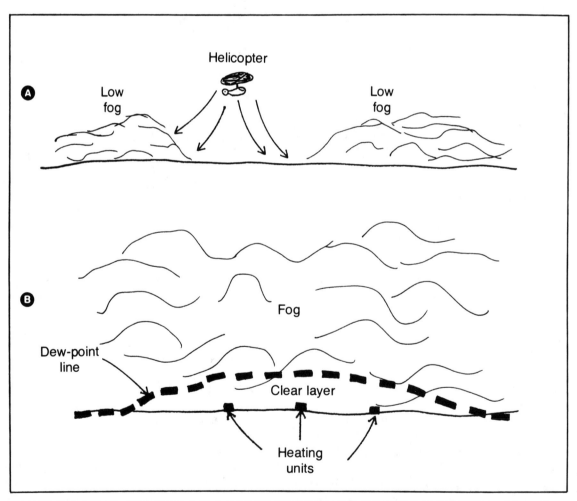

Fig. 7-12. Two methods of fog dispersal. At A, low fog is blown away; at B, higher fog is burned off from underneath.

another, perhaps more important function, however; it helps nature put back what people have taken away. If this was not done, vast areas, previously wooded, would be devoid of trees. This could change the impact over a region hundreds of times larger than the deforested area itself. Rainfall and temperature distribution patterns would probably be altered, and topsoil might be blown away by surface winds of increased speed.

If enough trees are removed from the world, say some scientists, there could be a significant effect on the amounts of oxygen and carbon dioxide in the atmosphere. Trees convert carbon dioxide into oxygen. So efficient is this process that plants have been seriously suggested as oxygen-making apparatus on board space vessels of the future. We have already seen what might happen if the atmospheric carbon dioxide concentration were to rise. If such a change were accompanied by a large-scale loss of trees, the tendency for climatic change might be accentuated. Previously fertile land would, perhaps, become desertified. In some places, this process is already underway.

Desertification

The world's deserts appear to be generally expanding, probably because of natural climatic changes. When a desert expands relentlessly into surrounding, less arid regions, the process is called *desertification*. The desert literally invades nearby land, just as a rising ocean swallows up low-lying terrain (Fig. 7-13). Agriculture is driven out, and because most of the world's societies depend on farming, the people are forced to move. In Africa, expanding deserts have led to mass migrations with resulting quarrels among the affected nations. On an extreme, worldwide scale, desertification could lead to major wars.

Some desertification, certainly an unintentional form of climate modification, is the result of the activities of people. The process goes something like this on a small scale: we decide to put a residential development on semiarid land; trees are cut down and other types of vegetation removed to make room for streets, sidewalks, parking lots, shopping centers, and houses. The albedo and

water-retaining characteristics change; the temperature rises, and the relative humidity falls; the hotter, drier climate affects vegetation in surrounding areas. The residential community is a man-made "desert seed," planted in a desertification-prone area. The man-made desert expands into the natural desert. Multiply this small-scale desertification process by a few hundred, and the result is a major problem.

Man-made desertification can perhaps be prevented by appropriately designing cities and residential areas when they are built in desertification-prone places. If the proper measures are taken, it might in fact be possible to undesertify large regions by modifying the local climate in a way that would favor the growth of vegetation. This has already been done in parts of the southwestern United States.

The Effects of Landscape Modification

Sometimes it is difficult for us to tell exactly how our activities affect the local climate. We can get some idea of the effects of cities and landscape alterations by means of infrared photographs taken from airplanes or from space.

Infrared photography is a fairly old art; using special film, ordinary cameras can be used to take infrared pictures. The energy efficiency of a building or house can be ascertained by means of this technique; in cold weather, "hot spots" on the photograph indicate places where energy is leaking. In some municipalities, infrared photographs have been taken from airplanes, allowing each homeowner to see how much heat is radiated by the roof of his house. On a larger scale, infrared photography may provide a way for us to figure out how we can optimize our environment without reverting to the Stone Age.

An infrared photograph, when taken from space, gives a view of a large area all at once. Figure 7-14 shows two examples. The San Francisco Bay area (A) and the California Imperial Valley (B) are highly developed parts of the United States west coast. In the photographs, the dark areas are the hottest, and the light areas are the coolest. The darker regions radiate more heat into

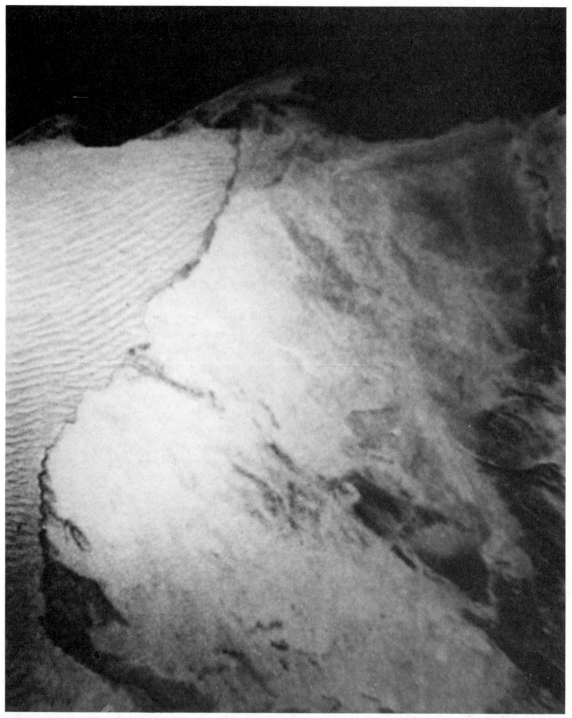

Fig. 7-13. A desert creeps into less arid regions. The boundary line is visible near the center; sand dunes can be seen at left (courtesy NASA).

space, conduct more heat into the air near the surface, and result in more intense thermal updrafts than the lighter areas.

The environment at San Francisco is considerably different from that in the Imperial Valley, as can be seen from the photographs. In San Francisco, developed areas are represented by lighter shades; they absorb less solar heat than the surrounding countryside. In the Imperial Valley, the populated places appear dark because they absorb more solar heat than the desert sand, which is nearly white in color. The activities of people can be expected to have different small-scale climatic effects in the Imperial Valley, as compared with the San Francisco area. Precisely what these effects are, and what we can do to make them more desirable or undesirable, will have to be learned from experience and from continued scientific research. This is true not only for San Francisco and the Imperial Valley, but for every place where human beings settle.

Man-made Disaster

One of the most frightening climate modification activities, according to scientists like Carl Sagan, would be the unthinkable, but dangerously possible, global nuclear war. A large-scale nuclear holocaust would do more than just kill about 100 million people in the United States within the span of a few minutes. The fallout would, say the scientists, cool the planet by reducing the amount of solar light and heat reaching the surface. The effect would be similar to that of thousands of volcanoes all erupting at the same time. This cooling could perhaps bring on a prolonged ice age by upsetting the fragile balance of nature.

We all harbor in the backs of our minds our own versions of the nuclear nightmare. As we sip cool drinks on a summer evening, sirens begin to wail. We switch on the radio, rather casually, and hear the unbelievable announcement that an all-out attack has been launched by the "other side." We have about 30 minutes before all of our major cities will be destroyed by temperatures hotter than the interior of a broiler oven and winds of the speed of sound. We run to the basement and cower, waiting

for the brilliant flash that signifies the end. It comes. The shock wave levels our home. Perhaps we live, or maybe we die.

Researchers have said that about half the population of the United States would die in a nuclear holocaust. But what about the rest? What kind of environment would be left to them? Apparently the survivors would have to endure worldwide freezing as well as radioactivity. The ironic thing about it is that the "nuclear winter" would, in fact, be a worldwide phenomenon. A country's own nuclear weapons would contribute to its climatic ruin.

A typical nuclear bomb releases about the same amount of energy as 10 million tons of dynamite. Today's fantastic weapons are a thousand times more powerful than those that leveled Hiroshima and Nagasaki in 1945. A detonation near the ground would dig a crater as much as ¼ mile wide and 200 feet deep. All of the earth previously contained in this crater would be circulated around the globe, some of it staying aloft for months or even years. In an all-out nuclear war, several hundred such explosions would take place. The prevailing winds would carry the radioactive fallout all over the northern hemisphere.

Once the cooling began, according to the "nuclear winter" proponents, there would be more snow, and existing snow packs would melt more slowly than before. This would increase the albedo of the earth to such an extent that the cooling would persist long after the fallout had settled to the surface. Previously absorbed solar energy would be reflected back into space; cooling would beget cooling. The ice age induced by the nuclear war might last a hundred years, or perhaps a hundred centuries.

WHAT TO EXPECT BY THE YEAR 2000

Assuming that the scenario just described does not take place, what will our climate be like by the year 2000? Long-term climatic change is of scientific interest, but people have a tendency to care less about conditions a millenium from now than about events that will take place within their own lifetimes. Most of us will be alive in the year 2000, and climatic changes that occur by then are of immediate concern.

Ⓐ

Fig. 7-14. Infrared photographs, taken from space, show the difference in heat distribution around San Francisco Bay, at A, as compared with the Imperial Valley, at B (courtesy NASA).

238

B

239

In 1977, as winters seemed to be getting colder and summers more hot and dry, the National Defense University conducted a study to determine the likelihood of various climatic changes between then and the end of the century. Of special concern were temperature change, precipitation variability, and fluctuations in the length of the growing season. The project was conceived by Joseph W. Willett, of the United States Department of Agriculture. A panel of scientists was asked various questions concerning climatic change, both natural and man-made. The responses were tallied and analyzed.

The predicted possible temperature changes, along with the probability for each, are shown in the graphs of Fig. 7-15. Opinions varied considerably for climate in both hemispheres and at all latitudes. Some scientists predicted no change at all, while others thought our globe would warm up or cool down by as much as 5 degrees Celsius (9 degrees Fahrenheit). Overall, the consensus was that a slight warming will occur all over the world by the year 2000. This can be seen by noting that the areas under the curves are somewhat greater on the "warmer" side than on the "colder" side of each graph. The main factor was the expected increase in atmospheric carbon dioxide.

The panelists' opinions were more diverse for the polar regions than for any other part of the world. In Fig. 7-15, the probability distribution is low and flat for the highest latitudes and becomes more narrow for progressively lower latitudes. Some panelists believed that the poles would get much warmer, possibly resulting in a rise of the sea level because of ice cap melting.

The scientists were also asked what they thought would happen to the length of the growing season between now and the end of the twentieth century. Three possible scenarios were presented: an increase of at least 10 days, a decrease of at least 10 days, and a change of less than 10 days either way. Figure 7-16 shows the results based on five temperature-change scenarios: large cooling (LC), moderate cooling (MC), static (S), moderate warming (MW), and large warming (LW). While the panelists disagreed on what would take place, their individual opinions were based mainly on what they thought would happen to the global temperature. Global warming, they concluded, would prolong the growing season; global cooling would shorten it.

Because global warming seems more likely than global cooling, we might be lucky enough to experience a slight increase in the length of the growing season. Before we get overconfident, however, we have to consider other factors. For example, global warming might cause a reduction in the amount of arable land if deserts expand poleward, or if the sea level rises a few feet. Then, even if the growing season did become longer, we might still have less food to eat. Agricultural belts will certainly shift if the climate changes significantly. This could augment a lengthening of the growing season, or it could offset it.

One of the most important climatic factors is the extent to which precipitation varies from year to year. Droughts are more likely in areas where the amount of precipitation fluctuates greatly, as compared to areas where the rainfall is relatively constant. The panelists had some specific statements to make regarding precipitation variability as a function of global cooling or warming:

". . . A temperature change per se does not imply increased climatic variability . . ."
". . . Precipitation variability is probably generally greatest during cooling periods and least during warming periods . . ."
". . . Since my inference is for temperatures as warm, or warmer, than now by 2000, the precipitation variability should not tend to increase. Precipitation variability is likely to increase overall in association with decreasing amounts . . ."
". . . Decreasing temperature trend will bring more variability . . ."
". . . It seems intuitively reasonable that a decrease in the equator-pole temperature gradient could cause a more "summertime" condition and less variability . . ."

From this, and the preference of the panelists for a slight global warming scenario, we can surmise that

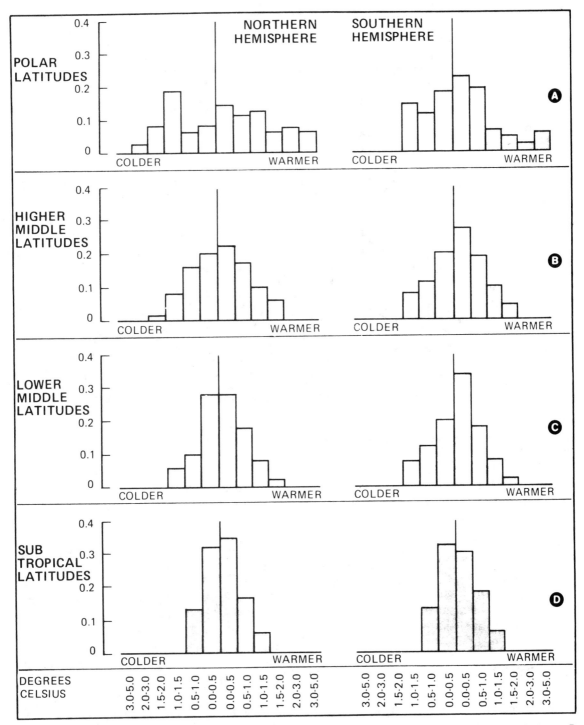

Fig. 7-15. Expected change in mean temperature for various parts of the world by the year 2000. At A, polar latitudes; at B, higher middle latitudes; at C, lower middle latitudes; at D, sub-tropical latitudes (after NOAA/National Defense University).

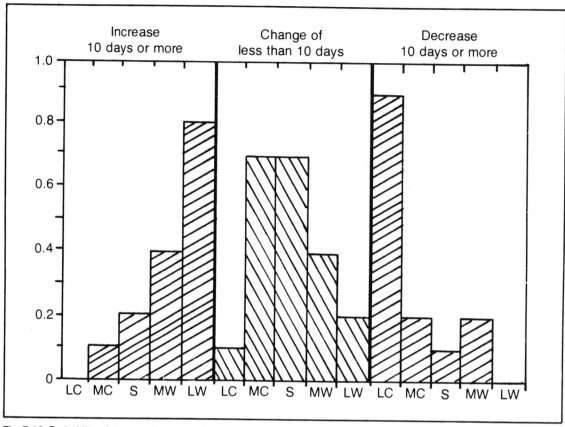

Fig. 7-16. Probability of changes in the growing season as a function of temperature change by the year 2000. Abbreviations are as follows: LC = large cooling; MS = moderate cooling; S = static; MW = moderate warming; LW = large warming (after NOAA/National Defense University).

our precipitation may become less variable by the year 2000. As two panelists pointed out, however, it's not necessarily that simple:

"... I do not expect any radical changes. The variability is induced by extreme events. A single tropical storm rainfall (has a considerable influence) . . ."

"... Probability of certain extreme events might be more important (than general warming or cooling) . . ."*

TRIAL BY FIRE

There may be uncertainty about short-term, medium-term, and long-term climatic trends, but when it comes to the extreme distant future, global warming is inevitable. This is guaranteed by fundamental changes that will occur in the structure of our parent star.

According to contemporary astronomers, the sun has at least several hundred million, and probably over a billion, more years' worth of hydrogen fuel remaining with which to produce energy at a constant rate. The sun is not infinitely large, however. Every second, some of its hydrogen is converted into helium by nuclear fusion. When the supply starts to run low, the sun will expand. The surface temperature of the sun will cool, but the diameter will increase. This will cause a gradual, but inexorable, warming of the earth.

---

* From *Climate Change to the Year 2000* (National Defense University, 1978), pp. 50-51.

Carl Sagan graphically describes the death of the sun, and the effects it will have on our planet, in his book *Cosmos*. There will be a "last perfect day" before the onset of climatic change. The effects will appear almost imperceptible at first: shorter winters, probably an increase in rainfall, and an acceleration of storm activity. More hurricanes will rage across the oceans, and the maelstroms will reach progressively higher latitudes. The tornado season will begin earlier each year. The polar ice caps, if they still exist by the "last perfect day," will begin to melt, and the oceans will rise hundreds of feet. The locations of the jungles, savannas, steppes, farmlands, and deserts will shift.

The final storms on our planet will be more violent than any since its birth. The seas, lakes, and rivers will boil. The wind will blow hot and wild as the atmosphere escapes into space. Volcanic and seismic activity will probably shake our planet and flood it with molten rock. The scene will truly resemble many people's visions of the Judgement Day, but these final storms will not be the result of the wrath of God or any other supreme being. They will be a natural consequence of the death of a medium-sized star. On a cosmic scale, the event will be inconsequential, and it could be far more violent. Many astonomers believe that if the sun were about half again as large as it actually is, it would explode abruptly in a cataclysm known as a *supernova*. In that case, we would not have thousands of years of advance notice before the sun died, but only a few hours or days. We are lucky that our parent star is relatively small; we have a chance to get away.

As eons pass following the "last perfect day," the sun will expand until it practically fills the sky. As the surface of the sun cools, it will become redder and less well defined, but it will appear much brighter because of its vastly larger angular diameter as seen from the earth. Some astronomers think that the sun will bloat so much that the earth, and possibly even Mars, will be engulfed and vaporized. Today, the sun measures 864,000 miles in diameter. That is about a half percent the size of the earth's orbit. When our parent star becomes a red giant, it might become 200 million miles across

(Fig. 7-17).

At first—for a few tens of centuries after the "last perfect day"—humans will survive by moving toward the poles. Eventually, they will be faced with two alternatives: leave or die.

Fortunately, we have plenty of time before the final, ultimate heat wave. Right now, we are tempted to dismiss the space program as a waste of money; other problems seem more important. Yet, when the "last perfect day" arrives—and it will—we will be forced to find a new home. This will probably be easy if we have been preparing for a billion years or so. We can begin by looking at the other planets in our solar system as they are today.

Presently, only one planet, Mars, bears even a slight resemblance to our Earth. Mercury has no atmosphere, and temperatures are extreme. Venus is also far too hot, and the atmosphere is too dense for us to survive. Jupiter, Saturn, Uranus, and Neptune are shrouded in noxious gases and are ravaged by storms of unimaginable violence. Pluto is a desolate piece of rock with no atmosphere and temperatures approaching absolute zero.

Mars, although not a paradise, can accomodate us. We could perhaps use Mars as a stepping stone to other solar systems when our sun dies. As the sun grows larger, the climate of Mars will remain endurable for a while longer than the climate of the earth.

Climate of Mars

Mars is about 50 percent farther from the sun than Earth. For this reason, and also because of its thin atmosphere, Mars has a cold climate by our standards. Rain never falls, although a thin layer of frost occasionally forms in the polar regions in the winter. We would have no trouble getting used to the length of the day on Mars: 24 hours and 37 minutes Earth time. The axis of Mars is tilted to about the same extent as the axis of our planet, but the year is 687 Earth days long. We would have to get used to slower seasonal changes.

The normal barometric pressure on Mars is too low for humans to survive without an artificial environment, but this is perhaps a blessing in disguise, for winds on Mars can blow at speeds of up to 300 miles per hour. Because the air pressure is only about 1/50 of Earth's, the force of the wind is much less than it would be on our planet. Blowing sand, however, would occasionally present a hazard.

Most of the Martian air is carbon dioxide, and most of the surface is a desert of red sand. Astronomers have long wondered why Mars is so red; some scientists think that Mars once had an atmosphere containing abundant oxygen, but iron in the

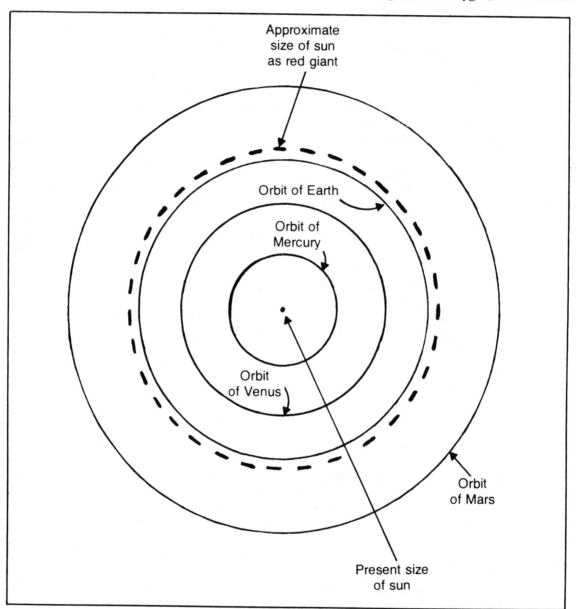

Fig. 7-17. The sun will someday grow huge by comparison to its present size. It might engulf the three inner planets and perhaps even Mars. In this scale drawing, the sun is shown as it is today and as it would be as a red giant 200 million miles across.

planet's soil locked up the potentially life-giving gas. If that is true, then there is a plentiful, and usable, supply of oxygen on Mars.

Parts of Mars appear greenish in color through telescopes. These areas shift with the seasons. Before the space probes visited Mars, some astronomers thought that the green areas were great fields of strange plants. That theory was proved wrong by the unmanned craft that landed on Mars. We still do not know precisely what is responsible for these shifting green features. Perhaps red sand intermittently covers up areas of copper oxide.

The greatest mystery of Mars is its so-called canals. More than a century ago, Mars watchers claimed to see remarkably straight, dark lines crisscrossing the planet when the earth's atmosphere was exceptionally clear and calm. The Martian canals were thought by some people to be plain evidence that civilizations existed there. (This is probably why the word "Martian" sounds as familiar as "Earthling" when we speak of living beings!) Space probes have not detected any evidence of these canals, and we still have no idea what they are, or even whether they exist at all.

There is a good possibility that Mars has experienced periods of glaciation, as evidenced by terrain that bears a striking resemblance to previously glacier-covered areas of the earth (Fig. 7-18). River beds, now dry, exist on Mars (Fig. 7-19), virtually proving that there once was water there.

Even before the space probes flew by the planet and eventually landed there, we could see evidence of storms by looking at Mars through telescopes. The wind blows the Martian sand into dunes that look hauntingly like those of the deserts on the earth (Fig. 7-20). Sandstorms sometimes cover the entire planet, obscuring all observable detail.

The surface of the red planet is heavily cratered. This fact was revealed by the first probe that flew by. Mars lies closer than the earth to the asteroid belt and is probably subjected to more meteorite impacts. Once such catastrophe might have radically altered the climate sometime in the past.

Mars has at least one volcano: Mount Olym-pus, larger than any mountain on our planet. This great peak rises 17 miles above the surrounding plains and is 300 miles wide at its base. It is possible that a massive eruption of this volcano was responsible for changing the climate of Mars for the worse, thousands or millions of years ago.

Mars today is indeed a windy, cold, dry planet, but it can be colonized. It would be possible to construct a whole city within a pair of huge thick plastic domes supported by internal air pressure (Fig. 7-21). The double-dome structure would prevent pressure loss in case one of the plastic bubbles burst. The inner dome could be supplied with oxygenated air at a pressure of 20 inches of mercury, a comfortable and breathable concentration for humans. The outer dome would be pressurized at about half that level.

Inside the colony, oxygen might be extracted from the surface material, much of which is believed to be iron oxide (ordinary rust). Some oxygen could also be manufactured by food plants grown within the domes. There is no free water on Mars, but some might be obtained from the polar ice caps. The temperature on Mars sometimes rises to levels that we would consider comfortable, but usually it is below freezing. Heating systems, perhaps powered by the sun, would be a necessity.

Mars will not give us a permanent solution to our solar problems. When the sun reaches its maximum size, even Mars will be extremely hot and could be vaporized. We will have a little extra time, however, to get packed for the ultimate journey we must someday make: a trip to another solar system. While the sun is bloated but still shining, we might escape to one of the outer planets for a while, but even this will be a temporary respite. For someday the sun will completely run down, leaving the solar system with no source of heat and light whatsoever. The final heat wave, deadly as it may be, will be followed by permanent cold and darkness. Those planets not vaporized during the red giant phase will continue to obediently move around the dead sun, locked in an everlasting deep freeze of about -450 degrees Fahrenheit. The solar system will no longer be capable of supporting any kind of life.

Fig. 7-18. Some Martian mountains show evidence of past glaciation (courtesy NASA).

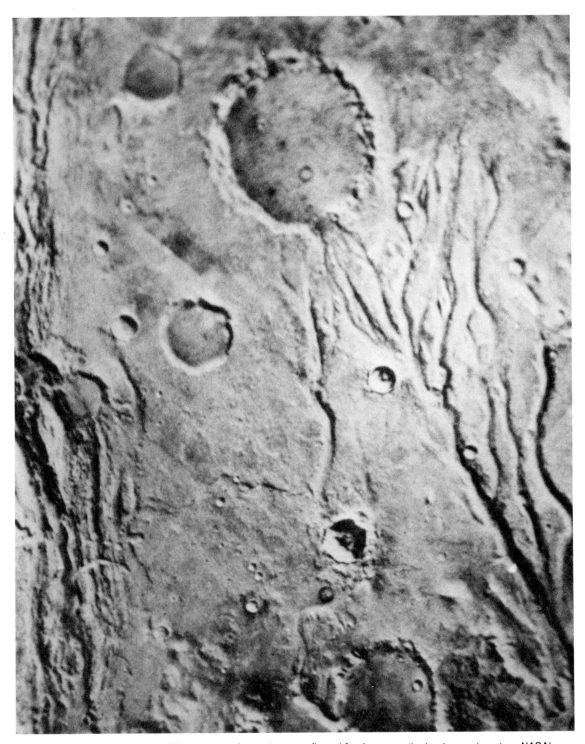

Fig. 7-19, Dried-up riverbeds on Mars suggest that water once flowed freely across the landscape (courtesy NASA).

Fig. 7-20. Windswept dunes in a Martian desert (courtesy NASA).

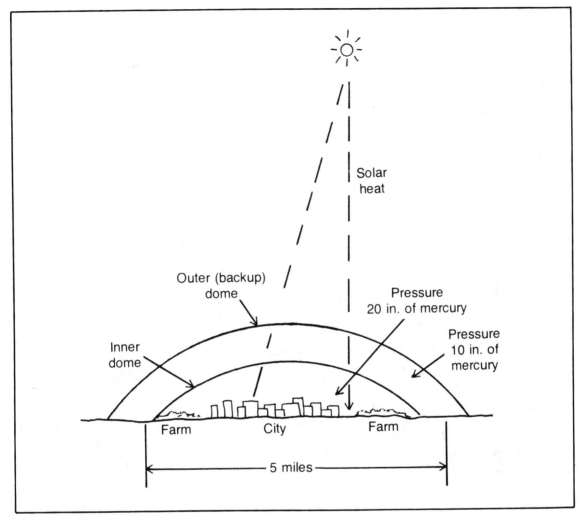

Fig. 7-21. A simplified illustration of one possible method of constructing a city on Mars. Two thick plastic domes, perhaps 5 miles in diameter, are supported by air pressure. Heat is supplied via the greenhouse effect.

Finding a New Home

Science fiction writers have, on occasion, reminded us of a haunting possibility. We are inclined to consider it a bit farfetched, but if we are to survive after the sun dies, we will end up acting out this legend.

Are we the descendants of a people that fled their dying star, searched for a new home, found this particular planet hospitable, landed, and settled? If the human species can survive until the death of the sun, and if we can find a habitable planet

in some other solar system, it is possible that we did it before. It is not my purpose here to prove or disprove this theory, but it is comforting to think that we might have gotten to earth that way. It gives us hope for the future: if we made the ultimate journey once, then we can make it again when it becomes necessary.

As we accelerate past the orbit of Pluto on our way to another star system, we will ride more comfortably if we know of several colonies we have already set up on distant planets. If we have no colonies to which we can move, then we will have a variety of different types of stars from which to choose. Double and multiple star systems would be undesirable because their planets would probably have irregular climates. A planet in orbit around a double star might move in a figure-eight path. First one star and then the other would dominate the climate of the planet. The days would vary in length tremendously. Such a planet might at times endure temperatures of 200 degrees Fahrenheit with constant daylight, and at other times be plunged into a deep freeze with black nights and dim days. In a triple or quadruple star system, the effect would be even more pronounced.

When we "adopt" a parent star, we will have to be selective. We will be looking for a single star rather than a double or multiple star. Small stars will be preferable to larger ones, since massive stars have short lives (less than a billion years) and have a propensity for exploding with very little warning. Many stars fluctuate in brightness and temperature at regular or irregular intervals; conditions would not be favorable on planets in orbit around such stars. Ideally, we will find a fairly young star similar to our old sun in its early days. Our computers will have already searched for, and found, at least a few hundred such stars in our galaxy. We will then begin looking for a suitable planet.

If we think seriously about the problems of finding another planet that can support our form of life without an artificial environment, the enormity of the task seems almost overwhelming. We might never find such a place. If we did happen to encounter an inhabitable planet, we would have to examine it closely to be sure that it met our needs.

Parts of our own Earth look forbidding when viewed from space (Fig. 7-22), and we might not

Fig. 7-22. Some of the earth's deserts look so hostile that space travelers, searching for a new home, might pass our planet up. We must not commit that kind of mistake when we are forced to leave the solar system.

observe a planet carefully enough. We would have to land in several different places on a planet in order to determine its suitability for supporting life. Suppose some aliens, used to conditions similar to those on our planet, were to visit Earth with the intention of settling here. What if they made a miscalculation and landed in Antarctica, or in the desolate sand sea of Fig. 7-22, but nowhere else? They might conclude that Earth was a completely inhospitable place, and that it could never support life. Having checked all of the other planets in the solar system and found them hostile as well, the aliens would abandon the sun for another star. When we are looking for a new home, we do not want to make that kind of error. In order to learn about the climate of a planet, we will have to do extensive research.

Our new home need not be exactly the same size as Earth; it might be somewhat larger or smaller. As long as the gravitational field is not too strong or too weak, we will be able to adapt to a change in weight. The new planet will not necessarily need to have the same average temperature as Earth. Ideally, this would be the case, but a slightly warmer or cooler place will be inhabitable. The most technologically advanced societies on our planet have evolved about midway between the poles and the equator, adapting to average conditions on Earth. On a cooler planet, we could survive well enough at the equator. On a hotter planet, we would find conditions acceptable near the poles.

We could get used to certain astronomical differences on a new planet, but only to a limited extent. The day might be much longer or shorter than an Earth day or Mars day. We might end up sleeping once every two or three days, or two or three times every day. The axis might be tilted more or less than the axis of Earth or Mars. The seasons would then be more or less pronounced than those of Earth and Mars. It is not likely, however, that we could tolerate a planet that always keeps one side facing the sun, or that has an axis tilted by 90 degrees. Imagine what the climate of

the earth would be like if either of those extremes were reality!

Three things will be absolutely necessary in order for us to survive on a planet. First, there will have to be a breathable atmosphere. If there is too little or too much oxygen, or if there are any poisonous gases present, we will not be able to live. Second, there will have to be water in some form, or at least the hydrogen from which we can make water by means of reactions with oxygen. Third, there must be some way to grow or obtain food. A lifeless planet will probably not have the soil necessary to grow plants.

Although there will be other complicating factors as we search for a new world on which to live, we cannot do without these three necessities. We are sometimes reminded of that bitter lesson right here on Earth when we pollute our air or water, or when the topsoil blows away during a drought.

The whole business of finding a new planet certainly sounds like a lot of trouble, and we can be sure that it will be difficult. We have plenty of time in which to develop the necessary technology to accomplish the task, however, assuming that we take care of the home planet we have now.

Violent natural phenomena are a part of the universe, and they will exist wherever we go and whatever we do. Our species has endured the worst storms and climate shifts that nature has been able to deal us. We actually thrive, in some ways, on severe weather and climate. Such conditions force us to move ahead, to do things. If the weather and climate were always ideal, progress might completely stop. We would probably never have come into existence at all if some natural cataclysm had not eliminated the dinosaurs. If the weather and climate had always been perfect since the Stone Age, we might still be throwing rocks at animals to obtain food and making our shelters in caves and forests.

The challenge of violent weather and adverse climate will always be with us. We will continue to survive and improve because of it.

Bibliography

Clark, Champ and editors of Time-Life Books. *Planet Earth: Flood.* Alexandria, VA: Time-Life Books, Inc., 1982.

Dunn, Gordon E. and Miller, Banner I. *Atlantic Hurricanes.* Baton Rouge, LA: Louisiana State University Press, 1964.

Eagleman, Joe R. *Severe and Unusual Weather.* New York: Van Nostrand Reinhold Company, 1983.

Gribbin, John. *Weather Force.* New York: G. P. Putnam's Sons, 1979.

Halacy, D. S., Jr. *Ice or Fire?* New York: Harper & Row, Publishers, 1978.

Kirk, Ruth. *Snow.* New York: William Morrow and Company, Inc., 1978.

Wendt, Herbert. *Before the Deluge.* New York: Doubleday & Company, Inc., 1968.

Whipple, A. B. C. and editors of Time-Life Books. *Planet Earth: Storm.* Alexandria, VA: Time-Life Books, Inc., 1982.

Winkless, Nels III and Browning, Iben. *Climate and the Affairs of Men.* New York: Harper's Magazine Press, 1975.

Index

Index

258

259

OTHER POPULAR TAB BOOKS OF INTEREST